HR FORECASTING AND PLANNING

Paul Turner

Chartered Institute of Personnel and Development

This book is dedicated to Gail, Jane Marie and Annette

© Paul Turner 2002

Design by Paperweight
Typesetting by Intype London Ltd
Printed in Great Britain by The Cromwell Press,
Trowbridge, Wiltshire

British Library Cataloguing in Publication Data
A catalogue record for this book is available from the British Library

ISBN 0–85292–933–1

The views expressed in this book are the author's own and
may not necessarily reflect those of the CIPD.

Chartered Institute of Personnel and Development. CIPD House,
Camp Road, London SW19 4UX
Tel: 020–8971 9000   Fax: 020–8263 3333
E-mail: cipd@cipd.co.uk Website: www.cipd.co.uk
Incorporated by Royal Charter. Registered charity no. 1079797

CONTENTS

ACKNOWLEDGEMENTS

I would like to acknowledge the help and support of the following people in the research for and writing of this book: John Philpott, Sandra Lowe, Caroline Jankowska, John Whitehead, Tony Garnett, Neil Hasson, Phil Thomas, Rob Aldridge, Eric Linin, Rory Campbell, Catryn Hemlock, Jennifer Schramm, Martyn Sloman, Mike Cannell, John Stevens, Eila Rana, Norman Mitchinson, Bernard O'Driscoll, Audrey Lucy, Peter Cornwall, Peter Empringham, Theresa Barnett, Alex Mayall, Lesley James, and Vicky Wright.

Thanks are due also to Annette Turner for her invaluable help in referencing, and to Robert Foss of the CIPD for his expert guidance and counsel and for having the patience of a Portsmouth fan.

INTRODUCTION

We wanted a seat at the table. Well, it's the hot seat.

Libby Sartain
Chair of the American Society for Human Resource
Management, 53rd Annual Conference, San Francisco,
2001

People management professionals should not be seen only as the people who mop the brows of the wounded. They are uniquely placed to design and operate organisations and practices that build on continually regenerated contributions from the people who invest themselves in their employer's success.

Geoff Armstrong
Director General of the CIPD, 2001

Those who work in HR nowadays need the imagination of Steven Spielberg, the incisiveness of Jeremy Paxman, the interviewing skills of Oprah Winfrey and the skin of a rhinoceros. While for tiptoeing between the political sensitivities of managers, the grace of Darcey Bussell is hardly any less essential. An organisation's tendency to demand so much from HR professionals requires a broad range of competencies, more than most functions in the organisation. There are not too many departments that serve hot tea to the troops in shock (rather like the Red Cross) while at the same time planning global campaigns for the effective deployment of people (like Caesar, or at least Caesar's HR director, probably called Brutus).

Two of the attributes that do not get nearly enough attention, though, are strategy and planning. We have all heard criticisms of HR as not being sufficiently strategic, as focusing too much on the tactical, as not having a voice on the board. Some of these are justified; others less so.

Nevertheless, if these are the perceptions, then we should do something about putting them right.

One thing we can do is contribute to strategy-setting in a way that is seen as adding value. This book attempts to demonstrate how to do so by dealing with the subjects of:

☐ strategic human resource forecasting (SHRF) – in which we look at the 'radar' of the organisation and start joining up the dots as they appear on the screen

☐ human resource planning (HRP) – in which we take these patterns and convert them into meaningful activity.

These are two areas in which we can make real progress. The demand for HR input at strategic level is there: chief executive officers increasingly see people issues as critical to competitive advantage. And the supply is there: there is the basis for a methodology for HR to excel at strategy and planning. What we have to do is to pull everything together in a consistent and professional way.

The basis of the model that is included in this book is shown in Figure 1. The processes that will be outlined are intended to raise the profile of critical people issues. Among the most important of these are performance management, knowledge management, individual and organisational learning, and how to manage change. All of these elements are within the domain of HR, and dealing with them will determine how successful those responsible for HR will become. Taking a strategic view across the organisation is essential.

In essence the book will answer the questions:

☐ How can I help my organisation to be more successful through the best use of HR?

☐ How can I get HR on to the strategic agenda?

☐ How do I deal with the end-to-end process of HR forecasting and planning?

☐ How do I persuade my organisation to take these models on board and include them in its own strategy-setting process?

☐ How do I implement the processes?

Figure 1 **SHRF, HRP AND ORGANISATIONAL STRATEGY**

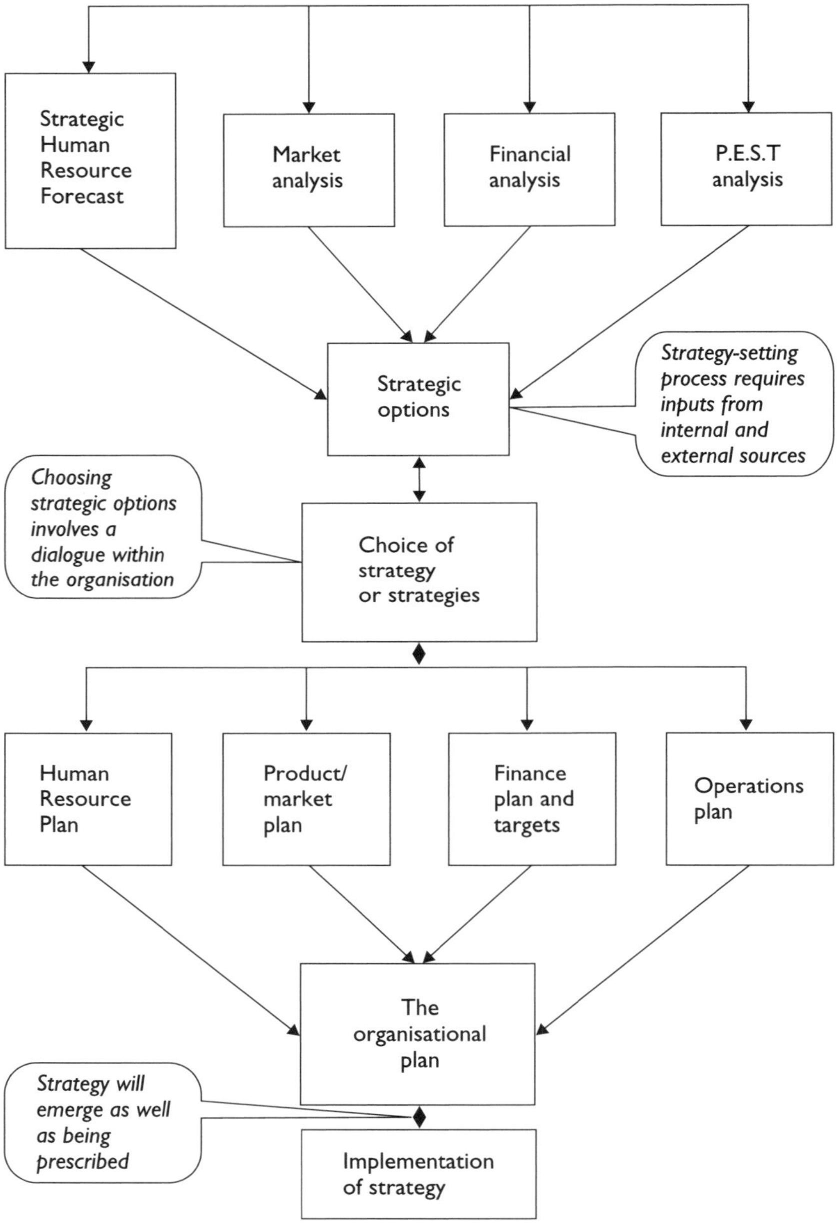

Strategic Human Resource Forecast	Market analysis	Financial analysis	P.E.S.T analysis

Strategic options

Strategy-setting process requires inputs from internal and external sources

Choosing strategic options involves a dialogue within the organisation

Choice of strategy or strategies

Human Resource Plan	Product/ market plan	Finance plan and targets	Operations plan

The organisational plan

Strategy will emerge as well as being prescribed

Implementation of strategy

☐ How do I manage them on an ongoing basis?

To help in this, the book is divided into three parts.

Part One is a review of the issues around forecasting, strategy and planning, and the role of HR in these. Chapters 1 to 3 address the subject in a generic form, exploring the different points of view about strategy and the options available to organisations as they set strategy. This is an essential precursor to the actual processes in an HR context. The chapters pull together strategy and HR by outlining the strengths and weaknesses of traditional approaches to the subject – with particular reference to manpower planning. Finally, they address the strategic role of HR, how this has evolved, and how it may do so in future.

Part Two deals with the component parts of the strategic human resource forecast (SHRF). Chapters 4 to 10 look at business strategy, its application in HR, and the type of scenarios that might arise in the future. Demand and supply of people in both society as a whole and the organisation in particular are also analysed. Ideas about the nature and impact of culture on the organisation's strategy are examined, with provision for a gap analysis. This section enables the reader to develop a SHRF for input into the strategy-setting process.

Part Three is concerned with the human resource plan (HRP), which is outlined in Chapters 11 to 17. This deals with most of the HR implications of strategy and represents the output for the HR 'business plan.' It provides an analysis of the quantitative elements of the HRP (these should not be new to anyone who has done manpower planning). Further discussion follows on the organisation's design and how to resource it once agreed, as well as the constituent parts of the learning, training and development plan. The strategic aspects of learning in its broadest sense are also covered here. Two further chapters cover the detail behind reward and employee relations.

In dealing with the subject in this way, it is possible to take best practice from those parts of manpower planning that have worked while developing new themes in response to the changing demands of the current business environment. The key differentiators of the SHRF and HRP processes from other types of approach (eg manpower planning) therefore are:

- [ ] SHRF and HRP are dynamic, not static, entities.
- [ ] They are part of an integrated approach to knowledge management within the organisation which embraces the dynamic, creative use of information (rather than the creation and storage of it).
- [ ] They feature during the input stage of the strategy-setting process and at the output stage.
- [ ] They are based on the assumption that people are key to the achievement of sustained competitive success rather than a resource to be deployed. The development of business strategy recognises that 'human capability' is a strategic issue.
- [ ] SHRF and HRP contain elements that are 'soft', such as culture management and organisation development, as well as the harder aspects of headcount forecasting.
- [ ] HR is regarded as having a valid contribution to make to strategy-setting in the organisation.

The models proposed are not meant as a panacea but as contributions to the challenges that we all face. This means that further adaptation to the unique circumstances of the reader's own organisation will be fundamental.

So may I together with Kalil Gibran enjoin you to remember to 'sow seeds with tenderness and reap the harvest with joy.'

PART I

STRATEGY, FORECASTING, PLANNING AND PEOPLE

1 HR AND ITS CONTRIBUTION TO STRATEGY

Strategic human resources

'Strategic' is a word we overuse. Yet the human resources within a business are one of the few areas that are capable of being truly strategic.

What decides whether in fact the human resource of an organisation is used strategically is how much the people of the organisation – their attributes, motivation, development, priorities and performance – directly support the company's strategic goals. But the process should not be a uni-directional response to a chosen business strategy – the human aspects of a business will often be critical to the viability of that strategy, and must be fully considered as it is formulated and implemented.

How, then, can human resources be used strategically? Firstly, the people of a business must be genuinely recognised as critical to it. Secondly, the human resources function has to be an integral part of the strategic planning and thinking within the business, and business managers need to incorporate people issues into their strategic and tactical activities. Thirdly, the HR strategy must not only support current business requirements but must also prepare the business and its people for the growing demand for talent, and competition for the best human resource. This requires innovative approaches to every link in the HR value chain – recruitment, development, motivation, performance management and reward.

Human resources (with the talent it incorporates) is likely to become the key differentiator for innovation, for understanding customers, for managing human relationships and for developing the business. Small wonder, then, that any

> company that aspires to success – or any manager within such a company – has to recognise and respond to the strategic power of human resources.
>
> *Norman Mitchinson*
> *Director of Human Resources, Lloyds TSB*

HR – how do we make a positive contribution to strategy?

A great deal is expected of people who work in HR. Not only are we asked to deliver six-sigma quality in recruitment and training, reward, industrial relations, employee communications and organisation design, we also have to be strategists, employee champions and business partners. We are then expected to deliver self-service through web-enabled HR systems while reducing headcount through outsourcing. On top of all that we are still regarded as the safe house for everyone's problems.

HR is a very diverse, challenging and satisfying profession. It helps considerably in responding to these multiple challenges that there is a growing recognition of the importance of good HR practice as a major contributor to an organisation's competitiveness. This is because human effort is increasingly seen as the key ingredient in achieving long-term success. The management of this effort combined with investment in new technology is a significant contributor to growth and prosperity. HR professionals play an important part in the development of this approach. The positive link between HR and organisational performance has been demonstrated by a good deal of research. A model of this is shown in Figure 2.

So how is HR evolving into a function that can make the positive contribution required? Well, first it is getting its own house in order. HR people generally have their fingers on the pulse of fashion. This is a good quality, and it is why we are regarded as among the most innovative people in organisations. Three things are very fashionable at the moment and seem to be on everyone's agenda:

- [ ] web enablement
- [ ] outsourcing
- [ ] organisational strategy.

Figure 2 **MODEL OF THE LINK BETWEEN HRM AND PERFORMANCE**

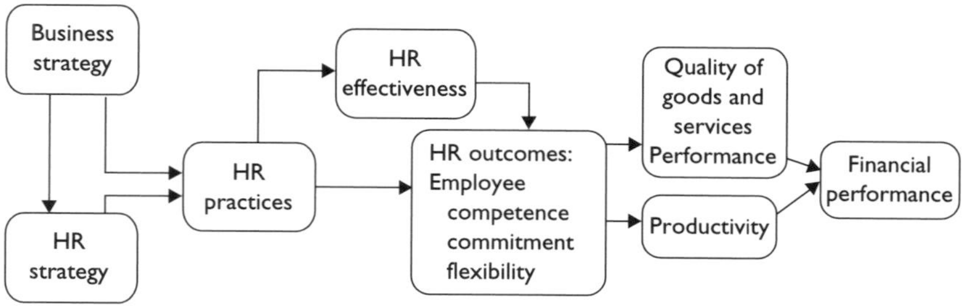

```
┌───────────┐                    ┌───────────┐        ┌───────────┐
│ Business  │              ┌────▶│    HR     │        │ Quality of│
│ strategy  │              │     │effectiveness│      │ goods and │
└───────────┘              │     └───────────┘        │ services  │
      │                    │            │             │Performance│       ┌───────────┐
      │        ┌───────────┐            ▼             └───────────┘──────▶│ Financial │
      ├───────▶│    HR     │     ┌───────────┐                            │performance│
      │        │ practices │────▶│HR outcomes:│────▶                      └───────────┘
      ▼        └───────────┘     │ Employee  │     ┌───────────┐──────────▶
┌───────────┐                    │competence │     │Productivity│
│    HR     │                    │commitment │────▶└───────────┘
│ strategy  │                    │flexibility│
└───────────┘                    └───────────┘
```

Source: CIPD, 2001

Web enablement

We should all, apparently, be installing HR information systems and putting a whole range of HR things on the web. This will have the effect of liberating both the profession and the workforce. People will manage their own human resource needs through technology, for example by changing their reward package, doing training programmes and tracking career options. Using enterprise-wide information systems they will be able to access a wide range of services that sit traditionally in the files and manuals of HR.

Does this liberate those who work in HR? Conventional wisdom talks of the disintermediating effect of technology freeing up HR from transactions and moving to more strategic work. But some are already talking of reintermediation through technology-based collaborative enterprises. It doesn't matter whether we are disintermediating or reintermediating (or even just plain old mediating) – the effect of technology on transactional work will indeed enable HR to focus on both operations and strategy.

Just one note of caution about this powerful use of technology in HR. In many organisations such an initiative tends to be cost-driven. In this respect HR is no different from any other part of the organisation, being subject to the same business forces. However, the idea that technology somehow replaces HR is an absurd one. Imagine if all advice about people was available only via technological means – akin to the synthesised voice from *OK Computer* – distant and scary. It would be a mistake for organisations to disintermediate at the expense of employee satisfaction. Live, up-close and personal interaction will remain at the core of HR.

Outsourcing

The second fashion accessory is the outsourcing of HR in one of a variety of joint-venture or alliance services arrangements. BP Amoco and Exult have set the trend in the UK. It is assumed that we will all follow – and given the number of consultancies forecasting that we will, the assumption is more than likely to prove right! These two topics are *zeitgeist* in HR: they are the things that people debate about. Sooner or later, though, they will have been dealt with. We will all be web-enabled and we will all have made the decision to outsource or not. That decision may not be too far off. If the rest of the world follows the pattern of the USA, the web-enabled outsourced HR business will be the norm.

Organisational strategy

The final area of fashion is that of organisational strategy and the role HR plays in it. Increasingly, HR professionals are joining in the strategy-setting process at an early stage.

Whereas once the marketing plan was key, and some clever financial engineering could make money out of money, people strategies are now among the most important. Leading-edge supply chain management in such industries as pharmaceuticals and aerospace, and the development of new business paradigms in retailing and professional services, demand a different response from HR. HR has to work more collaboratively, more strategically. But – to paraphrase an e-business saying – 'the hard part isn't getting strategic HR off the ground, it is getting it out of the door.' Converting very fine words about strategic HR into practical working tools is as valid an objective as developing new theories of HR. SHRF and HRP are two of these tools.

A new paradigm for HR

HR is becoming multi-disciplinary and has to embrace new concepts as it strives to succeed in its overall 'strategic' direction. For example, the US *Journal of Cost Management* recently contained an article about skills-based human capital budgeting. Written by two of Computer Science Corporation's leading business process specialists, J. Lehr McKenzie and Gary L. Melling, this excellent article forecasts that human capital planning would become a strategic driver because a key issue facing organisations was 'ensuring that the right people with the right skills are in the right jobs at the right time'. This was to avoid low productivity, excess capacity and insufficient resources to meet the demands of value-added work (McKenzie and Melling, 2001). Surely that is a part of strategic human resource management. If we are to make the strategic contribution we so desire to, we have to understand and know how to operate such innovative tools and techniques in our own organisations. We also have to deal with the concepts of knowledge management, workforce scenario planning, effective diversity management, and vision and values alignment.

HR cannot afford to have a restricted view of the future. It has to be expansive in its outlook. Right now, imagination is as important as knowledge for HR professionals. The professionals who work in the function are expected to be both operational and strategic – and to be able to deliver added value to the strategic debate. Organisations can no longer afford to say 'You're in the wrong room, my friend,' when HR makes to join in the strategic debate. But one of the problems for HR is that too much of its defining research is presented in an abstract way, as though HR was philosophy. The subject lends itself to such analysis – after all, it is concerned with that most complex form, the person and his or her behaviour. Although much of this output is interesting, it does not always help in the war for talent or the people aspects of a merger. The role of HR is to make sure that people receive all the consideration possible in times of organisational decision-making. Techniques for doing so are now mandatory for HR. We need to mould both research and practice into something that is coherent.

The problem is that the definition of HR is still evolving, in spite of its many years of development and excellent track record in delivering both business and individual needs. It is worth exploring why this is the case, and deciding on a way forward so that HR can be best placed when called upon to make its strategic contribution.

'Should we do away with HR?'

That is a good question. After all, in these days of intense competition, organisations are focusing on their core business, and all other parts are being cost-reduced or outsourced. This is particularly true of support areas such as HR and finance.

But we have seen evidence that people are key to achieving competitive advantage, and that models of strategy-setting require a high level of input from HR. The question that this evokes is 'Exactly what should HR do to achieve this level of input?' Unfortunately, there is a vast range of views and opinions about what HR should and should not do. What is it about HR that attracts such descriptions as 'the dog that didn't bark'? Maybe it is that we are not clear about our role in the organisation, or that we have not been loud enough in articulating the vital work we do in the organisation. Whatever the reason, there is some way to go in improving the standing of HR. Unless this is dealt with, we will not be admitted to the strategic debate necessary for the successful delivery of SHRF and HRP.

An area for concern is that our tools and techniques are not consistently applied. Finance have balance sheets and P&L accounts, marketers have Boston boxes and STP, strategists have 'five-forces analysis,' GE strategic positioning matrices and value chains, and so on. HR tools needed for strategic input vary from organisation to organisation – there is not even an agreed way of reporting headcount (staff working flexible hours, for example). This means that a common understanding of how HR should intervene does not exist, making for a fragmented and inconsistent approach. We could rectify this by having a generic form of strategic intervention – at the very least, some tools and techniques that we can agree as best practice. Then we will be able to make a difference.

But a question often asked by sceptics is '*Can* HR become strategic?' Many have tried to find the answer. The sheer diversity of views is overwhelming. Some are genuinely innovative; others make it look as though someone has just 'rearranged the faces and given them new names'. This lack of agreement about the value of HR, personnel, training, development or people management permeates much of the output. One analysis of the role of personnel management, for example, saw it as 'an instrument and victim of the dilemmas of capital' (Legge, 1995), and one of its roles as managing a contradiction in capitalist systems, which was the need to obtain both the control and the consent of employees. Legge concluded that for most line managers, HRM remained rhetoric – that it had not been translated into reality. There were pejorative views. 'HR was regarded as normative and optimistic. . .[Commentators] thought they were missionaries and that social sciences should be used to improve society' (Warner, 1997). The issue was not a new one. Skinner raised the question of the role of HR in his article 'Big Hat, No Cattle' (Skinner, 1981). Perhaps it is not surprising, then, that Ulrich asked the question 'Should we do away with HR?' (Ulrich, 1998).

People management is becoming more important

There is a very good reason not to do away with HR: people are becoming more important in the achievement of organisational success, and we have evidence to prove it. Furthermore, those who have chosen HR as a profession have spent their careers developing people competencies that are unique and can add significant value, as organisations try to achieve sustained success through people.

This is important, because by the beginning of the 21st century national industry and commerce was engaged in the battle of global competition in a way very different from the position of 20 years earlier. The sources of competitive advantage of the 1980s and 1990s – technology, finance and marketing – are not going to be enough to provide organisations with sustained business success in the 'noughties'. These competencies are now the price of admission to the competitive arena. Technology proved to be a great leveller in the world of industry and commerce. In response, new business policies were needed in order to give organisations a better chance for long-term success in the 21st century. It was recognition of this that brought people to the fore, and effective human resourcing strategy, processes and practice in modern organisations have in turn become recognised as critical success factors.

There is an increasing body of research that supports this and demonstrates the positive links between effective people factors and company performance. A CIPD-sponsored study (Patterson, West *et al*, 1997) for example concluded that

- ☐ Job satisfaction could explain 5 per cent of the variation between companies in change in profitability.
- ☐ Organisational commitment on behalf of people explained some 7 per cent of variation in performance between companies.
- ☐ Cultural factors accounted for some 10 per cent in variation in the profitability between companies.
- ☐ Human resources management practices together explain 19 per cent of the variation between companies in change in profitability.
- ☐ HRM practices taken together account for 18 per cent of the variation between companies in change in productivity.

These results are striking when compared to the findings for the percentage change in profitability caused by other business factors:

- ☐ Some 2 per cent of change in profitability and less than 3 per cent of the change in productivity is explained by the generic term 'strategy'.
- ☐ Emphasis on quality accounts for less than 1 per cent in the change in profitability.

- ☐ Emphasis on technology explains only 1 per cent of the variation between companies in change in productivity over time.

- ☐ Expenditure on research and development accounts for 6 per cent of the variation in productivity and 8 per cent in variation in profitability.

So there is a great case for saying that HR rather than becoming obsolete is actually becoming more important.

So is the message being heard?

In spite of a good deal of evidence about the positive effects of good people management practices on profitability and productivity, there is less evidence for the complementary conclusion that an organisation might want to integrate the work of its human resources professionals into the setting and practice of strategy. David Guest has suggested reasons why this might be the case (Guest 1999). He gave a number of possible explanations:

- ☐ The message is not being heard by personnel managers.
- ☐ The message is not being believed.
- ☐ Personnel managers believe the message but cannot sell it.
- ☐ Personnel managers do not know how to introduce HRM.
- ☐ Personnel managers are too busy managing turbulence and change to develop a sustained human resource strategy.
- ☐ Academic messages are muddled and contradictory.

There are other reasons for the less than effective strategic contribution. One of these is the lack of clarity about the role of HR because of the diversity of its involvement in the organisation. In the past HR has had many focal points – in one direction implementing hard business decisions (dealing with people fallout, employment and industrial relations and pay negotiations), and in the other direction operating in seemingly ephemeral areas (culture change and values). This diversity and ambiguity has created an environment in which an enormous amount of energy has gone into defining the role of HR. There has been a plenitude of academic debate.

Equally, HR professionals themselves have adopted a variety of positions along a broad spectrum. Last of all, line managers have different approaches when using the professional services of HR.

If those in HR are to become involved with the processes of SHRF and HRP, then they have to rescind some of the negative perceptions and take up a different position, both in the organisation and with strategic decision-makers. It is about time we did so. John Purcell has recently noted that the debates about HR's role and position have become a 'mix of guilt and boredom – guilt because of the inevitability of the accusation of limited influence and a function unable to hold its own in the corridors of power, boredom as the seemingly endless debate continues on whether HRM is different from personnel management' (Purcell, 2001). It is hard not to agree with Purcell's argument.

So what can we do about it?

If we are to focus HR on the need to make strategic interventions, we have to decide exactly what role we should play. Now is the time for HR to make the change from being a deliverer of transactions to a deliverer of strategy. As Lynda Gratton notes, unless those in HR get to grips with the new demands of strategy, the corporate HR function will die (Gratton, 2000).

We can make this step change. Indeed, a good deal of progress has already been made. HR is going through a revolution. Three things are happening simultaneously:

☐ the 'strategisation' (not a real word, but you get the drift) of HR

☐ the industrialisation of HR processes

☐ the commercialisation of HR.

These are the HR responses to the recognition that people are critical to competitive success. This view is backed up by leading-edge thinking that has been ensuring that HR becomes more aligned to business need and at the same time more businesslike itself in how it is managed. The result is an increasing commercialisation of HR and the industrialisation of its processes in response to business demands. There are many examples of this. Philips, the Amsterdam-based electronics corporation, recently introduced 'performance-focused HR' worldwide to improve the organisation's business orientation. Lloyds TSB set up an HR call centre to channel transactional queries throughout the organisation, and followed this up with a direct-access website that by 2001 had received more than 2 million requests for information. Swiss Life's intranet allows 500 employees to choose their benefits flexibly. And so on. Undoubtedly, one of the main drivers behind these trends is the notion of freeing up HR expertise.

We are pushing at an open door. SHRF and HRP should be part of a virtuous circle of dialogue and iteration producing outputs that can be used to inform human resource strategy and policy ensuring that human resources actions are aligned to business or organisational strategy.

A way forward for HR

These views lead to the belief that the role of human resources in the achievement of long-term success is recognised. There are plenty of opportunities for organisations to take the concept on board and invest in such measures as will enable the human advantage to be achieved. Such a model would have a corporate pay-back since 'human resource executives working in the more admired firms [as identified by *Fortune* magazine's annual corporate reputation survey] appear to place more emphasis on treating employees fairly than do HR executives working in less admired firms' (Koys, 1997). HR professionals need to be more prepared to champion people at senior management level. And we need to reach a position in which 'HR will speak with a more confident voice within the organisation. HR's role has to be one of consultancy, co-ordination and maintaining fairness' (Ulrich, 1998). Ulrich has outlined the deliverables and activities associated, as shown in Table 1.

HR must stand up and be counted as a strategic partner to business managers. To do so we have to develop a new paradigm and new competencies to back it up. Employers are

Table 1 **KEY HR DELIVERABLES AND ACTIVITIES**

Role/Cell	Deliverable/ Outcome	Metaphor	Activity
Management of strategic human resources	Executing strategy	Strategic partner	Aligning HR and business strategy: organisational diagnosis
Management of firm's infrastructure	Building an efficient infrastructure	Administrative expert	Re-engineering organisation processes: shared services
Management of employee contribution	Increasing employee commitment and capability	Employee champion	Listening and responding to employees: providing employees with resources
Management of transformation and change	Creating a renewed organisation	Change agent	Managing transformation and change: ensuring capacity for change

Reprinted by permission of Harvard Business School Press, from *Human Resource Champions* by D Ulrich, 1996.

shifting their HR department's focus from administrative and risk management functions to more strategic and business-critical functions such as employee selection, retention and development (*HR Magazine,* 2000.) In addition, other areas in which HR will become involved include, *inter alia,* knowledge management (to facilitate cross-corporate knowledge-sharing), M&A selection (scanning the environment for strong M&A candidates), workforce scenario planning; strategic/OD consulting, and continuous change management (Corporate Leadership Council, 1999).

In order to make the necessary advances, an approach to HR might combine HRD and HRM with customer relationship management (CRM), so necessary for effective business partnering. Such an HR model that linked all these various component parts might then be expressed in the formula:

$$\text{New HR model} = f\text{HRM} + \text{HRD} + \text{CRM}$$

If we are to be involved in these new challenges, we have to join up our thinking, add strategic capability to our armoury and ensure a high level of interface with business managers. By adopting a more sophisticated approach to the segmentation of the needs of a heterogenous workforce we might *also* move to offering HR products and services to a segmented customer base. We will thus be moving away from a one-size-fits-all approach to HR that focuses on groups of employees with similar needs, or, ultimately, to the situation in which every employee gets an HR service that meets his or her own unique needs. To elaborate on this further, a move towards shared services is a positive one based on the desire for the HR function to 'be more professional in the work it [does], achieve greater consistency and accuracy, be more aware of best practice, use better processes to complete its work, and deliver work on time and to budget' (Reilly, 2000).

These ideas are based on a sound rationale and are in line with a partnering approach to HR that is becoming more commonplace in organisations – backed, of course, by a mix of insourced and outsourced administrative services. There is also a view that HR should be concerned with 'processes such as leadership, motivation and consultation' (Hendry, 1995). Furthermore, it has been argued that HRM should come together with HRD at a nexus as a series of integrated proposals 'linking together different combinations of organisational variables such as communications and involvement; structure, shape and empowerment; resourcing strategies and flexibility; organisation development strategies; employment strategies; and conflict' (Stewart and McGoldrick, 1996). A combination of these positive views of HR would result in a function that has earned a strategic role in the organisation based on the fact that it has proven operational capability and business or organisational alignment.

Conclusion

The role of HR is moving away from that of a function that does only transactional work to one that makes a strategic contribution as well. Strategic human resource forecasting and human resource planning will require interventions on the part of HR professionals that are both integrated and aligned with the organisation's overall strategic intent. These interventions will be part of a process and a system. They will be made at the highest level of the organisation's strategy-setting structure, and will require a dialogue based on an understanding of strategy in general and strategy as it applies to the specific organisation.

The above demonstrates that people can be shown to be a key source of competitive advantage or sustained organisational success. Given such a proposition, the need to achieve excellence in HR strategy and management is a critical objective for organisations. In the modern organisation HR can provide the link between core competencies, shared learning and successful strategy – in short, harnessing the organisation's intellectual capital, converting it into organisational learning, and most importantly ensuring excellent implementation of the outcomes (Conference Board, 1997).

2 MODELS OF STRATEGY: THE GROWING IMPORTANCE OF PEOPLE

What is strategy, planning and forecasting?

This is a fascinating question! Let me offer a couple of different and, in some sense, opposing explanations or motives for why the Guidance Council does these things at all.

The first explanation is all about the ability to use evidence in order to predict outcomes. It is the value we derive from being able to assess the implications of our environment and how that informs the actions we need to take. Indeed, a step before that is to use an analysis of our environment to determine – if only to some extent – what our objectives ought to be. We are trying to guarantee success.

There is in this view an assumption that formal strategic development is good – be it used in business towards a profit objective, or be it as individuals in order to get the most from life. There is some truth in this, and the Guidance Council does have strategic plans. But that is not all. The all-pervasive sense that strategy-planning and forecasting is a necessary part of 'knowing where you're going and knowing how to get there' seems more dominant today than ever before.

The other explanation is closer to the experience of effective careers guidance. It is that strategy-planning and forecasting arise from something much more fundamental in human nature: the need for security and the need for reassurance that we are making the right choices. This is much less analytical, and centres strongly on the values and desires of the individual (or enterprise).

The Guidance Council is, therefore, always alert to the need for proper business disciplines. But it also recognises that 'choice' is not the same as making a decision.

> Strategy, planning and forecasting have a role to play in determining the direction and success of an enterprise – but they are not the whole story.
>
> *Bernard O'Driscoll*
> *Chair of the Careers and Education Guidance Council*

The importance of people to organisational success

As we have seen in Chapter 1, there is an acceptance that organisations have to get the people things right. If they fail to, the people walk away, there is customer dissatisfaction, the organisation suffers, and shareholder value falls. This raised profile of people issues in organisations is something of a double-edged sword for the HR profession. At long last they are getting the recognition that has long been denied – but now they also have to deliver on the strategic stage and come up with more contribution than the excellent trans-actional activity for which they are respected. Chief executive officers and the board expect HR to fulfil a much broader brief than ever before. So the challenge for all of us today is how to make sure that in turbulent times we get the people things right. This chapter looks at the case for HR to have a more proactive role in the strategy, planning and forecasting processes of the organisation. In addition it outlines some of the strategic models that might be encountered in these processes.

In the new business paradigm by which people are the enablers of long-term organisational success, HR professionals play an important role. We have to deliver not only operational excellence in our traditional roles of personnel and training, but also strategic value added through our unique knowledge of people dynamics. This is a combination of practical efficiency and professional insight. Given the current levels of change, though, especially the raised (or dashed) expectations of the new economy, we might start with the question 'Is it realistic even to consider strategy, planning and forecasting in a dynamic and unpredictable world?' These things do not seem to sit easily with some of the short-term dislocation that has been a feature of our economy for the past few years.

In defence of strategy

It seems that the moment HR is accepted as having a role to play at strategic level, the function risks having the prize snatched from its grasp. How can we advocate strategy in such an unpredictable business world? There are two schools of thought:

☐ There are those who say it is useless trying to plan. No one can predict what is going to happen. Let things evolve. Make sure you are flexible and fleet of foot so that whatever happens you can cope with it.

☐ And there are those who would claim that it is now more than ever necessary to plan. 'Resource is scarce, budgets are tight. You have to make sure that you put your resources in the right places. You need a strategy and a long-term plan. You have to know where you are going.' For those who work in organisations it is hard to know what to do for the best.

Where can we start, then, in searching for the answer to this conundrum? And what should HR be doing in solving it? The answer for HR may lie in the more established realms of business strategy and forecasting

But what does this debate about strategy mean to the HR professional? It means quite a lot, actually. Establishing that we can and, indeed, should maximise the use of strategy and forecasting is only the first stage in the process. Having a strategy or a strategic human resource forecast (SHRF) are not themselves passports to success. 'Strategies can be good or bad. A bad strategy would either specify inappropriate or inconsistent objectives, or propose a plan of action that was seriously deficient' (Richardson and Thompson, 1997).

In order to minimise the risk of inappropriate strategy due to the misunderstanding or understatement of the people implications, HR professionals' interventions must be made at an early stage. They must be integrated with the overall process of strategy-setting and add value in a way that is perceived and is different from that which can be obtained from general or functional managers involved in the process. This means that those responsible for HR will be expected to make a value-adding contribution to the strategy-setting process, and will therefore need the knowledge, skills, attitudes and behaviours to participate at this level. They will also need the tools and techniques associated with participation at this level.

There are two reasons for this. First, strategic human capital management is increasingly being used to describe the investment in the people elements of an organisation's operations. Second, the 'new era of labour' is different from previous eras. This is because of the nature of the modern workforce. Demographic and attitudinal changes have precipitated this new era. HR has to be aware of this, and adapt its profile accordingly.

Strategic human capital management

This concept seems to be growing in popularity as the more transactional aspects of HR get disintermediated. Strategic human capital management includes such aspects as 'strategic human capital planning, organisational consulting/high-level organisation development, accelerated talent development, and sourcing' (Corporate Leadership Council, 1999). Figure 3 shows the many inputs that contribute to the need for HR to grasp this concept. As we shall see in later chapters, the idea of human capital management takes HR on to a different strategic plane. The figure shows that the management of human resources has been affected to a considerable degree by a large number of internal and external factors that bring with them the demand for a more strategic focus and holistic resolution.

The people implications of any of these activities require a strategic perspective on the part of management in general and HR in particular. The joining up of HR activity to make sure that employee relations, reward, training and recruitment/redundancy are integrated – always a fundamental challenge to those in HR – is now a mandatory objective.

What this shows is that some important influences are forcing organisations to regard the management of their people as more than the processing of transactional hygiene factors such as pay or skills training. Instead, organisations

Figure 3 **FACTORS CONTRIBUTING TO THE NEED FOR STRATEGIC HUMAN CAPITAL MANAGEMENT**

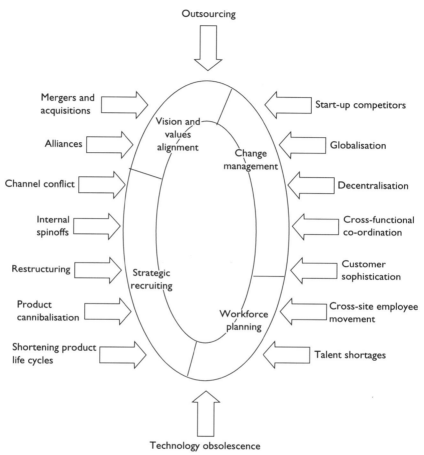

Source: Corporate Leadership Council, (1999)

are having to adopt a more holistic view by which people are seen as a source of competitive advantage, and to acknowledge that sustained organisational success will have demands that transcend the 'normal' packages that constituted the traditional psychological contract.

The 'new era of labour'

This new era presents challenges for the people, for society as a whole, and for the organisations in which they work. There is the challenge of generational complexity. Organisations have to deal with different forces as they try to balance the needs of the four generations of workers they are likely to employ. There is the challenge of aligning the needs of individuals and organisations. And there is the challenge of managing work-flows that transcend the old-order silos of marketing, production, finance, and so on. A very complex model of organisations is emerging, and those responsible for HR will need to be match fit to deal with this new game. They will need new skills and new tools – HR tools that allow a strategic contribution to the organisation.

The main characteristics of this new era (Corporate Leadership Council, 1999) are:

- □ demographic diversity within organisations – the four generations: X, Y, Baby-boomers and 'Matures'
- □ attitudinal change on the part of employees – this leads to an inversion of the traditional approach: rather than organisations' having jobs to offer to potential recruits, now people have careers to which they attach organisations
- □ raised expectations of the new economy – people are living 'portfolio' lives
- □ a greater emphasis on equality and diversity that is derived from sound business arguments as well as from legislative requirements
- □ demand from employees for a better work–life balance
- □ demand from organisations for greater flexibility in their workforces.

The evolution of 'eras' of labour determines the evolution of approach to people management within those eras. Figure 4, for example, shows how the labour market has evolved, and how the approach to recruitment and retention has changed accordingly – the third age being subjected to a more scientific approach to labour market practice. It is possible to replicate these changes in practice against almost any aspect of HR.

Figure 4 **ERAS OF LABOUR MARKET PRACTICE**

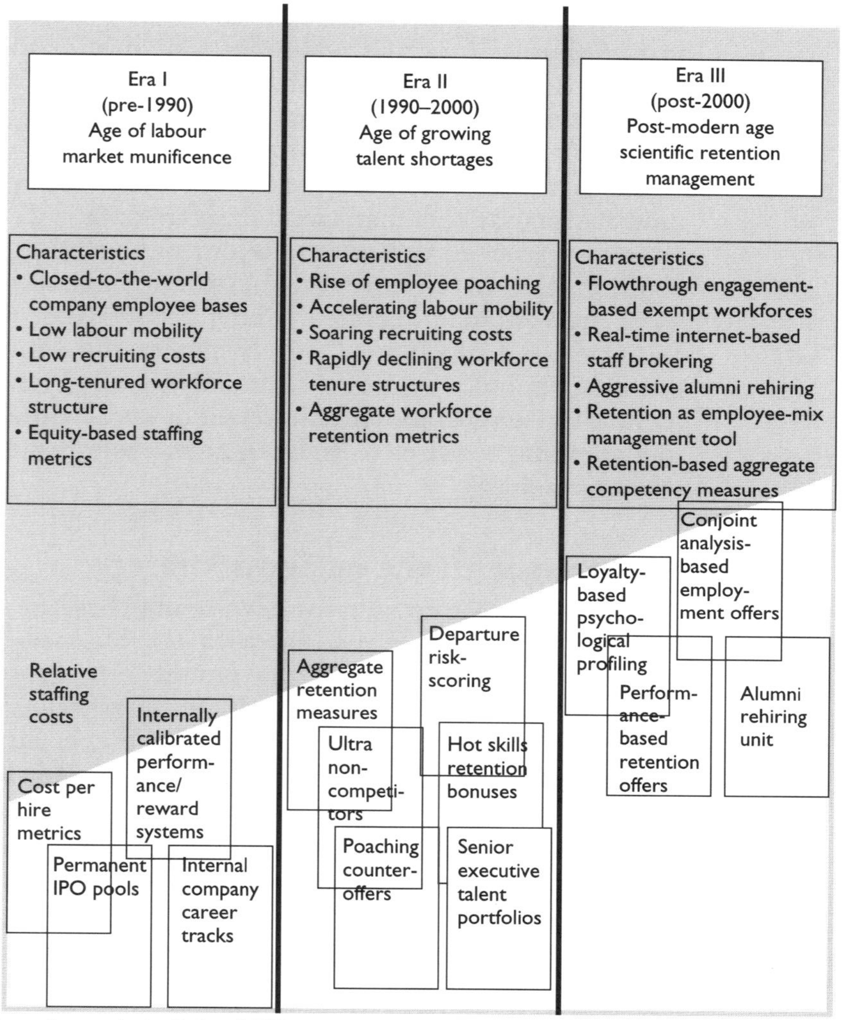

Era I (pre-1990) Age of labour market munificence	Era II (1990–2000) Age of growing talent shortages	Era III (post-2000) Post-modern age scientific retention management
Characteristics • Closed-to-the-world company employee bases • Low labour mobility • Low recruiting costs • Long-tenured workforce structure • Equity-based staffing metrics	**Characteristics** • Rise of employee poaching • Accelerating labour mobility • Soaring recruiting costs • Rapidly declining workforce tenure structures • Aggregate workforce retention metrics	**Characteristics** • Flowthrough engagement-based exempt workforces • Real-time internet-based staff brokering • Aggressive alumni rehiring • Retention as employee-mix management tool • Retention-based aggregate competency measures

Relative staffing costs

Cost per hire metrics

Internally calibrated performance/ reward systems

Permanent IPO pools

Internal company career tracks

Aggregate retention measures

Ultra non-competitors

Poaching counter-offers

Departure risk-scoring

Hot skills retention bonuses

Senior executive talent portfolios

Loyalty-based psychological profiling

Conjoint analysis-based employment offers

Performance-based retention offers

Alumni rehiring unit

Source: Corporate Leadership Council, 1998

Those responsible for HR will need to meet new demands at both individual and organisational level if they are to remain at the forefront of the management of the organisation. Getting to grips with Era III will require new skills. These skills are no longer ones of transactional ability alone. Instead, they are about the need to take a strategic view of the people of an organisation now reflected in the language of human capital. This means a long-term high-level joined-up approach to HRM that features in the organisation's strategic debate as much as technology, finance or marketing. It requires a mindset shift for the HR profession. The ability to contribute forecasts and strategies from a people perspective is now an essential skill for those in HR.

We in the HR profession need to know about how these new factors in the management of people will impact on strategy. We need to know how our organisation is going to position itself in whatever business or organisational environment in which it operates. The role of HR is itself being transformed from one of purely processing transactions to one that includes strategic value adding. Our new tools and techniques will complement those of those other functions in a way that requires us to be in at the very beginning of the strategic debate.

HR strategy starts with the business strategy

An obvious place to start in developing these new tools and techniques would seem to be with the business or organisational strategy. At least this would give those in HR a framework against which to evaluate the people implications of what the organisation is trying to achieve. But even here we might not get the straight answers we are looking for. Organisations have many choices over how they tackle competition or service in their markets. The conventional methodologies of strategic decision-making may not be enough. There are too many contradictions.

Not too long ago I had a meeting with a businessman on Wall Street. I asked him, 'What is the secret of your success?'

He answered, like a character out of *New Yorker* magazine, 'That's easy. I look for a trend in the market going that way.' He raised his arm and pointed over Battery Park, over those beautiful twin towers, towards the Statue of Liberty. He then turned and pointed in exactly the opposite direction, over Brooklyn Bridge. – And then I go that way.'

Back at my desk in a large corporate environment, I looked at the strategic planning documents I had to complete to get a budget for the next three years. The strategic planning process was based on a philosophy that was the opposite of my New Yorker's. Clearly the person who had designed our planning process was a classical scholar – the process was undoubtedly based on the Stoic logic of ancient Greek philosophers. Our strategic plan was based on the assumption that if the organisation applied reason (rather than emotion and passion) to the future, everything else would fall into place.

I now had two diametrically opposing views of how to be successful. And it seemed to me that both were valid. So here I was, faced with clear-cut but almost contradictory choices. This was not very helpful, and even more frustratingly, the dichotomy applies equally to HR strategy.

What should we do in HR when asked to make a contribution to the strategic debate, then? Do we answer 'We must make plans,' or do we leave ourselves in the hands of the goddess Fortuna? Given the importance of people to the achievement of organisational success, though, HR has to take a position. Although we cannot predict the future, we cannot operate in a strategic vacuum. We will be called upon to participate in a process in which we are likely to face some difficult questions about the people implications of strategy. We cannot just walk away to the dark end of the street and whistle.

A mistake often made is to see the intuitive approach of the New Yorker in the example above and the systematic approach of my own organisation at the time as mutually exclusive. Perhaps they were, in the past. Large organisations had to have formal approaches to their resource allocation decisions, often involving millions of dollars. The entrepreneurism of the smaller organisation was difficult to achieve in this large-scale environment. So formal strategy processes were put in place. To balance the formality, such things as intrapreneurism, skunk works and chaos management were encouraged (or tolerated). These were only three of a range of innovative approaches that tried to turn these ocean liners into speedboats. They had mixed success. Nowadays, however, the gap between the extremes of strategy has narrowed because of the changes in organisational structures and decision-making processes. There are likely to be flatter structures, virtual organisations and a mix of approaches.

Larger organisations have tried to emulate some of the practices of their smaller counterparts. Small and medium-sized enterprises (SMEs) have picked up some of the techniques of larger organisations. So the formal strategy versus entrepreneurism approach is not as polarised as it used to be.

In this environment – often confusing, never straightforward – the HR approach might be to combine enough direction to allow us to make plans in line with the business strategy, but at the same time to allow flexibility in the people strategies to take account of other, unexpected, factors. In fact the HR strategy is often a hybrid – a combination of 'prescriptive' economically rational approaches and 'descriptive' cognitive, visionary approaches. This will be examined in greater detail in later chapters.

So what happened to my three-year planning document? Not surprisingly, I completed it. I think I still have it. Somewhere. I never really used it, of course. But I made sure that I influenced the process in future. The experience convinced me that strategy was not about completing documentation but about taking genuine stock of what was going on in the external environment (good and bad) and trying to align all of the processes of the organisation in a way that would maximise opportunity and minimise risk.

Strategy in the new (or knowledge) economy

Today there is a greater recognition for forecasting and planning, which has been precipitated by the economic adjustment that came about when the New Economy turned out to be something different from what we expected. The readjustment converged with other economic and social trends to force a rethink about strategy. As that *zeitgeist* journal of the New Economy *Fast Company* noted (in December 2000):

> We all thought we had it figured out – the New Deal of the new economy. Jump on the fast track. Work your ass off. Make it work for the short term. Grab the payoff. Breathe. Then came the New Economy mid-course correction. All of a sudden we found ourselves making mid-career corrections to our work

and lives. Companies can no longer play the game as a short-term sprint to the payoff counter.

Soon after the 'dot.com readjustment', *Fast Company* included Michael Porter in its hip New Economy pages with an article about 'Big Ideas'. The world's most famous Business School Professor was regarded as a key player in deciding which way was next in this new age (*Fast Company*, March 2001). Porter's foray into strategy and the Internet presented a powerful economic case for strategy and strategic planning processes even in the rollercoaster world of the dot.com. He urged a return to strategic fundamentals, and emphasised the need for them by noting that 'Internet technology provides better opportunities for companies to establish distinctive strategic positionings than did previous generations of information technology' (Porter, 2001).

Certainly, this is a single example of the application of strategy-setting and forecasting principles to the 'unpredictable' world of the New Economy, but Porter's credibility as a strategist has helped those who believe in trying to set direction and plan accordingly. His intervention has added legitimacy to the arguments.

What I want to do is to pass on some ideas about how we might prepare our organisations to deal with the very real people challenges that they will face in the 21st century. I want to propose that the way we do this is through the use of strategic human resource forecasting (SHRF) that is the input to the strategy process, and human resource planning (HRP) that is the output. Both of these are based on the fundamental assumption that HR strategy is aligned to the business strategy. If it is not, then the HR strategy will exist in a vacuum that will ultimately have a deleterious effect on the whole organisation. Later in the chapter I will present some of the models of strategy that might be used to achieve this objective.

HR forecasting and planning starts with business forecasting and planning

The ambivalence we noted in the strategy debate applies equally to that in forecasting and planning. As we have seen, many believe that planning and forecasting are irrelevant: the environment is too unpredictable to be able to plan effectively. There is evidence for this view. The great strategic planning constructions set up in large organisations during the 1960s and 1970s gave strategy and strategic planning a bureaucratic edge that lost touch with the reality of running a business or organisation. Strategic planning lost its credibility. The process became the main objective, and getting the strategic planning documents completed within the timescales was more important than the quality of the output – which invariably went in the bottom drawer (or on to the C-drive) until the time came round again for the next year's submission. It was a strategic merry-go-round that kept planners employed but added little to shareholder value or stakeholder satisfaction.

Business forecasting has been described as 'the study of historical data to discover their underlying tendencies and patterns, and the use of this knowledge to project the data into future time periods. As the world of business has become more complex, the need to assess the future on some rational basis has grown, and forecasting has assumed a prominent position in the business administration process' (Hanke and Reitsch, 1989). The use of forecasting varies from organisation to organisation. It is possible to be successful at forecasting the outcome of a particular situation. It is also possible for forecasting to go wrong – horribly so, in some cases (Rhinehart, 1993):

> I might never have gone on a quest for my father if it hadn't been for unexpectedly light rain in Iowa. I was long three hundred futures contracts of December wheat based on a forecast of torrential rains in the mid-West. I expected the heavy rains to ruin the harvest and raise the price of wheat. Unfortunately, the rains didn't fall mainly on the plain. They fell primarily on Cleveland, Chicago and Detroit, where very little wheat is grown. The price of wheat plummeted the next day and I lost about two million dollars for my clients. My employer called me in for a chat. My clients phoned me for chats. My employees and colleagues avoided me. The only people who phoned or dropped by were people who wanted to shoot me.

It is rarely possible to be completely accurate about business forecasting. As Yale Professor Paul Kennedy has noted, 'Nothing one can say about the future has. . .certainty. Unforeseen happenings, sheer accidents, the halting of a trend, can ruin the most plausible of forecasts. If they do not, then the forecaster is merely lucky' (Kennedy, 1988). Dealing with the future from past experience is thus bound to be 'provisional and conjectural'. But in an age of scarce resource it is essential to try and forecast possible scenarios for their impact on business strategy. This is particularly important now for the impact of human resources forecasts on the strategy and vice versa. The whole question of strategic human resource forecasting should therefore comprise much more than a linear extrapolation of past events.

Business forecasting comes in a variety of shapes and sizes, and there are a number of different methods that those in HR are likely to come across during the organisation's strategy-setting process. An article in the *Sunday Times* noted that leading businesspeople read the 'signs of the times' in different ways (Smith and Rushdie, 2001). These varied from Sir Terence Conran's view that 'restaurants and shops are very firmly on the pulse of public spending,' to that of Sir Richard Branson, who said, 'I use a junk mail index to judge the health of the economy. Last year I received a record amount of junk mail.'

These examples demonstrate the rich nature of forecasting in business and the economy. It can be argued that the unpredictability of the environment means that organisations, and the individuals who run them, will take their direction from both instinct and statistical analysis. But at the same time, forecasting is something that is becoming more sophisticated through the application of new technological tools and techniques.

Models of business and organisational strategy-planning and forecasting

There is a good case to suggest that HR people need to know about strategy. If they do not know, they will not be able to participate in the organisation's strategy-setting process. The organisation's success depends on an HR contribution that is as much about strategy as it is about tactics. So understanding the concept of strategy is a prerequisite of effective strategic human resource forecasting and human resource planning.

HR strategy should be aligned to the business strategy. Because of that it is important that HR professionals know enough about strategy to be able to engage in dialogue with their own business partners. 'Strategic human resource planning and development, which entails the close integration of thinking about future HR needs with thinking about competitive strategy, organisational strategy and the business environment, can and should play a key role in the evolution of specific competitive strategies' (Hamlin *et al*, 2001).

There is no one universal strategy that is relevant to all organisations – no strategic 'theory of everything'. Models of strategy have proliferated over the past 20 years or so, and this makes the choice of strategic process a complicated one. Henry Mintzberg (Mintzberg *et al*, 1998) has identified 10 schools of strategy in two broad groupings, as shown in Table 2. The two groupings are:

- *prescriptive approaches* which tend to be formal and analytical: this type of strategy-setting was predominant during the 1970s and 1980s and, indeed, is still adopted in modified formats

- *descriptive approaches* which involve visioning, emergent and transforming processes, and are based on interaction within the organisation as well as on external analysis: this type of model came into prominence during the 1990s.

Given a wide choice of credible alternatives, the factors that impact on an organisation's choice of strategy will include its history and past experience, its present market position, the amount of change anticipated, and the personal preferences of the chief executive officer! Before HR can expect to participate in the strategic debate, the function will have to understand the particular process for the setting of strategy that is being used. This will inform the approach of the HR community to strategy. In fact, if those in HR misjudge the

Table 2 **THE 10 SCHOOLS OF STRATEGY**

School	Key words	Strategy	Process
Prescriptive schools			
1 Design *a process of conception*	congruence fit distinctive competence competitive advantage	Planned perspective, unique	Simple, informal, judgemental
2 Planning *a formal process*	programming budgeting scheduling scenarios	Plans decomposed into substrategies and programmes	Formal, deliberate
3 Positioning *an analytical process*	generic strategy competitive analysis portfolio	Planned generic positions	Analytical, systemic
Descriptive schools			
4 Entrepreneurial *a visionary process*	bold stroke vision insight	Personal, unique perspective	Visionary, intuitive, emergent
5 Cognitive *a mental process*	map frame concept bounded rationality	Mental perspective	Mental, emergent
6 Learning *an emergent process*	incrementalism emergent	Patterns, unique	Emergent, informal, messy
7 Power *a process of negotiation*	bargaining conflict coalition political game collective strategy	Political and co- operative patterns	Conflictive aggressive
8 Cultural *a collective process*	values beliefs, culture ideology	Collective perspective	Ideological, constrained, collective
9 Environmental *a reactive process*	adaptation evolution	Specific positions	Passive imposed, emergent
10 Configuration *a process of transformation*	configuration stage life cycle turnaround revitalisation	Any of the above, in context	Integrative, episodic, sequenced

After Mintzberg et al, 1998

main acceptance criteria for strategic participation, they are unlikely to be able to influence the people elements at all.

It is worth looking at some of the more prominent strategic models in more detail. Out of the many alternatives, the views of Michael Porter and Henry Mintzberg would seem to exemplify different approaches.

Michael Porter's view of strategy

Without doubt Michael Porter has been one of the foremost experts on business strategy during the past 20 years. His work on competitive strategy and competitive advantage set the agenda for the business debate on the subjects. He has defined the strategy-setting process as 'the search for a favourable competitive position in an industry. . .Competitive strategy aims to establish a profitable and sustainable position against the forces that determine industry competition' (Porter, 1985). It is 'a broad formula for how a business is going to compete, what its goals should be, and what policies will be needed to carry out those goals'. The six principles on which the fundamentals of strategy can be achieved are given (Porter, 2001) as:

□ Start with the right goal.
□ A company's strategy must enable it to deliver a value proposition or set of benefits.
□ Strategy needs to be reflected in a distinctive value chain.
□ Robust strategies must involve trade-offs.
□ Strategy defines how all elements of what a company does fit together.
□ Strategy involves continuity of direction.

In Porter's terms an organisation has to take a clear strategic position, understand that position, and then make sure that its activities along the value chain (sales, marketing, production, HR, and so on) are aimed at achieving or enhancing the strategy. Porter gave three potential positions as 'generic strategies':

□ *Cost leadership*, as the name implies, involves an

organisation's becoming the lowest-cost provider in its industry sector, and competing on that basis in a broad market.

☐ *Differentiation* means achieving a position that has different or unique characteristics in relation to the competition in a narrow market.

☐ *Focus* means achieving competitive advantage in narrow-market segments.

In presenting this clear view of strategy, based on a rational choice of competitive positioning, Porter gave guidelines on how companies could both analyse their strategic possibilities and then apply the outcome to the choice of strategy. The approach was taught extensively in Business Schools around the world, and has been used by countless chief executive officers in their own organisations.

The purpose behind formulating strategy in this way was to achieve an advantageous position for the organisation in its chosen market. If the strategy was successful, it would (according to Hamel and Prahalad, 1994) enable an organisation to generate:

☐ an understanding of how competition for the future is different

☐ a process for finding and gaining insight into tomorrow's opportunities

☐ an ability to energise the company top-to-bottom for what may be a long and arduous journey toward the future

☐ the capacity to outrun competitors and get to the future first, without taking undue risks.

Ultimately, successful strategy would ensure that shareholder value was maximised – 'By estimating the future cash flows associated with each strategy, a company can assess the economic value to shareholders of alternative strategies at the business unit and corporate levels' (Rappaport, 1986).

This, then, is the economic rationally-based case for strategy-setting in commercial organisations.

Evolving views of strategy

Porter's definitions of and objectives for strategy seem straightforward. The problem, of course, is that there are innumerable combinations of goals, objectives, policies and practices. All organisations are different. They have different structures, cultures and values. They have different histories and backgrounds. To apply a rational economic basis alone might not be possible. Organisations also have different markets, customers and shareholder expectations. In these circumstances it is difficult to achieve a simple strategic 'theory of everything'.

Given this stark assumption, then, one of the most difficult challenges facing contemporary organisations, whether they are public or private, is to try to find strategies and strategy-setting processes that are right for them – ones that lead to ways to take some control of their destiny so they are not exclusively subject to the whim of fortune. And in the light of the complexity of organisations and their interactions with markets and customers, views of strategy alternative to those of the rational economically-based school of thought have evolved. A critique of the idea of achieving competitive advantage that perhaps summarises some of the thinking behind these alternatives noted that 'competitive advantage is a concept that often inspires in strategists a form of idol worship – a desire to imitate the strategies that make the most successful companies successful. Every competitive advantage is predicated upon a particular set of conditions that exist at a particular point in time for particular reasons. Many of history's seemingly unassailable advantages have proved transitory because the underlying factors changed. The very existence of competitive advantage sets in motion creative innovations that as competitors strive to level the playing-field, cause the advantage to dissipate' (Christensen, 2001).

There were views less sympathetic to the inherently rational approach. Strategy-setting was not always the result of economic analysis, countered other academics and practitioners. Strategy-setting could be bound up with emotion as well. The chief executive's personal preferences were as powerful as any 'five-forces analysis'.

The alternatives contained views about processes and turbulence and chaos. In particular, the work of Henry Mintzberg and the approach to 'crafting strategy' (Mintzberg, 1987) recognised other forces at work when strategy was being formulated.

Henry Mintzberg's view of strategy

Henry Mintzberg described strategic planning as an oxymoron – which makes his position clear on the subject. In an attempt to guide those whose job it is to put strategy into practice, he described the process of a 'strategy safari' and has identified 10 schools of thought in respect of strategy development. These schools have varied in popularity over time. It is argued that three 'prescriptive' schools were largely dominant during the 1970s and 1980s, but that other 'descriptive' schools rose to the fore in the 1990s. An outline of what might be encompassed in each of these 'schools' is included in Table 2. Mintzberg *et al* then show how they have all fared on a temporal basis, although the conclusion is that 'we have to get beyond the narrowness of each school; we need to know how this beast called strategy formation – which combines all of these schools and more – really lives its life' (Mintzberg *et al*, 1998).

Bob Garratt's work with the leaders of many organisations led him to support such a view. He noted that 'many organisations using strategic planning. . .waste valuable resources in ineffective strategic processes' (Garratt, 2000). Garratt then argues in favour of 'strategic thinking as seeing', an approach very consistent with that put forward by Mintzberg. This view of strategy as an emergent process to be crafted with a broad framework is one that has struck a chord with many who are involved in strategy-setting. The advice to see strategy-setting as a 'safari', and not to adopt a specific school, resonates with many who have been concerned with the unpredictability of strategic decision-making in organisations.

Which strategy to choose?

It should be clear from the above that organisations have choices in how they set business strategy. These cover a broad spectrum ranging from the economic-rational to the visionary. Those in HR will of course have an opinion about which is the right way to set strategy. But the most important thing is for them to find out exactly how the organisation is undertaking its strategy-setting, and to ensure that they conform to it by way of gaining admittance.

These opposing views create an interesting challenge for practitioners. According to the laws of physics, in a head-on collision between two forces, the most powerful force usually prevails. And to date no one view of strategy has proved so powerful that it has become the dominant strategic hypothesis. This creates a problem for those practitioners looking to set strategy in their own organisations.

So where does this leave us in the thorny debate about which strategic process or forecasting methodology to use, and more importantly, which strategy? There is a broad set of views on which path to follow in business or organisational strategy, and on the validity of using forecasting as a tool. Unfortunately, an interesting academic argument may not go down too well with the chief executive who wishes to know in which projects the company should invest or in which markets he or she should develop. He or she is increasingly looking to those who are responsible for human resource management to provide some guidance about the likely trends in the people aspects of the organisation. He or she will also expect some indications about what should be done to ensure that people are a key source of sustainable organisational success. Presenting dilemmas, polarised options or theoretical constructs will not get HR onto the strategic agenda.

It is incumbent on those directing an organisation to take responsibility for evaluating strategic choices on behalf of the employees, shareholders, other stakeholders and themselves. If those strategic choices can be made in a rational way, every effort should be made to do so. Those responsible for HR will be able to use the outcomes of these in their own forecasting and planning. If the strategic choices involve something other than or additional to the rational, then judgmental, political and social influences come to bear. HR will have to participate in the economic, social and political debates over strategy.

In reality, though, the strategy-setting process is not likely to be a linear one based on a clear sequence. It is likely to be more iterative. A way forward is to temper the econometric method for strategy evaluation or forecasting with experiential realism. This principle applies as much to human resource strategy as to business strategy-setting. It will certainly be an important factor in the development of strategic human resource forecasts and human resource plans. Those setting strategy in organisations will make decisions based on personal judgement, emotion and socio-political influences. This should not stop those who have the responsibility for making such decisions from taking account of all other types of rational information and analysis. The role of those responsible for human resources in an organisation is to provide this rationally-derived information in respect of the people implications of strategy, and to combine it with their own unique insight into the people aspects.

It is a requirement of strategic human resource forecasting that some basic questions are answered:

- [ ] how many people the organisation needs to achieve its business or organisational strategy
- [ ] what kind of skills those people need
- [ ] what kind of management culture should prevail in the quest for sustained organisational success
- [ ] how leaders can provide direction in a prevailing culture or, indeed, how culture should be changed
- [ ] how employees can be engaged within the organisation's mission.

Furthermore, once these questions have been answered it is then the role of HR to convert the outcome into HR plans.

What would be useful is to know how SHRF and HRP can make a difference. After all, manpower planning has hardly set the world alight in recent times. . .

3 FROM MANPOWER PLANNING TO STRATEGIC HUMAN RESOURCE FORECASTING

The manpower planning record

Having presented the case for strategy and planning in the previous chapters, the next logical step is to look at the specific tools and techniques by which those in HR can make their contribution.

Yet I sometimes think that another review of manpower planning will do no more than confuse an already bad situation. We all need some form of manpower planning, though – maybe not some of the traditional forms of manpower planning that added little value because they went out of date almost as soon as they were written. But a new improved formula would help. The problem is that such a formula, in the singular, is difficult to create, given the complexity and diversity of our working environment. And yet, as we have seen from the previous chapters, the need for forecasts, strategy and plans has never been greater. Nor has the pressure been on HR as much as it is today to provide expert people input on strategy and planning.

This chapter looks at what we can do to position HR both strategically and operationally by providing input into the strategy debate via the SHRF and HRP. A starting-point will be to review what has worked and what has not worked in the planning arena, and to take this learning into the future by converting it into something that is of practical use. The result should be clear definitions for both strategic human resource forecasting and human resource planning which form the rest of this book.

Unfortunately, we cannot ignore the track record for manpower planning. It has not been very good. There are some exceptions to this sweeping generalisation, of course. At the HR 'summit' in Montreux, early in 2001, the senior Vice-President of Ericsson described the successful approach that had allowed them to recruit 80,000 people in eight years. Likewise the head of HR research at Deutsche Bank spoke of the plans they had put in place to make sure that their human resources activity enhanced employee commitment. In both cases human resource planning in its broadest sense had contributed to success (Britt Reigo and Dr Silvia Steffens Duch, 2001).

Learning from experience

By the end of the 1990s the unprecedented pace of change in organisations led to criticism of the traditional approach to manpower planning as being 'prescriptive, over-centralised and lacking in flexibility in planning for people under turbulent conditions' (bin Idris and Eldridge, 1998). This was a fairly widespread overview. Two reasons for so much negative press towards manpower planning might be put forward:

☐ the inflexibility of traditional approaches

☐ the sheer amount of change that has gone on in the external environment, making it difficult to plan with oldfashioned tools and techniques.

This is a problem for all those who work in organisations. Thornton May summarised the issue rather succinctly when he noted that 'In the old economy, executives had a choice. They could be fast or they could be smart. They could "do" or they could "think". They could not do both. The function of planning (the equivalent of organisational learning) was structurally separated from the operation of the enterprise' (*Fast Company*, FC learning, Core curriculum). This observation is as true for manpower planning as it is for any other type of business planning, and it is one we need to deal with if we are to advance the role of HR into a strategic one. Our human resource plans need to be strategic with an operational edge.

The evolution of manpower planning

Manpower planning is not a new concept. It has a long history. The ability to mobilise human resource in a planned way was even a feature of the success of the Roman Empire more than 2,000 years ago. So much so that when Hannibal arrived at the gates of Rome, 'he found three armies in order of battle prepared to receive him.' This was in spite of other military campaigns elsewhere. The way the Romans were able to do this was by training every citizen 'in the discipline of the soldier' (Gibbon, 1781) and making sure that senators were trained in the art of generalship. In Roman terms, the planning and creation of a succession of leaders and a flexible workforce, albeit a military one, was an attribute of their sense of anticipation of and planning for untoward circumstances. Until the decline and fall, that is.

But what is important here is that manpower planning in the Roman Empire was not a static entity that bore no relation to experience. It was dynamic. Circumstances were reviewed constantly and strategies adapted accordingly. The same principles of challenge and response can also be applied to human resource planning. It should be the foundation on which good business and organisational performance depends. This is so obvious that it is difficult to believe people have queried the need to plan. Perhaps it is because the traditional approaches to planning have not delivered what they promised.

Modern manpower planning (in its various guises, for example human resource planning, strategic manpower planning, and corporate manpower planning) has been treated to a mixed reception. It has been seen as a tactical rather than a strategic activity, as no more than a numerical analysis. Research has shown that 'traditional approaches to manpower planning have tended to delimit and define it as a central personnel activity, which attempts to reconcile an organisation's need for labour with the available supply in local and national labour markets' (Beardwell and Holden, 1997).

Traditional manpower planning tended to adopt a mechanical approach, with the objective of perfect equilibrium, to be reached by analysing shortfalls and surfeits of labour. In an ideal world this would provide a logical, rational basis to people issues during the planning process. And that is perhaps the primary problem with traditional manpower planning approaches – we do not live in an ideal world. The manpower plan of an organisation has to be adaptable and flexible (within a framework).

Manpower planning appears to have been borne out of the economic need to ensure that there were enough people to satisfy a rationally-derived business or organisational strategy. This sentiment can be seen in definitions of manpower planning over the past 20 years or so:

☐ *1970s* – 'Manpower planning has been defined as a strategy for the acquisition, utilisation, improvement and preservation of an enterprise's human resources' (Stainer 1971).

☐ *1980s* – 'Corporate manpower planning is the planning of personnel for large organisations. . .manpower planning is the process of forecasting manpower requirement and manpower availability, and matching their demand and supply' (Verhoeven, 1982).

☐ *1990s* – 'The purpose of manpower planning is to provide continuity of efficient manning for the total business, and optimum use of manpower resources, although that optimum utilisation of people is heavily influenced by organisation and corporate culture' (McBeath, 1992).

Attempts were made to achieve more of a dialogue in its preparation, but in spite of the inclusiveness of the process and the evolution of the concept of manpower planning through the decades, there was still scepticism about its effectiveness. More often than not, it did not fit together at all.

One of the leading authors on the subject of manpower and human resource planning is John Bramham. His framework for manpower control was one that articulated the 'matching' approach inherent in the manpower plan (see Figure 5). Manpower planning in this form seems to be at its most effective when put alongside the rational approach to strategy-setting as an economic process of identifying market opportunities and filling them with organisational responses. However, its weaknesses are also derived from this close correlation with a largely rational, economic-based approach. There was perhaps an inherent instability in business plans derived in this way, given the unpredictability of market forces and the sheer dynamics of organisations that questioned the traditional approach to manpower planning. Furthermore, it has been argued that manpower planning in this way did not – and, indeed, could not – take enough account of the

Figure 5 FRAMEWORK FOR MANPOWER CONTROL (THE 'MANPOWER PLAN')

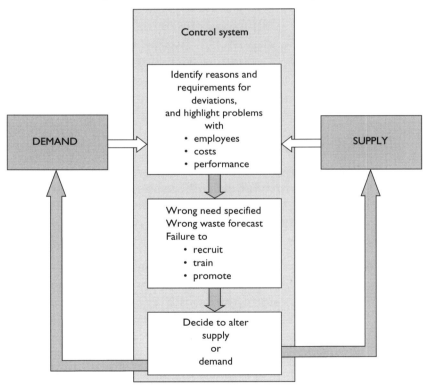

After Bramham, 1988

complexity of both external and internal factors: it was too rigid. But, in large organisations this was (and still is) a fairly normal approach.

Human resource planning

So a different approach, 'human resource planning', was born. It was an attempt to make the process a more dynamic and iterative one. According to this view the human resource plan 'consists of a range of tasks designed to ensure that the appropriate number of the right people are in the right place at the right time. In essence it involves assessing the current levels and utilisation of staff and skills, relating the internal elements to the market demand for the organisation's products, and providing alternatives to match human resources with anticipated demand' (Zeffane and Mayo, 1994). But most importantly it is 'fundamentally a dynamic process that endeavours to monitor and manage the flow of people into, through, and out of the organisation.' It is the use of the language of movement that is the key indicator of the nature of human resource planning in this definition.

Nevertheless it remains a moot point whether manpower planning has made the transition to a more strategic level. As Lundy and Cowling (1996) say:

> There is still some debate on the extent to which manpower planning has successfully transferred into human resource planning (HRP). In HRP the manager is concerned with motivating people – a process in which costs, numbers, controls and systems interact and play a part. In manpower planning the manager is concerned with the numerical elements of forecasting supply, demand matching and control, in which people are a part. There are therefore important areas of overlap and interconnections – but there is a fundamental difference in underlying approach.

In the light of the inherent problems associated with matching the demand and supply of labour in the type of turbulent environment of the recent past, the credibility of manpower planning has been reduced. A recent study concluded that manpower planning was a 'tedious mathematical technique, largely ignored' (Rothwell, 1995).

Human resource planning in practice

Manpower planning can be best summarised as a principle based on good intentions and sound logic, undermined by an external environment that rarely follows logic and by internal organisational forces that are constantly on the move. And yet organisations have continued to do some sort of planning in spite of its limitations, almost regardless of what academic research says they should or should not do. Studies have shown that over time the use of manpower or human resource planning has prevailed, in spite of many perceived and actual limitations. A 1988 survey showed that at the time 60 per cent of respondents used manpower planning to identify future training needs, 50 per cent to analyse labour costs and productivity, and 40 per cent to review changes in the labour market (Cowling and Walters, 1988). By 1999, Tyson and Doherty's report on 'Human Resource Excellence' showed that in the 50 organisations surveyed there was a considerable 'planning presence' (Tyson and Doherty, 1999).

What these two studies show was that in the organisations surveyed, HR strategy and planning were present either as entire processes or as processes to deal with particular aspects of HR (such as training). Of course, this is not comparing like for like, and so makes any conclusion circumstantial at best. But what the studies suggest is that manpower or human resource planning in some form has endured. We can conclude from Tyson and Doherty's study that in those organisations surveyed, the majority had a long-term human resource strategy, and that it carried with it longer-term human resource planning activity. Leaving aside the possibility that this strategic HR activity might have been a mere formality, then, those who advocated the death of the 'five-year plan' must have been shocked at these findings. How was it possible for organisations to ignore the research, which showed that the plans over three to five years were flawed because of the fast-moving and unpredictable environment?

Actually, it is not so surprising. Organisations often feel they must show that they have some idea how they should deploy their resources over time. For most, it is not enough to let things evolve. Stakeholders require the senior management of the organisation to demonstrate that they have objectives and plans for future directions. There is no doubt that flexibility is a necessary requirement for all organisations in the 21st century, but there is a big difference between flexibility and anarchy.

Shareholders, employees and managers are aware of the need to deploy scarce resources effectively. Hence the continuing preparation of strategic plans in a modified form (ie not the great complex constructions of a previous age). The SHRF and HRP processes should therefore take the learning from these previous eras and lend themselves to adaptation accordingly. Turbulence and unpredictability are not mutually exclusive to the need to allocate resources in the best way for the organisation. Human resource planning continues to be a useful HR tool. Indeed, a recent study of the HR implications of the new economy highlighted 'global workforce management' and 'long-range workforce planning' as two key components of the human capital model (Corporate Leadership Council, 1999). But surely this case should not rest on some of the rather flimsy mechanical approaches that led to the demise of manpower planning. So what can be learned from such previous experiences?

A successful approach to human resource planning

We have seen above that manpower planning in its traditional form was not 100-per-cent successful and that a new approach was called for. Nonetheless, an effective 'processual' perspective of HR planning, outlined by Carole Tansley, might be one that is a useful guide. The key considerations for successful human resource planning might be listed as:

☐ HR planning must always be seen within the strategy-making context.

☐ In particular, human resource planning can most usefully be defined as the relatively specific element of HR strategy-making that proposes appropriate actions with regard to human resourcing.

☐ HR planning involves the creation of formal and explicit

sets of proposals intended to achieve actions that will help achieve long-term organisational performance.

☐ The challenge for those undertaking HR planning is therefore to propose actions that contribute to long-term corporate success, not only by being prepared to take into account surprise circumstances but also by introducing new ways of thinking.

☐ This requires that there is sufficient openness or flexibility about the direction proposed.

☐ It also requires that there are opportunities for the variety of individuals and groups that make up an organisation to have an input into both the *thinking* and the *action* implicit in planning.

☐ The *systems* and *processual* perspectives provide two different ways of viewing the relationship between an organisation and the individuals who constitute that organisation.

☐ HR planning involves a combination of thinking and acting, so can usefully be seen in process terms. This involves the incorporation of continual experimentation, revision and rethinking in which processes of argument, debate and conflict between different managers and interest groups play a part.

Can the previous dialogue provide the basis for decision-making on which type of planning process to advocate in an organisation? These conclusions certainly provide an excellent backdrop to SHRF and HRP. They recognise that the 'soft' processual approach is the contemporary view and has features that are appropriate to the type of environment in which many (if not most) organisations operate. However, it may not always be the case that such an approach is feasible. The rigidity of the strategic planning process may prevent new interventions, as mentioned above. In such an event the HR community invariably offers a hybrid approach combining softer aspects with the hard realities of traditional planning.

We can certainly learn enough from the detritus of historical manpower planning to be able to formulate something that is meaningful, adds value and incorporates both thinking and doing. The strategies for doing so are twofold:

☐ Make strategic human resource forecasting an integral part of the strategy-setting process in business or public sector organisations.

☐ Ensure that the human resource plan is an integral part of the overall strategic plan in those organisations.

This might be achieved by providing a means of ensuring that strategy takes account of the human dimension of an organisation such that human resources are regarded as a potential source of sustained organisational success – and by ensuring that the allocation of resources to people considerations are helped by having a coherent plan.

Strategy, planning and forecasting for HR professionals

The previous chapters have outlined the main arguments in favour of a new approach to strategy-planning and forecasting for HR professionals, as well as the strategic models that are likely to be encountered during this process. The main reasons for the use of strategic human resource forecasting and human resource planning are:

☐ to ensure that an organisation takes account of people as contributors to its success by recognising their unique contribution to strategic direction and performance

☐ to align and integrate people strategies with organisational strategies

☐ to ensure that the demand for people numbers, knowledge, skills, attitudes and values are matched with the supply of these attributes

☐ to provide a process by which people considerations are raised early in the strategy-setting debate and to ensure that business-based plans are put in place for the people outcomes of this debate.

Strategic human resource forecasting and human resource planning should go beyond the application of quantitative methods to 'headcount' management if they are to achieve the important objective of alignment to business strategy. Although headcount forecasting and management will continue to play a key part in both strategic human resource forecasting and human resource planning, other considerations will be as relevant to the contemporary view. These considerations will include organisational culture, organisational development and organisational 'well-being', amongst other things. Particular importance will be attached to the development and retention of talent and, significantly, the nature and application of leadership in the achievement of strategic goals. These 'softer' aspects of human resource management have come to assume an increasing prominence in the successful implementation of strategy. Even though they are categorised as 'soft', they are often the hardest to deal with, and the process of SHRF and HRP will have to provide a framework for doing so.

What is needed, then, are some tools and techniques that will enable us to convert these theoretical constructs into something that can be used in the workplace. The two processes recommended are those of strategic human resource forecasting and human resource planning, and these are defined below.

A definition of strategic human resource forecasting

For the purposes of this book strategic human resource forecasting may be defined as:

☐ a process by which an organisation looks ahead at the people implications of business and organisational strategy, and facilitates a dialogue within the organisation about these implications. Its objective is to give direction to the people decisions to be made at strategic level that will enable the organisation to achieve sustained success. It is concerned with external commercial, political and technological forces and their effect on people in the organisation. It is also concerned with the internal behavioural or sociological dynamic of both the individual and the organisation as a whole. The SHRF deals with the quantification of the people implications of business or organisational strategy and the likely qualitative inputs or outputs of the strategy.

The SHRF comprises a process intended to form an intervention into the strategic planning process or the strategy-setting process of the organisation. It consists of groups of strategic HR activities:

□ dialogue with strategy-makers

□ scenario planning aligned to the business or organisational strategy

□ demand-and-supply forecasts for the people aspects of strategy

□ gap analysis

□ input to the HR plan.

Once SHRF has become an input to the strategy-setting process in an organisation, the output will need to be converted into something that will enable those in HR to allocate their own resources in a way aligned to business or organisational strategy. This is shown in Figure 6.

A definition of human resource planning

The human resource plan (Figure 7) may be defined as:

□ the output that arises from the process of business or organisational strategy-setting as it affects the people in an organisation. It contains quantitative analyses of HR data ranging from headcount and costs to qualitative analyses about culture, learning and knowledge management. The HRP is a dynamic entity that can be changed if turbulence or unpredicted extraneous factors affect the business strategy.

It consists of a range of plans within the key HR activities. These can be grouped as follows:

□ resourcing through specific organisational design, quantified HR plans and resource allocation

□ employee commitment and relations

Figure 6 **THE STRATEGIC HUMAN RESOURCE FORECAST – THE PROCESS**

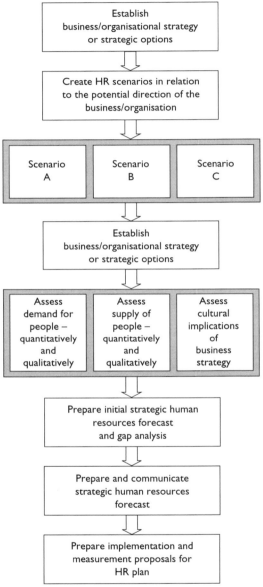

Figure 7 **THE HUMAN RESOURCE PLAN**

The human resource plan					
Organisational design and development	Resourcing plan	Training and development plan	Quantified resource plan	Reward plan	Employee relations plan

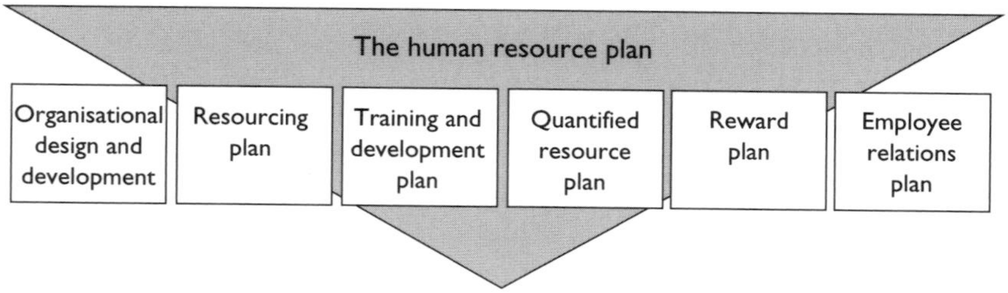

- ☐ learning, training and development
- ☐ reward and recognition.

The component parts of these models will be used to form the basis of succeeding chapters.

PART II

THE STRATEGIC HUMAN RESOURCE FORECAST

4 THE COMPONENT PARTS OF THE STRATEGIC HUMAN RESOURCE FORECAST

We have already seen that business or organisational strategy-setting is an iterative process that has a number of inputs – including financial or marketing data, political or techno-logical analysis, and an assessment of the core competencies of the organisation. The objective is to give a direction to the organisation that enables resources to be allocated to the most appropriate areas. Such a process allows stakeholders to see how their 'investment' is being utilised and whether they are getting the best returns for this investment. In business this might be a financial stake; in public sector or not-for-profit organisations it might be through services to the community.

Further significant inputs into this process are the people implications of strategy. Again, we have defined the strategic human resource forecast (SHRF) in a comprehensive way that embraces a wide spectrum of people issues – with the result that the SHRF is HR's key input during the strategy-setting process. It is worth noting that the SHRF is not a plan. It is not the human resource plan (HRP), which is an output of the strategic debate. The two should not be confused.

As Garratt has noted, 'Directing an organisation is very different from managing one...planning is a process after strategic thinking' (Garratt, 1995). The SHRF is a contribution to the direction of the organisation, not its subsequent man-agement. It is a contribution to the strategic thinking that takes place during the strategy-setting process.

The process of forecasting

The SHRF is based on an iterative process that takes its initial feed from the business or organisational strategy and works through the strategic dialogue to the HRP, the people output of strategic planning. The component parts of the SHRF are included in Figure 6, but a checklist summarises succinctly:

- establishing business or organisational strategy or strategic options
- creating HR scenarios
- assessing demand
- assessing supply
- assessing the cultural implications of the business strategy
- preparing the initial SHRF
- moving to the HRP.

A summary of what is included in each of these components follows – each is dealt with in more detail in subsequent chapters – and represents proposals only. They are not intended to provide a planning panacea. Instead, the later chapters present options that will undoubtedly have to be adapted to the individual needs and culture of the organisation.

Establishing business or organisational strategy or strategic options

This will involve those responsible for HRM in the organisation 'sitting at the top table' during the strategic debates that take place. It requires a good understanding of the business implications of the strategies that are being proposed – for example:

- If these are about taking the business into new markets, then the implications relating to the competencies of people must be identified.
- If these are about the acquisition of a company, then the implications relating to the cultural compatibility of both organisations will have to be understood.
- If the strategy is to downsize or outsource to reduce costs,

then the implications for industrial relations must be included as part of the SHRF process.

The involvement of HR at this point is an increasingly accepted part of the business planning cycle because of the recognition that inappropriate skill sets, organisation design or culture can impair the chances of strategic success. Once theoretical concepts, such as the war for talent, are now very real challenges to most organisations – the bulk of which will fall on HR to resolve. Those responsible for HR must draw attention to the labour implications of any particular strategy and will therefore have to have a full understanding of that strategy.

Creating HR scenarios

Scenario planning is something that is well established at organisations like Shell, who have used the process for many years. It is also something that could be applied by HR in the SHRF process. For each of the strategic options that are identified, a series of HR scenarios can be created. This means trying to anticipate the people implications of the possible strategic options. For example, the entry into new markets might require a recruitment campaign for new sales people, new production facilities to deal with increased output, and so on. These are the likely people outcomes of a strategic option.

Those responsible for HRM will need to raise the profile of the people issues around each of the scenarios so that the strategic debate can take these into account as they continue. The scenarios will include 'soft' issues of culture and competence as well as 'hard' issues of headcount management. If properly used, scenario planning can be a powerful wake-up call for those issues that tend to be 'off the radar'.

Assessing demand

In traditional manpower planning and forecasting, demand management has tended to be solely concerned with headcount. However, the idea would be better broadened to include other concepts that are critical to the people aspect of strategy. This relates to demand for skills as much as demand for numbers. The demand forecast will stem directly from the financial, sales or production forecasts.

This part of SHRF is likely to include a statistical input, and will require an understanding on the part of HR personnel of some basic techniques for calculating turnover and other factors that influence demand.

Assessing supply

Supply factors include an internal analysis of potential, but have a particular focus on external variables such as demographics, overall country or regional skills levels, and so on. At the very highest level the supply side of the SHRF will include information about 'labour' in the economy as a whole. It will take a macro-level view of the whole economic 'life cycle' of human resource, and how this is being dealt with at government level, since national policy will have an impact on the availability of numbers and skills.

An example of this would be the impact of the Learning and Skills Councils launched in 2001. The government was anxious to align skills development to the workplace and restructured the TECs into 47 LSCs working closely with the Regional Development Agencies. Any organisation that has to recruit and develop labour is influenced by this national initiative and needs to take it into account during the SHRF process.

Assessing the cultural implications of the business strategy

This is the area that is perhaps the most difficult to integrate into the strategy-setting process. Yet it is likely to be one of the most critical success factors of some strategies. For example, if a merger or acquisition is proposed, then the success of that strategy will be as much about cultural integration as economic integration. Of all the parts of the SHRF this area is the one where those responsible for HRM will find the most difficulty in including themselves in the strategic dialogue. It is also an area in which HRM has a unique insight and contribution, and such inclusion should therefore be promoted with vigour.

A recent study of the global Deutsche Bank demonstrated

the importance of culture to business success if 'commit-ment' was a part of the cultural mix. The study concluded that employee commitment was a distinctive feature between successful and less successful companies, and that 'employee commitment was a precondition for success' in the service profit chain (Steffens Duch, 2001). Furthermore, Ericsson, the global telecommunications provider, has recognised this critical aspect of success by appointing a senior Vice-President in charge of people and culture. The company developed a clear link between values, behaviours and culture. The values of professionalism, respect and perseverance were ultimately converted into the behaviours of 'passion to win, dedication to customer success, fast urgent creativity, value-adding teamwork' (Reigo, 2001).

Preparing the initial SHRF

It is possible to regard the SHRF as a single published docu-ment that enables the people input to strategy-setting to be well represented. In that case it results from the dialogue that takes place between HR and business managers about strategy. However, it is equally likely that the SHRF is not as structured as this implies. Instead, it may be an input that is constantly updated. The various options that are proposed will be refined as the debate progresses, and will eventually be narrowed to those with which the stakeholders of the organisation feel most comfortable. The SHRF then becomes more focused in its scope as the process moves towards its later stages.

Moving to the HRP

The preparation of a human resource plan comes after the natural outcome of the strategy-setting process. Once the debate has taken place about the strategic options that are favoured by the organisation, it becomes necessary to provide more detail about the people implications (and costs) of those strategic options. This is the point at which the human resource plan is developed. The HRP articulates the detailed requirements from each of the key areas of HR – recruitment and training, employee relations, and so on.

Who prepares the SHRF and HRP, and how it is done

The human resource function takes the lead in the preparation of the strategic human resource forecast and human resource plan. However, the nature of the process as it has evolved means that it is now by means of a dialogue rather than as a stand-alone activity within the confines of HR. It is important that those responsible for HR are proactive in getting their voice heard on the subject of strategy. It is no longer enough to 'sweep up' the human remnants of strategic plans. If we believe that people are key to competitive advantage, then people issues must be included in the strategy-setting process. This is something that those responsible for HR need to emphasise continually (it might not be the natural conclusion reached by all parts of the organisation). SHRF happens at the intersection of the various interest groups in strategy-setting, as shown in Figure 8.

What this Venn diagram depicts is the overlap of the various 'actors' in the SHRF process. The board of directors interfaces with the business managers in setting objectives,

Figure 8 **THE INTERACTION BETWEEN INTEREST GROUPS DURING THE SHRF PROCESS**

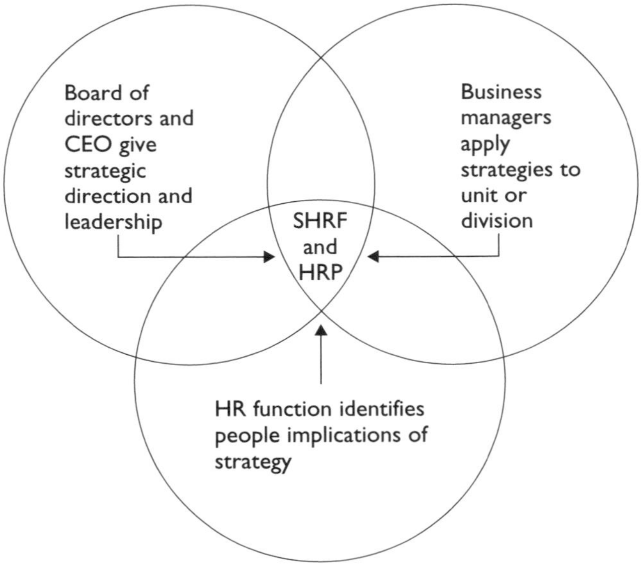

Board of directors and CEO give strategic direction and leadership

Business managers apply strategies to unit or division

SHRF and HRP

HR function identifies people implications of strategy

shareholder value or customer service targets and overall strategic direction. The board works with HR to establish the employment principles on such issues as diversity, remuneration and succession. HR works with the business managers on the people implications of their individual strategies. The board, HR and business managers then converge in an agreement on the eventual direction, strategy and human implications of how the business chooses to compete or how the organisation chooses to manage.

The facilitation of the preparation of the SHRF and HRP will be an HR activity. However, it is essential that consultation takes place with those who lead and manage those areas outside HR, including the chief executive officer and the directors of divisions, subsidiary businesses or functions within the organisation. Table 3 illustrates how the various parts of the process might evolve, who is involved in the process, and delineates the HR role. It is evident from the table that the HR director will be the main interface at each of the stages of the SHRF. He or she will provide a general input in the broader discussions of strategy but will draw on technical HR expertise for specialist areas (training, IR/ER, reward, and diversity). The HR director has a unique role to play, providing a 'people input' that does not fall specifically to any other functional director. However, in this model, the HR director is also a business director and will engage in strategic debate as an equal member of the board. The HR director's opinion on marketing or finance is one that is as valid as the marketing or finance director's view of human resources.

A project plan for the SHRF

The complexity of integrating the SHRF with other parts of the strategic planning process might imply the preparation of a project plan using whatever convention the organisation has in place for its project management methodology. Typically, the project plan would identify start and finish dates for each element of the SHRF, map these onto an overall programme, and highlight the links or dependencies between each activity. The successful delivery of such a complex set

Table 3 STRATEGIC HUMAN RESOURCE FORECASTING – ROLES AND RESPONSIBILITIES

Strategic human resource forecasting process	Who is involved	How they are involved	HR role
Business or organisational strategy-setting	• Chief executive officer – lead role • Managing directors • Functional directors • HR director	• General direction • Dialogue during strategic planning cycle • Strategic initiatives • Strategic projects	• Works with CEO and MDs to ensure that HR implications of business strategy are integral to process • Scans environment and adds input to process
Creating HR scenarios from business strategy	• HR director – lead role • Managing directors • Functional directors	• Dialogue between HR and business or functions • Dialogue with HR	• Joins in proactive dialogue with MDs
Assessing implications of business or organisational strategy on people	• HR director – lead role • HR policy staff • Personnel • Training • IR/ER • Reward • Diversity/equal opportunities	• Dialogue during HR strategic forecasting process	• Analyses business or organisation strategy and highlights issues
Assessing demand	• HR director – lead role • Local/regional personnel and training teams • Local and regional business managers	• Quantification of headcount • Quantification of skills	• Provides research and information

Assessing supply	• HR director – lead role • Local/regional personnel and training teams • Local and regional business managers	• Producing labour market data and feeding it into process	• Provides research and information
Assessing cultural implications	• HR director – lead role • External suppliers of cultural audit or staff attitude services	• Identification of new type of organisational culture required	• Undertakes cultural audit
Preparing strategic HR forecast	• HR director – lead role	• Strategic implications of people issues	• Prepares SHRF for inclusion in overall strategic plan
Implementation and measurement	• Chief executive officer – lead role • Managing directors • HR director	• Delivering measures of success and quantifying them	• Quantitative measurement of people aspects of strategy

of activities may be enhanced considerably by applying a rigorous methodology to project management. This is increasingly becoming a requirement of those in HR, for whom project skills should now be seen as an essential part of the armoury.

5 DEVELOPING ORGANISATIONAL STRATEGY AND STRATEGIC OPTIONS

> ## Strategy in organisations
>
> Culture changes slowly, whereas strategies – more concrete – are constantly refined. Nevertheless, strategy and culture go hand in hand.
>
> Change the name (as is now increasingly the custom, to an indefinite article or to a cast-off from the car manufacturers' model name handbook), change the logo, throw in a few coffee-tables and some ambient lighting if you must – but short cuts may change look and feel. They are unlikely to change the way a company enacts its business. Strategies, in general, require that to happen, and failing to recognise that the fabric is more influential than the fabrics can spike strategies just as surely as exchange rates, market conditions, or Acts of God.
>
> If we truly know our culture at all (and seeing ourselves as others see us is as difficult at company level as it is for the individual), then we have to know that strategy can be delivered by the kind of margins of change to which culture reacts. New processes, new people, new approaches to authority and responsibility can deliver change, but rarely at the pace or on the scale we may have anticipated or wished – and yet in reality, this *is* the pace and scale we should expect. Recognising this, and that the larger and more established the organisation, the less likely it is to leap wholeheartedly into a new cultural world, companies have begun to form conjoined but separate organisations when strategies call for a truly new approach, quickly.

The Prudential did not try to turn itself from Reliable Insurer into Online Bank – it gave birth to Egg: new people, new approach, new governance mechanics, and instant new culture. Dixons, high-street white-and-silver-goods retailer, became the UK's leading ISP by being something other than Dixons, giving the thirty-somethings free reign to be Freeserve.

If strategic goals can be delivered by the evolution of the culture you have, then it is possible to make yourself a better fit for the defined future. If the requirement is truly new, or counter-cultural, then either accept that you have a long road to travel or look to take the delivery away from where the embedded attitudes can swallow it up. As many major, established, culturally developed organisations have discovered in the rush to emulate the energies of the new millennium's briefly ascendant entrepreneurs, just taking off your tie and jacket does not turn you from Sow's Ear plc into Silkpurse.com.

Peter Empringham
Vice President, Concert

Developing strategy and strategic options

This chapter is intended to provide a practical view of HR's specific role in the development of organisational strategy and strategic options. Without an understanding of and participation in the organisation's strategy, those responsible for HR will not be able to provide the unique insights that form the core competence of the profession. The application of these insights is essential if the organisation is to achieve sustained competitive or service success. The process of developing organisational strategy is the entrée of HR into the development of competitive advantage. This entrée or intervention starts with the board and cascades down through all the strategic decision-making bodies of the organisation.

The process for developing strategic options and HR's role in it is outlined in Figure 9.

Each component of this process forms an important step. The parts are not necessarily sequential but often take place in a parallel process like so much of the organisation's strategic decision-making. However, before going into detail it is worth looking at the overall roles and responsibilities of key

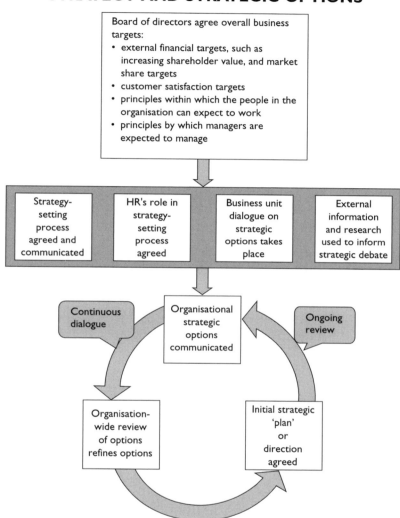

Figure 9 **DEVELOPING ORGANISATIONAL STRATEGY AND STRATEGIC OPTIONS**

players in the organisation to determine how those respons-ible for HR might interface during the process.

Strategy-setting and planning – a resumé

We have looked at the debate over strategy-setting and stra-tegic planning – and the arguments both for and against having some kind of formal process. My belief is that there should be a process, but that we must avoid the rigidity in making strategic plans that characterises some of the poorer examples and case studies.

In Alan West's excellent book on *Innovation Strategy* (1992) he articulated the case for strategy extremely well, and his words are ones that the HR community should take to heart lest we become culprits of the 'Let's just get on with it' school of management:

> Long-term studies show the value of strategic planning. For example, one investigation of small firms in the southern United States showed that planners are far more likely to survive than non-planners. Strategic planning, though not a universal road to riches, at least seemed to minimise the risks of failure.

The sentiment behind this particular statement has endured over the past decade and, indeed, has probably been reinforced by the dot.com rollercoaster ride. This is not planning as a rigid doctrine, but planning as a way of allocating resource to the most appropriate place in the organisation.

The key for organisations is not to make the strategic plan the objective of the strategy-setting process but a vehicle by which strategy is set. It is a tool of strategy and not its primary goal. In this respect those responsible for HR would be well advised to get to know the process, whatever it is, so that they can participate fully in inputs and influence any outputs.

HR and the board

To do so means that those in HR have to understand the role of the board in strategy-setting, since this forum is the ultimate arbiter of strategy. Bob Garratt, one of the UK's leading consultants on corporate governance, has described strategic thinking as a process by which directors 'can rise above the daily managerial processes and crises to gain different perspectives of the internal and external dynamics causing change in their environment and thereby give more effective direction to their organisation. Such perspectives should be both future-oriented and historically understood' (Garratt, 1995).

So what is the role of the board in this strategic thinking process, and how should HR be involved? The framework for analysing board activities is shown in Figure 10. This describes how boards of directors look outward to strategy formulation and inward to policy-making. There are significant people implications for both perspectives, and HR should be involved accordingly.

The board of directors will provide governance as to which strategies the organisation chooses. This process will include decisions on which markets the organisation should be competing in, the level of financial returns to shareholders, and the ratification of an organisational design that is best for both. It will, increasingly, provide a forum for people issues. These will include succession management, remuneration and diversity. Levels of staff satisfaction, now that these are closely correlated with customer satisfaction, will also be on the corporate agenda. It will be a requirement for HR to provide the board with information and advice on these issues. As a further output, the board will be very interested

Figure 10 **FRAMEWORK FOR ANALYSING BOARD ACTIVITIES**

	Past- and present-oriented	Future-oriented
Outward-looking	Providing accountability	Formulating strategy
	Approve and work with and through the CEO	
Inward-looking	Monitoring and supervising	Policy-making

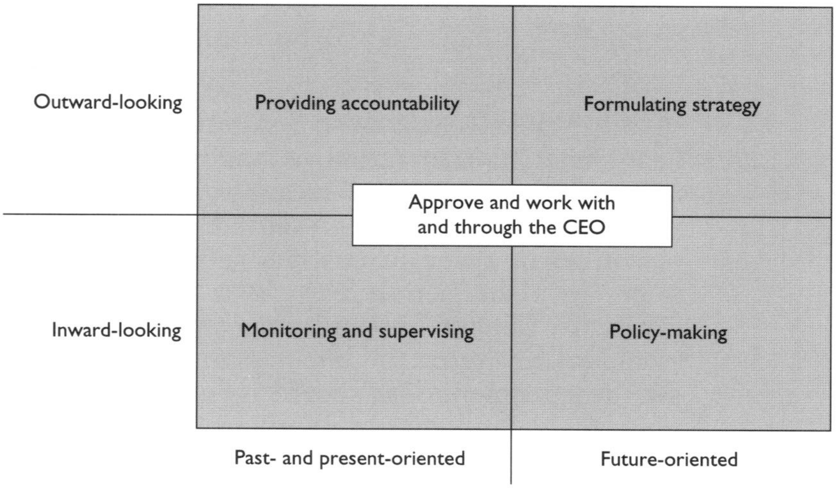

Source: Tricker, 1995

in functional policies which impact on shareholder value. These now include HR policy.

Everybody is aware of the argument that HR should be on the board, and that if there is no HR representation, then the function cannot be genuinely effective. This is only partly true. The fact is that the members of the board themselves will be *de facto* people experts: they must be to have achieved the level of success that got them onto the board in the first place. If the HR director is also on the board, that is an added bonus. If not, then those in HR had better make sure that the people case is well represented at board-level debates. There are several ways of doing this:

☐ First and foremost understand what the board actually does, what its drivers are, and what its corporate governance objectives are. This is the basic information needed to gain a higher HR profile.

☐ Further raise the profile of HR on an issues basis by asking for board-level sign-off on specific policies – such as diversity.

☐ Ask for an annual board presentation on HR to ensure that there is high-level commitment to activity.

☐ Brief the chief executive officer on a regular basis, and ask him or her to represent HR initiatives.

☐ Seek other board-level champions for HR initiatives.

☐ Be the technical expert on complex HR matters such as remuneration. Use this as leverage for other activities.

In this way HR can raise its profile with or without HR board-level representation. Actually, this may seem rather Machiavellian. It is not meant to be. It is just that those in HR do not always represent themselves as forcefully as personnel in other areas when gaining the board's commitment to their activities – even though the board will invariably support any initiatives that improve the people element of running the business or organisation. HR should see the agreement of the board as confirmation of its strategic importance, and should do all in its power to obtain such agreement and confirmation.

HR and other strategic decision-making bodies

There is a *prima facie* case for HR to gain board-level commitment to its strategic initiatives. That case is equally strong in relation to other strategic processes and forums. In developing organisational strategy and strategic options there is a need for HR to make inputs in the form of the strategic human resource forecast and its component parts, and to contribute to the output via the HR plan.

It is essential therefore to make sure that if there is a strategic planning process in existence, there is an HR element to it. Now this seems fairly obvious, but it is surprising how often the HR section is subsumed exclusively within business strategy, and not raised as a separate issue. In this respect the commonalities of HR strategies may not receive the cross-functional or cross-divisional airing that is desirable. Given the importance of people to the achievement of competitive advantage or organisational success, it is necessary to include a separate section within the strategic planning process for HR issues *over and above functional or divisional requirements*. Such aspects of people management as diversity, reward and employee relations require a cross-organisational view, and the strategy-setting process should reflect this. It is not enough for human resources to be an appendix to the main process of strategy-setting. It should be fundamental and totally integrated. This is a key factor in the development of strategic objectives.

Second, it is important that those in HR are included in the dialogue of strategy-setting *at every stage*. The inclusion of HR in such a dialogue is currently patchy at best. The classic example of this is during a merger-and-acquisition (M&A) process, when it is rare for HR to be included at the 'due diligence' stage. Yet the real challenges of M&A tend to have much to do with the people elements. Indeed, the failure of many acquisitions is because of the failure to deal with the people elements appropriately. However it is achieved, those in HR need to ensure their representation in the dialogue of strategy-setting.

Finally, the role of HR as business partner should be, in essence, a strategic one. The HR business-partner concept is one that many organisations have adopted. Moving away from the transactional responsibilities of HR, the business partner is an equal member of the senior team of any division or function. The business partner's role is to ensure that strategy-setting in a particular division or business unit has a professional HR input beyond pay and rations. An example of this new role may help in pointing up the differences:

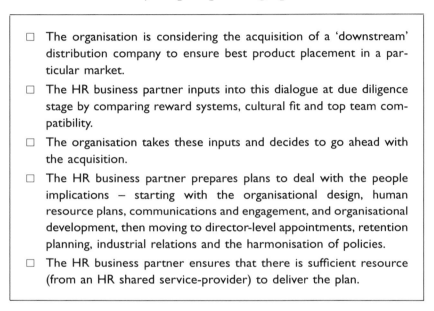

☐ The organisation is considering the acquisition of a 'downstream' distribution company to ensure best product placement in a particular market.

☐ The HR business partner inputs into this dialogue at due diligence stage by comparing reward systems, cultural fit and top team compatibility.

☐ The organisation takes these inputs and decides to go ahead with the acquisition.

☐ The HR business partner prepares plans to deal with the people implications – starting with the organisational design, human resource plans, communications and engagement, and organisational development, then moving to director-level appointments, retention planning, industrial relations and the harmonisation of policies.

☐ The HR business partner ensures that there is sufficient resource (from an HR shared service-provider) to deliver the plan.

The key thing to note here is the strategic level of the early parts of the process. Before getting into the transactions of pay and so on, the HR business partner starts with a strategy and a plan for people.

In this respect the inclusion of HR in the strategy-setting process is a key part of the job description and should be fulfilled accordingly. This of course raises the question of HR people's competence in the strategy area. As an issue, though, it is rather old-hat. For some time HR people have been developing their own strategic competencies to cope with the new demands. The CIPD's own qualifications have strategic inputs – its annual conferences include some of the world's leading thinkers on strategy, such as Michael Porter and

Robert Kaplan – and its outline for the development of HR people within an organisation increasingly includes a strategic element. In the USA, similarly, the 2001 SHRM conference included Norman Schwarzkopf and Gary Hamel as keynote speakers. If that is not enough to raise HR to the strategic level, nothing can be!

Developing organisational strategy and strategic options

The process of strategy-setting and the specifics of HR's involvement at the various levels have already been outlined (see Table 3 and Figure 9). The time has now come to look at it all in much more detail.

The board of directors sets overall business targets

In the first instance those responsible for HR will have to understand and be involved with the board-level strategy process – engaging in board-level dialogue is now part and parcel of the role of HR. One of the key functions of the board is to be outward-looking, to identify external opportunities by 'helicoptering' above the operational workings of the organisation. In this respect the board of directors will agree overall business targets – notably external and financial targets such as an increase in shareholder value, in market share or in customer satisfaction. The board's view on this may be different from that of personnel in the operational area – a point that anyone involved in strategy-setting must understand from the beginning. This is as true for HR as any other functional area.

The board will also want to agree the principles within which the people in the organisation can expect to work. These principles concern not just the economics of running the organisation but ethics, respect for colleagues and the overall governance of the organisation. This role of the board is growing in importance as external parties have an increasingly critical view of how organisations are run and how they interface with society. The environment is of course an example of such an interface, and most organisations are very aware of their environmental obligations. In HR terms the interface has been brought into sharp relief through the high profile of pensions management after the death of Robert Maxwell. It is likely that other areas will become an escalating concern of the board. Today, issues of diversity and equality of opportunity, reward and remuneration (especially of the organisation's senior management team) and leadership are regular board-level agenda items, and it is up to HR to make sure that its contribution is at an appropriate level.

Finally, the principles by which managers are expected to manage the organisation are naturally a board concern, and HR should be aware of this dialogue. Two recent initiatives provide good examples. The extensive attention given to diversity over the past 10 years has invariably been a board issue, and has led to organisational commitment at the highest level. More recently, the work of the Disability Rights Commission has attracted the attention of boards of directors (such as that of Lloyds TSB, which has made a policy commitment to its disabled staff). In both cases, principles of fairness have emerged from board-level dialogue.

The strategy-setting process is agreed and communicated

The strategy-setting process varies from organisation to organisation. Examples of different methods and styles include:

☐ *the strategic plan* – This is fairly common and involves individual managing directors' or directors of business units' participating in a consistent company-wide process. It is normally managed within set time-scales and includes an external market analysis for each business unit or function, a target business plan with financial and market share or customer service plans, and a technology or support-function plan. These are then referred to the overall corporate plan, and a challenge process begins to question the assumptions or the return on the organisation's investments.

☐ *ad hoc strategy-setting* – If we are to believe much of what is written about the current business environment, it is very difficult to plan forward. It is true that in some areas a specific plan like the one described above may not be feasible because of the unpredictability of the environment. In start-ups, for example, there has to be some fluidity in approach although that does not preclude the need for a plan. The role of HR in this process is as important as that in which it has is a more formal one.

☐ *no strategic planning process* – The best advice here is 'Good luck!' However, more practically, it is always worth raising the issue of strategy at every opportunity. When HR does this, of course, it will not win any popularity stakes – but emphasising the need for the organisation to have at least a framework within which resource allocation is made is a valid input to the running of the organisation (from whatever source).

Once the strategy-setting process has been established and agreed, it is up to all those in HR to make sure that they understand it.

HR's role in the strategy-setting process is agreed

So we have a process – but what is HR's role in it? This is where the serious negotiation starts. Earlier, the need to get access to board-level thinking – and, indeed, to try to influence that thinking – was emphasised. This is a primary element of the HR role and should accordingly be a priority objective.

The roles of each of the component parts of HR should then be agreed with those responsible for the strategy-setting process (starting with the CEO). Each role should comprise the input of an acknowledged expert first during the process of strategy-setting, and second during the implementation of the plan. It is as well to stress the word 'expert' just to emphasise that HR's role is no longer that of mere organisational policing to make sure that managers are doing the people things correctly. If we revert back to this view, we will never be admitted to the strategic debate. Instead, HR is a strategic partner in the debate. Its inputs are as valid and as valuable as those of any other faction on the strategy-setting 'team'. However, HR will have to earn its position by demonstrating that it can contribute at strategic level as well as being excellent at the implementation of operational matters.

Business unit dialogue on strategic options takes place

Once roles and processes have been agreed, the actual dialogue on strategy-setting takes place. There are two parts to this.

☐ The first is at business unit or functional level. In this, the HR business partner participates fully in the strategy debates that take place at the highest level in the unit, while other HR specialists make their own inputs at an appropriate time.

☐ There is then a wider debate on strategy that calls on HR to make contributions *over and above the needs of any one business unit or function*. It may have a bearing on important cross-organisation policy matters such as diversity, ageism, work–life balance, and so on.

This dual role is a difficult one for HR, since HR personnel wear two hats that might not always fit comfortably one on top of the other. The hats are those of business unit champion and organisation-wide people-sponsor. Sometimes the two roles conflict, and there is an immediate need to reconcile the two viewpoints.

A good example of this occasionally occurs in recruitment. In these days of the war for talent it is important for an organisation as a whole to have sophisticated recruitment strategies. They often include the development of an employer brand for the organisation as a whole. The HR business partner would contribute an input to this on a functional basis. But what if there were some specific requirements for the division, department or function into which the HR business partner reported that required something different from the employer brand? Niche markets for finance, marketing or technology staff, international recruitment and specialist graduates might demand a different approach. The HR business partner is in a difficult position, and must try to reconcile the contradictions between function and line.

External information and research are used to inform strategic debate

Strategy-setting relies on both external and internal information. At this stage in the process, external information about markets and competitors, or service requirements from the government, may help in strategic decision-making. HR has a role to play in providing such external information as:

☐ the state of the labour market

☐ legal or governmental frameworks

☐ global or international people considerations

☐ best practice on governance matters

☐ best practice on people strategies.

Accessing this type of information is important. Those in HR will be expected to provide an overview of labour markets, pay, legislation, and much else besides. There are many sources of information, and the Internet has made a good deal more readily accessible. Government websites provide valuable employment information. Best practice and benchmarking 'clubs' are also useful. This type of information is no longer an interesting option. It is almost mandatory for HR to be able to produce this information to hand. It may then be incorporated into the strategy-setting process. Those responsible for HR must ensure that this is the case.

Organisational strategic options are communicated

Relatively early in the strategy-setting process some strategic options will be put forward. In fact, it is likely that unless something is patently obvious, a whole range of options will be put forward. They can represent anything from stark yes-or-no questions, such as 'Should we expand into Italy?' to those that have more interpretation – 'Should we acquire a company on which to focus our expansion into Italy?' Such options will form the basis of the next stage of the dialogue as the organisation reviews its options about strategy, and are likely to be communicated to a larger audience than the board, although the debate is unlikely to go company-wide. Business unit or functional directors will discuss which options to choose, and it is important that, again, HR people are involved here, both at business unit and at company-wide level.

An organisation-wide review of options refines options

This review acts (in theory, at least) like a funnel. Options are poured in at one end, and some make it through and out of the other. Actually, to mix metaphors, those options that 'clear the hurdle' financially are the ones that will most probably go on to the next stage. In my experience there is always a problem in this process because of the need to evaluate each option and to produce the resources required for that evaluation. These resources are both technical and physical. (The problem surrounding the latter boils down to the question Do we have enough people around to do the work of evaluation when we are slimmed down to fighting weight already?) However, it is essential to participate fully in the review of strategic options in a way that adds value rather than in one that merely crunches the numbers of people affected. So it is incumbent on those who are responsible for resourcing HR itself to provide both skills and headcount for this process.

An initial strategic 'plan' or direction is agreed

Finally, a strategy – or at least a direction – should emerge from the maelstrom, and plans can begin to be made. At this stage those in HR will have participated in the dialogue and will have an understanding of the rationale, the objectives and the desired outcome of the strategy. This is priceless insight, and should be used to inform the direction of the HR strategy itself.

This has been an overview of the strategy-setting process. It is not intended to be definitive. Organisations may adopt these methods to a greater or lesser extent. One of the things that HR must do is spot when it has a valid role in intervening. Those responsible for HR should certainly be involved at every stage in the strategy-setting process, and in a variety of ways – at least in the first place as 'general managers' and in the second as technical experts in their field.

Subsequent sections look in more detail at the exact requirements and interventions for HR in the strategic human resource forecasting and human resource planning processes.

6 CREATING HR SCENARIOS

Scenario-planning

How do we get our organisations to leave behind the security-blanket of linear thinking and planning and take on something more radical? How do we get those who give direction in our organisations to imagine a world far away from the one they know and love? How do we in HR develop ideas about the future of employment that are not on today's agenda?

Perhaps the idea of future scenarios is a way of stepping out of the box. The second aspect of the strategic human resource forecasting process is to look at scenario-planning as a way of addressing some of these issues.

Scenario-planning is inexorably linked with creative thinking. Imaginative solutions to the problems created by expanding targets in a competitive world can be enhanced by instituting creativity as part of the intrinsic make-up of the organisation. Companies like Amazon.com, Federal Express, Fujifilm and Hewlett Packard use a variety of creative techniques to enhance their decision-making (McFadzean, 2001), and these can also be used in the process of scenario-planning.

In some organisations scenario-planning is a 'blue-sky' type of activity, in which those involved in the strategy-setting process think the unthinkable or dream up 'left-field' options for the organisation. This type of scenario-planning is as likely to take place outside of any formal planning process as within it. In most cases it remains a luxury for most organisations – although in the past year or so the urgency for innovation has seen a greater focus on diversification as a possible strategic option, and that is an environment in which scenario-planning thrives. If this type of thinking is possible within the culture of the organisation, then, so much the better. It is not always possible, however, for organisations to use this type of technique – mostly because of a lack of organisational slack that can be freed up to do it. (A high proportion of people in organisations these days have a job and a half just to keep business going as usual!) But scenario-planning can be a superb element to incorporate into the overall planning process as well.

It is possible all the same to include a modified form of scenario-planning in the overall planning process that projects an additional level of thinking on to what might otherwise be a one-level methodology. Such a modified scenario-planning approach works in a slightly less hypothetical way. Figure 11 illustrates the sequence of the process. Using this method a

Figure 11 **CREATING HR SCENARIOS**

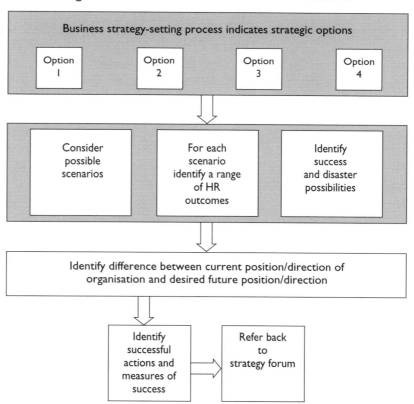

scenario is developed for each of the strategic options pro-posed. For example, if the option is to merge with a competitor, the scenarios envisaged might be:

☐ The merger exceeds original expectations, creating pres-sure on planned time-scales and resource allocation. What happens then? How does the organisation cope?

☐ The merger is a failure. Cultural differences are massive. What does the organisation do?

☐ Government intervention prevents the merger from going ahead. What are the alternatives?

Before embarking on scenario-planning, HR must ensure that the process fulfils two key criteria: 'First [the contingency scenarios] should be possible but extreme. More specifically, they should be sufficiently different for one option not to outshine the rest across all scenarios. Second, each scenario should be internally consistent' (Ghemawat, 1991). It is equally important for the process to lead somewhere, rather than being an expensive – but useless – roadshow. In other words, scenario-planning is a good vehicle for fostering stra-tegic debate, but it must aim for *workable* outcomes.

This process cannot begin, however, until we have a clear understanding of scenario-planning – and see it being success-fully employed in leading global organisations.

What is scenario-planning?

Patrick Dixon has urged people to take hold of the future or it will take hold of them. The reason: the world is undergoing enormous and unprecedented change. It is becoming FUTURE – that is, Fast, Urban, Tribal, Universal, Radical, and Ethical. Managers should prepare for the unexpected (Dixon, 1998). Scenario-planning *is* preparing for the unexpected. What would happen if an organisation was confronted with a radical and unexpected change in its business environment? What would it do if it found its business strategy completely derailed? What would happen, for example, if a significant business opportunity arose internationally, or the collapse of a market caused chaos in the core business? Most relevant for those in HR, what would be the people implications of these events, and how would we deal with them?

One way of dealing with such occurrences is to 'go into chaos mode'. All hands to the pumps. Deal with the change as a crisis on a day-to-day basis. Another is to put in place the contingency plans that many organisations have for dealing with the unexpected on a reactive basis. Yet another way, however, is to create an organisational frame of mind that is able to cope with the unexpected because it has already considered how to do so! It has already confronted various contingencies and their consequences, whether they are global and pervasive – such as an oil crisis, war, or stock market meltdown – or local and concentrated – such as unprecedented dot.com growth in a market, severe financial shock (as with Barings Bank), or whatever.

Scenario-planning is a way of building a mindset aimed at anticipation. It represents, according to Bob Garratt, 'an attempt to sidestep or circumvent the hazards of predicting, and in the process, to reap certain mental and practical gains that are commonly sacrificed in single-track predicting' (Garratt, 1995). Scenario-planning is not a new concept. As a means of avoiding surprises by addressing future possibilities, it has been used as a method alternative to anything included in the normal planning process. It has thus been summarised as a way of anticipating changes in the external environment that will 'impact positively or adversely on both the organisation's goals and the means of achieving them. The challenge would be easy to meet if only we could predict the future with a high degree. . .of accuracy' (Garratt, 1995).

A solution to the thorny problem of not being able to forecast the future accurately is to develop 'scenario-thinking' in organisations. This is as much the role of HR as it is of any other function. In this context scenario-thinking is a response to the fallibility of prediction-making in the business or organisational environment. At times of uncertainty those who 'think scenario' may be 'able to overcome the paralysis' of the situation (van der Heijden, 1997). It can help to prevent panic at the unexpected by presenting several possible future environments in light of which the business or organisation may find itself a 'safe house' in which to discuss and confront these outcomes. Although not referred to under the title used here, scenario-planning is used to some extent in HR, if on a more informal basis. The strategic human resource forecast presents an ideal opportunity to incorporate some scenario-planning into the people aspects of the strategy – some 'what-ifs' to stimulate the debate in an unpredictable world.

Examples of scenario-planning

There are a number of organisations that have excelled in the art of scenario-planning. Some of the best examples come from the Shell group of companies. Their definition (Shell, 1998–2000, at shell.com) sees scenarios as:

> plausible and challenging stories, not forecasts. They do not extrapolate from the past to predict what will happen in the future, but instead offer two very different stories of how the future might look. They help to prepare for discontinuities and sudden change; they help to create a common culture or language through which the future can be imagined and discussed; and they challenge the mental maps we all hold.

Shell use the scenario process to help them to understand better the complex situations they might encounter over a long planning period. They have used scenarios to concentrate on issues such as oil prices and the environment (naturally), but also on such issues as 'the post-Cold-War world order'. This use of scenario-planning came about because of the failure of the traditional planning process to engage managers in the need for change. Instead, scenarios were used to condition managers 'to be mentally prepared for a shift from low prices to high prices and from stability to instability' (Senge, 1990).

Other organisations have used scenario-planning in a different context, most notably in the technology sector. In one global technology company, strategy was seen to emerge from a number of scenarios ranging from defining outcomes for the company if it remained in its current state to 'exploring the implications for various combinations of emphasis in these sectors, or even abandoning involvement in one or the other sector' (Krombeen, 1988).

So what kind of scenarios might be developed in an organisation? Examples include:

☐ extremes of market conditions that force challenges different from those anticipated in areas of skill or resource supply

☐ effects of globalisation that create different cultural challenges

☐ merger or acquisition possibilities not previously anticipated

☐ political changes that require a strategic rethink.

Of course, each organisation will have its own future possibilities, and HR personnel will have to adapt their scenarios to their own unique circumstances.

Creating HR scenarios

In its purist sense scenario-planning tries to imagine the future at its most unpredictable. If a debate on it can then be instigated (most probably in a session facilitated by HR), it may well be of benefit to the organisation. For such a debate, any future is thus possible. What if the organisation became global market leader for its products? What if the source of raw material dried up and forced the organisation into a diversification strategy? What if the war for talent fizzled out? (There are those who say it has already – the employees won.) And so on.

We have already noted that scenario-planning in the advanced form used by, say, Shell may not be possible in all organisations. Yet there is another mode of scenario-planning that has virtually universal applications. This is scenario-planning within an option. It relies on using the same type of thinking involved in the broader definition of scenario-planning and positioning it within the framework of the strategy-setting process – that is, planning the scenarios for each of the strategic options derived. This can be very powerful from an HR perspective, since it can bring to the fore specific HR issues such as the war for talent and diversity.

As an example: for strategic option 'X' HR raises the

scenario that the organisation might not be able to deliver because there are not enough skilled people in the country to staff up the business units. That is a great stimulus to debate and can lead to a whole range of policy considerations that might not normally be pursued.

So even in a fairly neutered form scenario-planning can be undertaken as part of SHRF.

This description of scenario-planning is an adaptation of the approach that has been advocated in companies like Shell. It is an attempt to frame the people debate differently. If it is possible to get scenario-planning onto the agenda as a separate process, then that is a good achievement. If not, at least try to get it incorporated to the point where strategic options are being debated.

The business strategy-setting process indicates strategic options

In an earlier chapter it was advised that strategic options should be debated at an early stage in the strategy-setting process. It is important for HR to be involved in the debate at this stage, both to be able to add input to the strategy and to understand the output. This ensures that vital people issues are on the strategic agenda. At some point in the debate a series of strategic options will be considered. It is at this point that HR can look to scenario-planning to evaluate the strategic options in terms of contingencies that may promote or hinder their success.

I once saw this process take place in an informal way in an organisation that wanted to expand its US marketing potential. The strategic option was to the effect that acquisitions should take place from east coast to west coast. Indeed, acquisitions had already started before the strategy had actually been agreed – the organisation was distinctly a 'can do' one. The strategy raised the question of how to provide product support to the newly acquired US operations. It was scenario-planning that led to the previously unthinkable view of opening a company office in the USA. Very many other options for support were considered but were not satisfactory. The opening of the US office came about through a series of 'what-if' questions posed in a facilitated session with the board. It was scenario-planning in a primitive form, admittedly, but it was scenario-planning nonetheless. Opening the US office was a totally new scenario since product support had always before been provided from the UK. The scenario raised a whole series of HR issues about recruitment, organisation structure, and so on. The point is that scenario-planning brought up a possibility not previously considered.

Consider possible scenarios

Having looked at the possible options that might arise from the business strategy (these will be about growth through acquisition or organic methods, cost reduction, new products or services, and so on), it might be possible to plan out some scenarios for debate. Typically, these might be phrased in the form of questions and include:

☐ If our company became a global player, would we be able to manage it?

☐ Where are the main sources of competitive advantage through people? How can we strengthen them? What if they are lost through the attrition of key staff?

☐ Where in the organisation are the main sources of knowledge as a competitive weapon? Could we manage them better? What if they were jeopardised through radical change?

☐ What if we had a pan-organisational technology system in place for dealing with all aspects of human resource management – to facilitate web-enabled training, to extend flexible benefits and to contribute towards career management? How would this affect the management style?

☐ Could we cope if key members of the board left? What would we do? How would we manage succession?

☐ What if we moved from centralised to decentralised structures (or vice versa)? How would this affect the way we managed the organisation?

It is important to note that these are not planning tools. They are more free-form than that. Instead, they are stories about the future from which imaginative possibilities can be extrapolated. Then they can be converted into plans.

The process for raising these scenarios varies. Options include:

- putting scenario-planning on the agenda at strategy meetings – for example, if an option looks as though it might become the preferred one, then raise 'what-if' questions during the debate
- setting up focus groups of senior managers – this could be facilitated by those in HR, and would involve raising scenarios that the senior managers had not considered
- setting up brainstorming sessions with a mixed group
- allocating scenario-planning to a group of high-potential 'fast-trackers' to come up with some possible outcomes uncluttered by years of organisational culture or experience.

It should not be too difficult to introduce the idea of scenario-thinking. Then it will be up to those in HR to ensure that the idea gets followed through.

For each scenario identify a range of HR outcomes

Once the story is set up, the next stage will be for those who have had an input to the scenario to identify a range of possible outcomes. This is an exercise in broadening the vision beyond the organic and incremental. It is certainly an exercise in moving out of the box. How does this work, and what does it look like?

Let us take an example. The business strategy suggests a scenario that the organisation wins contracts in Asia-Pacific to set up joint-venture companies to manufacture products. The time-scale for putting these together is within two years of the planning period. It is essential that work starts on these projects immediately. The organisation has no office or representation in the Asia-Pacific region. What would be the HR outcomes of this scenario? Remember, the scenario is a story, not a forecast. It has to be beyond currently identifiable projections. The process for identifying HR outcomes is:

☐ Define some possible outcomes that are at the extreme – eg sales take off to 500 per cent of forecast, or sales do not take off at all; there is a political change that makes the venture possible/impossible; and so on.

☐ Define the general people requirements of the results of the ideas around these scenarios. In this case (for example) they might be: a resident team of expatriates in the Aspac region for start-up, emergency airlift because of political unrest, moving the head office from Birmingham to Beijing, recruitment of local experts for knowledge and technology transfer, identification of leadership, management structure and governance of the international venture. . .

☐ Define the specifics in relation to people issues – for example, pay and the terms and conditions of both the expatriate and local employees; employee relations issues in new territories; training needs from language to technology. . .

☐ Quantify the costs of such a venture in terms of increases to the pay bill, training spend, and so on.

☐ Prepare a human resource plan to ensure that all aspects of the venture are covered.

This is the type of general and specific outcomes with which each scenario should be furnished, and the process should be undertaken for every scenario that comes out of the strategy-setting process. The benefit of ensuring that each of the strategic options has a thorough grounding in alternative possibilities is the creation of a broader mindset than might otherwise be the case. Those responsible for HR could of course initiate their own scenarios to raise the level of awareness of business managers. Try saying to the senior management team, 'What would you do if we acquired X? How would we deal with the people issues?'

Identify success and disaster possibilities

Once the possible outcomes from the various scenarios have been identified, two important questions should be raised.

☐ What would success look like?

☐ What are the risks to and the possible show-stoppers of these outcomes?

In the Aspac example above, the success criteria might be:

☐ factories opened in China and Japan
☐ expatriate managers successfully located in territory for two years before passing over to a local management team
☐ the new venture successfully integrated into the group.

Some of the risks associated with the scenario might be:

☐ launch of project on proposed start date prevented by cultural and relocation issues thereby impacting on the overall delivery date
☐ delay of entire project by a year following failure to find suitable managers from within the company
☐ failure to transfer technology because of inappropriate training
☐ poaching of the team by a competitor who then sets up a rival joint venture.

Knowing what the risks to the people aspects of a scenario are, and then dealing with them, is an important part of the process but can require considerable sensitivity. Care is needed when raising the issue. Anything associated with possible failure or risk is not always viewed as an issue worth debating. It is, and organisations should be as much aware of the risks and their consequences as of success and its outcomes. Scenario-planning is a way of doing this in a safe environment.

Identify difference between current position of organisation and desired future position

One output of scenario-planning is to highlight gaps, again from a people perspective. It is at this point where interesting theoretical constructs begin to become interesting practical possibilities. So once a scenario has been created, once HR outcomes have been identified, and once some sort of plan is beginning to emerge, then the gap analysis should start.

Typical gaps (again exemplified using the Aspac scenario) include:

☐ lack of suitably trained staff to run joint-venture negotiations

☐ lack of trained staff to undertake technology transfers

☐ lack of international experience in the senior management team, giving only a 'current-business' view of the whole project (a real cultural issue).

As in the HR outcomes aspect of the scenario, the gap analysis will facilitate action-planning once one projected scenario becomes firm. If the scenario debate suggested that a skills gap would occur if the sales forecast was exceeded by, say, 20 per cent, then contingencies could be put in place to deal with it.

Identify successful actions and measures of success

At this point there will be several inputs to the scenario. From an HR perspective these will be a broad range of people possibilities, such as labour shortages or surfeits, skills gaps, reward that is too low (or too high), and so on. It is worth sanity-checking the whole process now with those responsible for establishing the scenario. The sanity check would be a strategic time-out in which to evaluate what the outcomes have been and how beneficial they are. If there is any sign that the scenario might turn into something that will require further action, then some action plans will have to be put in place. The action plans will consist of:

☐ aims and objectives for the venture outlined in the scenario

☐ an identification of the key people issues that arise out of the scenario

☐ headline proposals for dealing with the issues

☐ an estimate of time-scales for being able to deliver on the people

☐ some means of measuring success.

One of the most important aspects of this part of the scenario-planning process is time and timing. Too often the people issues of strategy are assumed – there will be enough trained staff, there will be enough money in the pot to reward appropriately, and so on. The time it takes to do some of the people parts of strategy is invariably underestimated. The scenario-planning exercise must not repeat this mistake.

Refer back to the strategy forum

Once the scenario has been worked through, it is essential to refer it back to the strategy forum for wider strategic debate. There is no right time to do this, since at this point in the strategy-setting process there will be debates taking place in parallel rather than in sequence. It all depends on the overall strategy-setting process that is being undertaken by the organisation. There is, however, likely to be a time-scale within which the process is being monitored, and those in HR should be aware of it for scenario-planning purposes. It is no use coming up with a brilliant people observation or proposal if the plan has already been submitted. Likewise, it is no use trying to persuade people of scenarios if their minds are already made up. Scenario-planning, like so much of the HR contribution to the strategy-setting process, is dependent on good timing.

7 ASSESSING THE DEMAND FOR PEOPLE

Strategic resourcing

Attracting, developing and retaining the right personnel for businesses today is what lies at the root of their success or their failure. All too often this is considered an area that is straightforward or incidental, yet until the true power of having the right people within a business is really understood, the business won't be able to face up to the challenges ahead from either the economy or the competition.

The alignment of corporate and personal values should lie at the root of any recruitment exercise, whether recruiting a CEO or a manual worker. The success of any business is largely reliant on the quality and commitment of its personnel.

But why is it that the strategy, values and vision of a business are only apparent to individuals once they are an intrinsic part of the organisation? Surely these are issues which if addressed correctly at the recruitment stage would increase the retention levels of personnel within organisations.

To grow our businesses, we have to focus on recruiting and developing people not just for our immediate requirements but for the future as well. In doing so, we must also offer them an environment that they want to be in, aspirational and inspirational goals, and personal development opportunities where they can thrive in a challenging situation.

There is a responsibility on everyone who is recruiting to devote sufficient time and attention to understand and clarify exactly what is required. We should also look forward to the development and retention of each recruited individual both in personal terms and in developing the business. The result then will not be a repetition of the recruitment process and a static or decreasing business.

Audrey Lucy
Managing Director, Jigsaw Consultancy

The demand for people

The demand and supply of people are the *yin* and *yang* of the SHRF: two complementary activities – not of Chinese philosophy but of the very real challenge of getting enough people to fill the posts created by strategy. Attaining equilibrium is a very desirable objective. To do so means having a good understanding of the labour market.

In theory, demand forecasting should be more straightforward than supply forecasting. After all, demand forecasting is based on an interpretation of the organisation's business plans. In reality, however, it is just as problematical. Business plans slip in time, get cancelled at the last minute, disappear amid the fervour of some new strategic objective (dot.com start-ups, dot.com wind-downs, mergers, etc), or just get scaled down. All the same, it should not be too much of a surprise to those who are working on the strategic human resource forecast to realise that understanding the demand for people is at the heart of so much that follows. It will ultimately determine the recruitment and redeployment strategy, and provide significant input into most areas of HR policy. Getting demand right is key. The objective of this part of the SHRF is to give some idea of the likely demands for labour in the period covered by the plan in terms of both 'business as usual' and the knock-on effects of any strategic projects that might be under consideration. This chapter focuses on how this demand might be determined.

The objective of this part of the forecast will be to give the organisation an evaluation of how the business strategy will affect both the numbers and types of employee needed. To do so will require both a quantitative and qualitative interpretation of business plans, and a dialogue with business managers about these conclusions. A process for undertaking this part of the forecast is presented in Figure 12.

The actual process will almost certainly be more fragmented than this approach implies, especially if there are multiple departments or divisions. But the objectives will be

Figure 12 ASSESSING THE DEMAND FOR PEOPLE

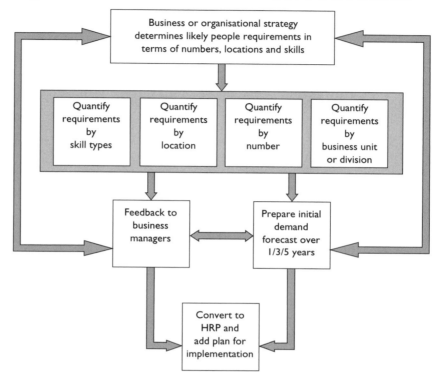

similar, regardless of the structure. The outputs of the demand forecast will also be consistent. These are likely to be:

☐ an estimate of the numbers required to achieve the business strategy in one to three to five years' time

☐ an understanding of where these employees will work, by division or by location

☐ an understanding of the types of skill that will be required, including an estimate of how many skilled people will be required within each skill type.

The change in approach to demand forecasting

Assessing the demand is not straightforward. As Chris Hendry has pointed out, 'the problem is how to convert volumes of work into numbers of people' (Hendry, 1995). He proposes two favoured methods for doing this: ratio-trend analysis and the use of work-study standards. Both of these methods are used in organisations, particularly in a factory or long-run process work pattern environment (fast food, for example.) In such circumstances the challenge becomes crewing up the shop or retail outlet or staffing the shop floor to meet anticipated demand. At the height of work-study and Organisation and Methods departments in the 1960s and 1970s such methods were commonplace. Nowadays, of course, modern workflow systems support such calculations using technology. The old brown-coated work-study engineers with their stopwatches and their plastic flowchart templates are rarely seen in the front offices of banks or stores. Furthermore, organisations have changed and in some circumstances make any such precision difficult. How do you measure productivity in a virtual organisation or a dot.com? How do home-workers get measured? In fact, senior HR people have been known to walk the floor doing manual headcount checks because of the complex nature of the organisation in which they are working. It is possible to use precise measurements in work-flow prediction (and this can be translated into headcount demand), but it is not always the best way. Likewise, it is possible to use some of the highly complex forecasting techniques based on advanced statistical methodologies. The role of those in human resources is to define the method for work forecasting and hence demand forecasting that is appropriate to their own organisations.

Obviously, there is no single IT solution that will suit every organisation, so there is no point in trying to recommend one. Rather, this chapter advocates the use of technology to facilitate – not to replace the need to have – a dialogue with business managers when gathering data about the demand for people. After all, the managers are the ones closest to the action and understand their own areas better than anyone else. So the data to be used will be a mix of statistical analysis and forecast, as well as interpretation based on discussion. In building up a database from which any projections can be made, data will therefore be derived from as many sources as possible. If the chief executive asks the question 'How many people work in head office?', those responsible for HR should be able to answer. Then when the question arises, '– and how many will be affected by strategy X?', the answer will be based on a reasoned analysis.

The nature of the demand information will be both qualitative and quantitative. Some of the information that should be prepared in the early stages of the demand forecast is listed in Table 4. Figure 13 gives a matrix against which both quantitative and qualitative demand factors can be plotted. It might be worth doing this as a simple brainstorming exercise in the first instance. The process described later in this chapter relies on viewing this type of simple analysis as complementing a business-aligned route to demand management. The two matrices can be updated as more information on demand comes to hand. The preparation of a demand forecast then will be a combination of formal methodologies and a less rational but equally rigorous dialogue with managers.

Table 4 INFORMATION REQUIRED FOR THE DEMAND FORECAST

Quantitative	Qualitative
Employee numbers and headcount	Skills and competencies
Geography:	Knowledge
• where employees are located	Training needs
• where they will be in future	M&A Skills
Demographics:	Functional skills
• age	
• gender	
• ethnic groupings	
Functions:	
• sales	
• customer service	
• technology	
• manufacturing	
• finance	
• support staff	
Ratios:	
• sales per salesperson	
• units manufactured per person	
• ratio of HR to total workforce	
Benchmarks against other organisations in sector	

Figure 13 **ASSESSING THE DEMAND FOR LABOUR**

	Short-term	Long-term
Quantitative factors	Current headcount – where people work – how many work in each location Current demographics Current business unit headcount Current divisional or functional headcount Benchmarking comparisons	Projected headcount totals Changing geographic patterns Forecast demographic changes Forecast changes in functions Future benchmarking targets
Qualitative factors	Current skills make-up Current attitudinal measures Current training levels	Future skills make-up Future training needs

The process for deriving a demand forecast

As with all other aspects of the SHRF and HRP, the process for evaluating demand is an iterative one. It involves initial interpretations of demand from HR's reading of the organisational strategy, modified in a dialogue with business managers. The main points of the process for compiling a demand forecast are examined sequentially below.

The business or organisational strategy determines the likely people requirements in terms of numbers, location, skills, etc

The first requirement is to ensure that a human resource presence is included in the dialogue about business strategy. Remember, this is not the human resource plan – which is the output – but a demand forecast – an input. The way to achieve this is:

☐ Where a dialogue is taking place in a business unit or function about the strategic options facing that unit, the HR 'business partner' should be involved.

☐ It will require the HR business partner to come up with an interpretation of the strategic option being debated in the form of a rough demand forecast.

For example, the business unit may decide to open a new distribution centre from which all products can be transferred to any part of a particular region. This would entail a demand for labour in the area planned for the distribution centre. For the purposes of this section, let us say that it is estimated that the unit will require 24/7 working and therefore the operation of a shift system. The rough demand forecast is for day, afternoon and night workers, in region X (or town X), comprising of, say, 30 distribution workers, three managers, and five administrators – a suggested total demand of 38 staff to be recruited. This guesstimate will then be discussed within each unit until a central view can be taken, a cross-fertilisation of ideas comes up with additional details, and a forecast may be prepared for further iteration.

Once these later discussions have been completed, an overview of demand in its basic form can be prepared. Such an overview will include a first pass at likely demands for labour that will form the basic building-block on which more detailed forecasts can be prepared. The stages below will add information to this demand forecast as it becomes more closely aligned to the strategic direction of the organisation.

Quantify people requirements by total number

This overview will need further refinement on two counts:

- □ via a dialogue with business managers to ensure that the interpretation made by HR is about right
- □ by applying known methods of calculation of staff turnover and other measures to give a more accurate forecast.

Taking the example started above, if staff turnover averages 10 per cent, then about four more people will be needed over the year, and the recruitment figure in the above example will increase from 38 to 42. If allowance is to be made for sickness absence at say, 3 per cent, then a further one member of staff will be needed. Holidays and suchlike mean another four staff. So in this case the headcount forecast at its roughest total of 38 staff will in reality be nearer 50.

Other methods that can be used to forecast demand for labour numerically include ratios and benchmarking.

Ratios

Ratios compare the relationship between two factors. The following – very simple – examples show how ratios can be used in demand forecasting.

☐ It takes 10 salespeople to sell 100 units. The ratio of sales-people to sales is thus 1:10. So if the intention is to sell 200 units, at a 1:10 ratio 20 salespeople will be needed. The demand forecast for salespeople is therefore 20, based on sales forecasts.

☐ There are currently 100 people in manufacturing to make 1,000 units. The ratio is 1:10. If the strategy is to buy a new piece of computerised manufacturing equipment which increases the ratio to 1:100, then it will take only 10 people to operate in the manufacture of 1,000 units. If the intention is to make 1,000 units, the forecast number required in manufacturing is 10.

In the first example, the demand forecast will have an implication for the resourcing plan in the form of a recruitment programme. In the second, there will be redundancy or redeployment implications by introducing new manufacturing technology. In the actual organisational strategy-setting process, each of the implications will have to be translated into demand estimates. Demand forecasting using ratios can be very helpful.

Benchmarking

Benchmarking is an equally good method for use in creating the demand forecast. However, the issue with benchmarking is the basis of comparison. It is important to make sure that information is provided on a like-for-like basis. A good example of this can be given using HR itself.

☐ The best practice international benchmark for HR is 1:100 (say). This means that one HR person has to be responsible for 100 people in employment. So if the labour force is 1,000, 10 HR professionals will be needed, according to the benchmark, and a demand forecast can be proposed using this figure. But the question arises, 'What is included in the HR figure?' In the USA, benchmarking statistics often exclude training (for example) from the figures. So to set a demand forecast for HR in Europe using the US benchmark might lead to some serious shortfalls in HR supply. Likewise, are pensions and payroll staff included in the best practice benchmark? Such questions must be thoroughly investigated if benchmarking alone is going to be used. Nonetheless, benchmarking continues to be a useful input to the demand forecasting process.

So this part of the demand forecast gives a quantified statement of staff requirements as a result of the interpretation by HR of the business strategy. Some of these measures will be firm – as in the sales forecast used to identify the number of salespeople – others less so, particularly in functional areas, staffing of which will be dependent upon where the business is in its development. This quantification process becomes particularly difficult when newer organisational forms are adopted. What about home-working? How are staff numbers forecast for these? Similarly, flexible working, split-shift patterns, contractors, and so on add a new dimension to the simple example outlined above. It is therefore a quite complex affair, and all factors have to be taken into account.

Quantify requirements by business unit or division

The assessment of demand has two important perspectives. The first is in relation to the whole of the company (and takes the form of a grand total), but the second is an analysis by business unit or division. Each of the strategic options for the business leads to a specific change to the demand for labour at a macro level. This is the base case on which a dialogue will take place by board members. The strategic human resource forecast will present a high-level view of the likely demands of the business strategy. It will tender a perspective on overall flows of human resource – in and out of the company – as well as between units. Quite clearly, this does not occur at business unit level.

In taking this bird's-eye view in the initial instance, then, policy and strategy implications can be monitored at an early stage before business unit plans are put in place. However, once this has happened, the business unit or divisional plans should be highlighted separately, giving the micro view as well. Each business unit or division will have different requirements, and each will have specific human resource responses. The overview of each business unit or division may then be refined further, and a total picture should begin to emerge. This will show the headcount requirements by number by division, giving all the alterations outlined above.

In preparing the strategic human resource forecast, those responsible for HR will therefore have to undertake two levels of dialogue. The first is at business unit or divisional level, and will allow a bottom-up picture to be built of the likely people requirements. The second is with the board, having presented a composite picture of demand.

Quantify requirements by location

In addition, the geographical implications of headcount demand will also have to be logged. This will enable the HR business partner to intervene and influence strategy. If, for example, the strategy was to open a call centre (or contact centre, as they are now called) in an expensive, low-unemployment part of the country, then the demand forecast would show this in numerical terms. It would be possible to influence the strategy by matching this to the supply forecast information and thereby square the circle. The advice from HR would be that 'It would be madness to open the call centre here. Demand for this type of call centre operative exceeds the known supply of labour in this area.' (This is HR being strategic, by the way.) The decision having thus been influenced, the geographical analysis will inform the supply chain decisions in the resourcing plan. The geographical analysis will also inform policy about pay, IR, and so on.

Quantify requirements by skill types

Demand forecasting is not just about the numerical analysis of headcount. It is also about the demand for skills. This part of the SHRF allows some dimensions to be put around any changes in required skills that might be anticipated, and this will then be used to inform the learning, training and development plan.

It is well known that there is an obsession about skill levels in the UK – as indeed there is in individual organisations. The creation of the LSCs was, in part, a national response to this issue. It is also likely that individual organisations will also have skills problems as they formulate their strategic plans. In the 1980s British organisations were concerned about international marketing, and this led to a wide-ranging review of marketing training in some organisations. British telecommunications companies, for example, saw the growing prominence of American and Japanese products as a threat in global markets and tried to adopt a marketing response to it, leading to the development of new products and marketing campaigns. Other skills changes occurred in banking during the 1990s, as the idea of turning a bank into a financial service retail organisation increasingly took hold. The real skills shortage came in retailing, and so retail experts were recruited in sales, marketing, customer service, and so on.

The demand forecast facilitates the identification of such skill changes by aligning the proposed strategic options with the current skill levels and thereby identifying gaps. The subsequent demand consists of both numbers and types of skill.

In preparing the demand forecast by skill types, those in HR will need a thorough understanding of the strategic options that the organisation is considering. Let us say, for example, that a sales strategy is being developed to work in partnership with the organisation's major or key accounts. A skills review will have to be undertaken to decide whether 'major account management' is something that can be achieved within the skills sets of the current workforce. If not, a gap will exist that will have to be filled through training or recruitment.

In a similar vein, let us say that 'procurement' is developing into a more strategic role than transactional purchasing. Fewer but larger contracts will be placed, and closer working relationships will be maintained with these partners. Are these skills in place? If not, can they be developed?

The skills review should cover the full span of the organisation.

Prepare an initial demand forecast

At this point a range of analyses of demand will have been completed covering numbers, geography, skills, and so on. Once all of these factors have been taken into account, an initial demand forecast can be prepared. The initial demand forecast will be both quantitative and qualitative in nature.

☐ In the first instance, it will contain a numerical forecast of headcount (both current and projected), by business unit, by division, and for the company as a whole.

☐ Secondly there will be an initial qualitative analysis, outlining future skills requirements, the gap from the present, and similar.

At this stage the initial demand forecast is a rough working estimate which will form the central subject of the dialogue with the business managers before further refinement. It is also possible that the initial demand forecast will be required in the form of 1- to 3- to 5-year forecasts, and this should be taken into account.

Feedback to business managers for initial dialogue

The conversion of strategic options into a demand forecast is a powerful HR contribution to the debate. At this point the initial findings can be taken back to the business managers responsible for the strategy and made the context of a dialogue. How might this be done for best effect, given that the strategies will be the desired outcomes of individual groups of business managers?

It takes a brave HR person to go back to a managing director and say, 'There will be problems if you do this.' We are in an age of 'can do' and zero defects. But no less a personage than General H. Norman Schwarzkopf, speaking at the SHRM conference in San Francisco in June 2001, said: 'Zero defects is a stupid model if you are in the people business'

(Schwarzkopf, 2001). It is an obligation to the strategic contribution of HR to the organisation to go back to the business managers and debate the findings from the demand forecast before they become firm. The type of findings might include competition for scarce resource from within the organisation (eg technology or marketing staff in different divisions), demand for skills that do not currently exist within the organisation, demand for labour in new geographical areas in which the organisation has no labour management experience (in international markets, for example), and a scale of demand that might be excessive. Each of these has implications for the human resources plan.

The key to this, however, is to go beyond analysis and critique and give proposed solutions. Examples might include:

☐ Ensure a realistic approach to the timing of the demand for labour by 'phasing'. So if there is to be a major sales drive that requires the recruitment of significant numbers of salespeople (and the HR professional knows that this will be difficult because of his or her knowledge of the supply side of labour), the dialogue will be about setting realistic recruitment dates. Such a proposal might be to phase in the recruits to allow time for the process of recruitment, induction and training. This is by far a better dialogue than a later one that might be about unattained sales targets because of the lack of recruits.

☐ Redeployment is a possibility often not exploited as it might be. So a demand in one part of the organisation can be met by a redeployment from another part. Some organisations – IBM and Lloyds TSB, to name but two – have specialist areas that are targeted with redeployment.

☐ Retraining is a further proposal to deal with demand for labour (where there are skills shortages, for example)

These are but a few of the suggestions that might be put forward as part of the dialogue. The point is for HR to add value through this dialogue, not simply to affect to comply with unattainable demands for labour.

Feed results into a quantified human resource plan

This dialogue should result in a finely-filtered demand forecast that will have highlighted issues and gaps. It will then be up to those responsible for HR to modify the demand forecast for inclusion into the overall human resource plan. A final point here is that the dialogue will not then stop but will be ongoing. No forecast is a one-off event. So as the organisation's strategic dialogue takes place it is likely that the demand forecast will change again and again. And even once it has been agreed it will probably change yet again. This is fairly normal because of the dynamic nature of any organisation and its interface with its environment. The whole point about the forecasting process is that is iterative. However, at some point there will have to be an agreed working plan to which subsequent HR plans are geared. The demand forecast should provide a major input to the resourcing plan.

The initial demand forecast will be debated for some time until a nearly final approach is determined. It is at this point that the forecast will start to be converted into plans and will therefore feed into the HRP.

8 ASSESSING THE SUPPLY OF PEOPLE IN ORGANISATIONS

by John Philpott, Chief Economist, Chartered Institute of Personnel and Development

HR would not be HR without its essential raw material – people. A forward look at the number and quality of people available in the jobs market is therefore a necessary prerequisite of strategic HR. This chapter focuses on the external factors that have an impact on an organisation's strategy and are therefore an essential part of the strategic human resource forecast.

The chapter has a format different from others' in that it comprises a précis rather than a detailed analysis. This is so as to focus on actual labour market supply trends from an economic perspective. It will enable the reader to obtain information on the markets, which can then be integrated into the supply side of the SHRF. The essence of the debate thus far is that strategy-setting should take account of both external and internal factors. People supply – in particular external supply – is an important determinant of whether an organisation will be able to deliver its required levels of performance. The inclusion of such an analysis in the SHRF, combined with the other steps in the supply forecast, is therefore critical to the success of HR's involvement in the strategy-setting process.

The process of delivering a supply forecast

The process by which the external supply of labour is analysed and integrated into the overall strategy and layout of the organisation, is included in Figure 14. Supply is generated by internal and external sources of labour and includes the supply of skills. The supply forecast should present these as discrete units in the first instance, but should also draw overall conclusions derived from a holistic supply perspective. So, for example, if the strategy is to open a new contact centre (call centre) in the north-east of England, individual supply elements will be analysed. Are there enough people available on the market to deliver the numbers? Does the labour force have potential for training in contact centre skills? Is there evidence of flexibility in the market? And so on. But once these individual elements of supply have been analysed, those in HR will want to draw some broad conclusions that will inform the strategy. In essence the conclusions will be about whether the supply of labour is sufficient in all respects to make the strategic option a feasible one.

The process by which a supply forecast is prepared is described below.

The business or organisational strategy informs internal supply of people

It was stated above that supply would be both internal and external. The business or organisational strategy can be used to generate a possible internal supply of labour. So it is necessary to understand how the business or organisational strategy is shaping up. This can be evaluated by dialogue with senior business managers, which should flag up at an early stage whether strategies are going to produce any fallout of people and therefore whether there is potential for redeployment as part of the supply side of the labour equation. It is a growing phenomenon in workforce management that it is necessary to redeploy scarce labour where possible. This part of the supply forecast will identify where decisions in one business unit to free up staff can be co-ordinated with another unit's demand for staff.

Figure 14 **ASSESSING THE SUPPLY OF PEOPLE FOR THE PURPOSES OF THE SHRF**

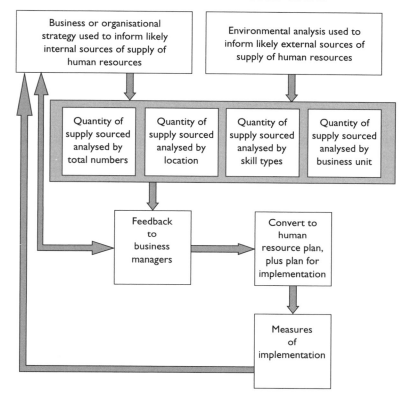

Environmental analysis used to inform likely external sources of supply

This section will largely be based on labour analysis from government sources. A significant amount of data is available on both actual labour and future forecasts. This is an indispensable part of the supply forecast, and those in HR will need to be fully conversant with the data. Much of the rest of this chapter is therefore dedicated to analysing the external supply of labour.

Quantity of supply analysed by total numbers

From the analysis it should be possible to gain an indication of the potential quantity of labour available for any particular type of work. This is inevitably an estimate – it is not feasible (for example) to forecast supply for more generically complex jobs such as 'sales' or 'administration' – but is becoming more critical. Indeed, in some areas knowing the potential numbers of employees is a vital part of forecasting. It may determine location, pay, training requirements, and even whether to go with the strategy or not.

The other important factor here is the internal source of supply. In the light of the war for talent, organisations are increasingly looking to redeploy people as one business unit downsizes. The blunt instrument of redundancy is no longer the only alternative.

Quantity of supply analysed by location

The geographical analysis is also an important characteristic of forecasting. Many locational decisions have been made in recent years on the availability of certain types of labour in certain geographical areas. The location of call centres in Glasgow is one such example. Others include technology location along the M4 corridor or 'silicon valley', specialist motor industry locations in the Midlands, and so on.

Quantity of supply analysed by skill types

Skills supply is a national issue. We saw earlier that there is a significant shift at policy level to provide the skills necessary for the economy to compete effectively. The understanding of labour availability by skill types is clearly something that is gaining in prominence. It is important that those in HR make this input into the strategy by understanding fully the issues about skills supply and how they might impact on the organisation's strategy.

Quantity of supply analysed by business unit

We also saw earlier that the supply forecast will be built up of individual components before taking a look at the bigger picture. Understanding the business unit requirements is one of these components. It will give those in HR a 'micro-analysis' of labour supply for a particular strategy emanating from a unit, and will inform the larger supply situation.

Feedback to business managers for debate and dialogue

Once the analysis has been prepared it can then be fed back to the business managers for discussion. The response to the information is likely to vary depending on circumstances. If, for example, the HR community points out that the feasibility of a strategy is brought into question because of the shortage of suitably skilled numbers of people in an area or business unit, that will require to be backed up by solid evidence. The output of this will be a modification of the business unit strategy to take account of the HR input.

Input to the human resource plan

At this point, what we will have is a composite picture making up a supply forecast that mirrors the strategy for the organisation as a whole and that for the individual business unit or function. Once the dialogue has taken place and strategy is agreed or changed, the process of planning can start. The supply forecast, when matched to demand (as discussed in Chapter 7), will inform a broad range of HR policies and practices that can be articulated in the HR plan. In particular, it will inform the basis of the resourcing plan that looks to match people to the requirements of the business strategy.

Measures of implementation set

Finally, some means of quantifying implementation will have to be agreed as part of the HR plan. Measurement will clearly be important in assessing the success or otherwise of the supply forecast, and will also provide valuable intelligence in assessing any changes to the supply situation. Measures can be set against all of the supply forecast indicators to give indications of achievement in terms of both quantity and quality.

Key to this process will of course be a thorough understanding of the actual labour market and trends therein. The paragraphs below indicate how to go about obtaining such an understanding.

The labour market in the UK

How is the UK's labour or people supply likely to develop in the coming years? To answer this question requires an examination of two broad types of supply projections:

☐ population and labour market activity projections, which taken together show trends in the potential *number* of people available and how many of these will be participating in the economy

☐ occupational and qualifications (or more broadly 'skill') projections, which offer an indication of trends in the *quality* of the labour supply.

This section of the chapter assesses projections of each of these trends in turn, although it is important at the outset to appreciate the significant interactions between them. For example, labour market activity rates vary by gender, age, race, etc. A shift in the underlying make-up of the population between groups with different activity rates can thus affect the overall number of people in the jobs market – the level of activity – without any change in trend in activity rates for any particular sub-group. Similarly, trends in full-time education and training can impact on the quantity as well as the quality of people available to employers insofar as this alters activity rates.

In addition – as the section will show – it is necessary to recognise that these trends are themselves influenced by wider economic forces, plus the impact of government policy and employer practices. State welfare and skills policies clearly have a bearing on the willingness of people to participate in the jobs market and the quality of the labour they supply. And the same is true of the way in which employers recruit, manage and develop people.

Labour supply projections should therefore not be viewed simplistically as a constraint on strategic HR planning but perceived rather as a planning parameter that HR professionals can themselves help to shift.

Population and activity projections

Most labour supply forecasts focus on people of working age (16–59/64 years). The population in Great Britain of working age currently stands at around 35 million, having risen from 32.6 million at the end of the 1970s. Change in the population results from the balance of births, deaths and net migration. Death rates are typically fairly stable, so population changes are driven by births and migration. On current official projections produced by the Government Actuary's Department, the total is set to rise to 36.3 million by 2011. This is an increase of 1.4 million on the base year for the projection (1998) – a rate of growth of 0.3 per cent per annum. Net inward migration accounts for about half the projected rise.

The population ages

Men comprise 52 per cent of the working-age population, and the numbers of men and women are projected to rise at similar rates. But with lower birth rates in recent decades against a background of stable death rates, the structure of the population is ageing. The number of people aged over 45 is projected to increase by 3.4 million between 1998 and 2011, whereas the number of 35–44-year-olds will be unchanged by the end of the projection period, while the number of 25–34-year-olds and 16–24-year-olds will fall by 1.6 million and 0.4 million respectively.

The UK activity rate

Although demographic change clearly has a bearing on the labour supply, the size and composition of the workforce depends primarily on the proportion of the population that participates in the economy and the characteristics of participants. This proportion – known as the economic activity rate – comprises people in work and those actively seeking work. At mid-2000 the rate stood at 79.1 per cent (28.7 million people). This is a high rate by EU standards, but lower than that of the USA. Of those in the workforce at that time, 27.1 million were employed and 1.6 million unemployed.

Female activity rates continue to rise

The activity rate is determined by a variety of economic and social factors. Over the long run the rate emerges from a combination of changes in the structure of employment and employer behaviour, trends in real incomes, and changes in social preferences. For example, the well-documented shift of employment from manufacturing to services, and from full-time to part-time work, has interacted with social change to raise the female activity rate relative to that of men: 74.8 per cent of working-age women were active in the labour market in mid-2000, compared with 56.8 per cent in 1971. And the rate is projected to rise still further to 75.4 per cent by 2011.

The effects of the economic cycle

In addition to structural change of this kind, the activity rate also responds to short-run fluctuations in the economic cycle by way of 'discouraged' and 'encouraged' worker effects. During economic downturns, more people tend to become discouraged about their job prospects and withdraw from the labour market. When the economy picks up, the opposite occurs as employment growth encourages people to look for jobs. Consequently, activity rate projections have to incorporate assumptions about the likely state of the economy – normally using the unemployment rate as a proxy – as well as taking longer-run factors into account.

Activity rate projections

Taking all such factors together, the Office for National Statistics publishes labour force projections broken down by age, gender and region. Current projections – which assume that claimant unemployment will remain at the low rate prevailing in recent years – indicate a small rise in the activity rate between now and 2011. Nonetheless, the overall growth in population will result in an extra 1.4 million people in the workforce – again taking 1998 as the base year – the labour supply growing at a slightly faster rate than the population (see Table 5). This outcome represents a marked improvement on the 1990s. The first half of that decade witnessed a contraction in the labour force in the wake of the recession of

Table 5 POPULATION AND LABOUR FORCE PROJECTION, GREAT BRITAIN, 1998–2011

	1998 (in millions)	2011 (in millions)	Change (in millions)	Per cent change per year
Population of working age	34.9	36.3	1.4	0.3
Activity rate	79.9%	80.7%	1.4%	0.4
Labour force:				
Men	15.5	15.7	0.2	
Women	12.4	13.6	1.2	
16–24 age-group	4.5	5.0	0.5	
25–34 age-group	7.1	6.4	−1.1	
35–44 age-group	6.9	6.9	–	
45–59 age-group	8.1	9.6	1.5	
60–64 age-group	1.0	1.5	0.5	
total	27.9	29.3	1.4	

Source: Government Actuary's Department and the Office for National Statistics

1990–92. Regional projections tend to show a similar overall outcome to that observed for Britain as a whole. Nationally, women account for almost 90 per cent of the projected increase.

Relatively fewer men in the workforce

Within this overall context, projected trends in male activity rates, and those for different age-groups, deserve particular attention. In contrast with the female rates, male activity rates have been in long-term decline. The rate for men has fallen from over 90 per cent in 1979 to 84.5 per cent in mid-2000. Indeed, the proportion of men active in the labour market fell throughout the 1990s despite the 'long boom' and rising employment. By 2000 there were 130,000 fewer men in the workforce than a decade earlier, even though the labour market nationally had moved back toward 'full employment'.

This outcome has been the result of two structural trends in the supply of labour that in conjunction have served to outweigh the positive effect of rising employment levels. First, along with their female contemporaries, younger men have been participating in greater numbers in full-time education. About two-thirds of all 16–19-year-olds are now engaged in full-time study, up from just one-third a generation ago. Second, older men – unlike their female contemporaries – have been leaving the workforce earlier, seemingly unable to benefit as well as women from change in the structure of employment. Some of these men have withdrawn voluntarily into early retirement, but most comprise a group of 'hidden' unemployed (the majority existing on state incapacity benefit). Significantly, the downward trend is projected to continue, albeit at a slower pace, the male activity rate dropping to 81.7 per cent by 2011. This will not prevent a small rise in the number of men in the workforce because growth in the male population of working age will offset the effect of a lower activity rate. When set alongside rising female activity rates, however, the fall in the male rate means that the gender gap in the workforce will continue to close. Women are thus projected to contribute 46 per cent of the total UK labour supply by 2011, up from 44 per cent in 2000.

An ageing workforce

The workforce, like the population, is ageing (a tendency most marked in regions with the lowest ethnic minority populations, since the latter have a younger age profile than the white population). The number of economically active people in the 45–59-year age-group is projected to rise by around 1.5 million between 1998 and 2011. At the same time the number of 35–44-year-olds in the workforce will remain roughly stable, while the number of 25–34-year-olds drops by over 1 million. Paradoxically, the number of economically active 16–24-year-olds is projected to rise, even though there will be fewer people in this age-group in the population and more of them will be participating in full-time education. By 2011 there will be 5 million 16–24-year-olds in the workforce, compared with 4.5 million in 1998.

The latter paradox is explained by a rise in the cost of education to the individual, resulting from a fall in the real value of student maintenance grants and the introduction of student loans. This has prompted students to combine part-time employment with full-time study. One in two students aged 16–19 is now active in the labour market, one in three in the case of 20–24-year-olds; a generation ago only one in 10 students was economically active.

The impact of policy and practice

It is of course necessary to apply caveats to projections of this kind when making strategic HR forecasts. Not only might unforeseen swings in the economic cycle alter the projected outcomes (as outlined above) but government policies and employer practices also have an impact on activity rates. Such an impact is difficult to predict with any accuracy, but the likelihood is that developments in policy and practice will serve to raise activity rates, all other things being equal.

Since the late 1980s, successive UK governments have sought to increase the size of the active labour pool by means of more work-focused welfare regimes, increased financial incentives to work, and efforts to encourage equal opportunities and workforce diversity. The present government has emphasised the importance of this approach and is starting to target its various welfare-to-work initiatives at groups with particularly low activity rates, such as lone parents, the female partners of jobless men, older people, and people with disabilities. Labour Force Survey data published each month by the Office for National Statistics show that individuals from these groups form the bulk of the 2.3 million people of working age in the UK who do not participate in the labour market but say that they want to work.

At the same time the government is also encouraging more employers to adopt current best practice in providing opportunities for groups who face barriers to employment that discourage them from actively seeking work. A good example is the voluntary Code on Age Diversity in Employment introduced in 1999. Against a background of a tight labour market and growing employer recognition of the need to access untapped sources of labour, the government is probably pushing on a gradually opening door in this respect. Assuming that the economy remains relatively buoyant, the chances are that the labour supply will therefore rise further by 2011 than current projections suggest as more previously marginal people are drawn into the labour market.

Skill projections

Activity rate projections offer primarily an indication of the quantitative aspect of the people supply. However, an assessment of the quality of supply is equally, if not more, important for strategic HR purposes because of the changing nature of the types of jobs that are available in the labour market.

The importance of 'employability'

It is ultimately supply quality – or the 'skill' or 'employability' of the workforce – that determines how quickly people can be recruited and deployed to meet shifting patterns of demand for products and services, and/or how easily people can be developed to improve product and service quality. The prevailing skill mix in the workforce therefore has profound consequences for business success. And from an economy-wide perspective, the mix also influences both the rate of growth of productivity and the sustainable rate of employment, which together determine income per head of population and thus overall living standards.

Measuring labour quality

Unfortunately, it is more difficult to measure the quality than the quantity of people in the labour force. The underlying problem is that 'skill' and 'employability' are loose concepts. For example, although qualifications are an indicator of formal skill they say little about people's experience or softer human skills. Moreover, nominally similar qualifications may have to be considered in the light of their vintage and/or differences in the degree of difficulty involved in attaining them. In practice, therefore, an examination of trends in the quality of the labour supply must consider a range of indicators. Principal among the latter are occupational trends and trends in the proportion of the workforce that is obtaining qualifications.

Occupational shifts and trends in qualifications

Occupational projections are currently available for the period to 2009 (see Table 6). These point to a continuation of a trend

Table 6 OCCUPATIONAL EMPLOYMENT TRENDS AND PROJECTIONS, UK, 1981–2009

	1981		1998		2009	
	000s	% share	000s	% share	000s	% share
Managers and senior officials	2,530	10.3	3,620	13.3	3,912	13.3
Professional occupations	1,968	8.0	2,936	10.8	3,803	12.9
Associate professional and technical	2,301	9.4	3,350	12.3	4,169	14.2
Administrative, clerical and secretarial	3,833	15.7	4,047	14.9	4,017	13.7
Skilled trades	4,256	17.4	3,738	13.8	3,473	11.8
Leisure and personal service	859	3.5	1,525	5.6	1,993	6.8
Customer service	1,452	5.9	1,801	6.6	1,988	6.8
Process, plant and machine operatives	2,967	12.1	2,455	9.0	2,421	8.2
Elementary occupations	4,321	17.6	3,671	13.5	3,613	12.3

Source: Projections of Occupations and Qualifications 1999–2000, Institute of Employment Research, 2000

that has prevailed since the early 1980s. The trend has a number of dominant features that highlight the changing skill mix of people at work. First, there is a rise in employment of people in managerial, professional or technical jobs – by the end of this decade their collective share in total employment will have increased from around 25 per cent to 40 per cent within a generation. Second, the rise continues in the numbers of people in sales, and customer and personal service occupations. Third, fewer people perform administrative, clerical and secretarial work. And fourth, there is a further marked decline in manual employment, skilled and unskilled. By 2009 just over one in 10 people will be performing skilled manual jobs, down from almost one in five in 1981.

These occupational trends – which reflect structural change in the pattern of demand for labour – are in turn having consequences for trends in qualifications. The key driving factors are a fall in demand for totally unskilled labour plus the fact that the fast-growing managerial, professional and technical occupations rely on formal qualifications to a far greater extent than do skilled manual occupations. These factors have placed a higher premium on the acquisition of formal skills, which is reflected in the higher rates of participation in full-time education referred to earlier plus a less marked but nonetheless growing tendency for older people to return to formal education and training. As a result, during the past 20 years the proportion of the workforce without qualifications has fallen from just under 50 per cent to around 10 per cent, as more qualified young people have entered the labour market while those retiring or withdrawing have tended to be less qualified (see Table 7). This trend is projected to continue. In the process, an interesting – and already clearly visible – side-effect will be a rise in *all* occupations of the share of people holding formal qualifications.

Continuing quality problems

On the face of things the rise in the incidence of qualifications suggests a fairly rapid and ongoing improvement in the quality of the labour supply. But will future improvement be rapid enough? And what about the overall quality of workforce skills?

Continuing quality problems in the labour force become apparent on examining more closely how the structure, rather than incidence, of UK qualifications has changed. The greatest improvement has been in the numbers of people with degree-level qualifications. The number with vocational qualifications has risen only modestly. And more than half the workforce (54 per cent) is still qualified at or below the equivalent of NVQ level 2 (almost one in three below that level). Moreover, it is well documented that some 7 million

Table 7 QUALIFICATIONS OF ECONOMICALLY-ACTIVE PEOPLE OF WORKING AGE, UK, 1979–200

	1979 %	1989 %	2000 %
No qualifications	46	28	11
NVQ 1 equivalent	14	21	20
NVQ 2 equivalent	17	23	23
NVQ 3 equivalent	10	13	19
NVQ 4/5 equivalent	12	15	27

Source: Department for Education and Skills

adults (one in five of the population of working age) experience significant deficiencies in basic skills. The least able
are either detached from the labour force, suffer long-term
unemployment, or capable of only low-quality and relatively
poorly-paid work. This leaves the UK at a distinct disadvan-
tage in comparison with its main EU competitors, France and
Germany. Although the UK compares favourably on higher-
degree-level qualifications, the country trails way behind
Germany in terms of intermediate-level qualifications – with
a 30 percentage point gap in the proportions qualified to NVQ
level 3 equivalent – and performs badly relative to both countries in terms of basic skills.

The glass half full or half empty?

The combination of a rising incidence of qualifications
against a backdrop of continuing skill deficiencies helps
explain mixed signals from business on the quality of the UK
labour supply. Regular survey evidence from industry groups
such as the CBI and British Chambers of Commerce indicate
that skill shortages at any one point in the economic cycle
are less of a problem than in past decades. This suggests
an overall improvement in the employability of UK labour.
However, government survey evidence shows that a substan-
tial proportion of businesses continue to cite a lack of suitably
skilled people as a source of difficulty in filling vacancies (one
in 12 establishments) and meeting current business objectives
(one in five establishments). Moreover, these supply
deficiencies reflect difficulties confronted by employers in
producing the current UK range of goods and services. Upgrading this range to meet ever more sophisticated consumer and
business requirements in an increasingly competitive market
environment will thus place even greater stress on the need
to improve the quality of the labour supply.

Raising the game

On current trends the UK workforce still appears to lack the
overall degree of quality necessary to meet the imperatives
of the emerging knowledge economy. This presents a challenge to policy-makers and people managers and developers

alike to raise their game. Improvement will depend crucially upon the efforts of the government to enhance basic skills in the population at large, through both formal education and remedial training for individuals already in the workforce.

Some of these efforts will be directed at groups with low rates of economic activity – by way of the various New Deal programmes – and if successful will serve to enhance both the quantity and quality of the workforce over and above current projections. In addition to this, measures directed at individuals – of which there have been many government initiatives – and employers – in the form of the Investors in People standard – should in principle raise the quality of workforce skills up to and beyond intermediate level. In both respects the supply trajectory should also be shifted by institutional reform, such as the newly established Learning and Skills Councils. Of considerable importance, however, will be the role of human resource development itself as a driver of improvement in the quality of the labour supply. This will be necessary in order to ensure that people are developed within the workplace in a volume and manner attuned to the high-performance requirements of the coming decades.

Much will hinge on spreading high-quality learning opportunities to all grades of employee. The government's quarterly Labour Force Survey continually records that one in three employees received no training from his or her current employer in the previous year. And already highly qualified people receive most of the training that is on offer – one in five of those qualified to NVQ level 4, compared with fewer than one in 10 of those qualified below NVQ level 2. This 'to him that hath' phenomenon is arguably as big a barrier to raising the overall quality of the labour supply in the UK as is inadequate investment in skills. If HR professionals can bring down this barrier, the quality of the people they have to work with and the quality of UK products and services will be much enhanced in the coming decade.

9 ASSESSING THE CULTURAL IMPLICATIONS OF STRATEGY

Culture in the strategy process

'Culture' is the context within which individuals and groups operate. For an organisation, it comprises the set of beliefs, values and emotions that enable its members to work effectively. The mutual trust that exists between the members of a fighting unit of the British Army is just as important as a shared understanding of Queen's Regulations. In most companies, the cultural context is assumed: newcomers absorb the unwritten rules through a process of observation, trial and error – otherwise, they face rejection.

Successful companies establish a culture that fits their operating model. A few years ago, the UK head of a global restaurant company told a newspaper reporter of the sheer pleasure and pride he felt in his company's ability to produce millions of identical hamburgers of consistent quality every day. This culture of consistency, which requires a centralised command-and-control model, would not suit companies whose competitive edge derives from product innovation or responsiveness to individual customer needs.

In an era of gradual change, the culture of a company adjusts over time to new market requirements and opportunities. Today, however, the pace of change in the economy – driven by the interlocking forces of globalisation, technological innovation, deregulation and government intervention – is such that companies are forced to adapt their operating models far more quickly to remain competitive.

> A business strategy encapsulates decisions on the markets in which a company competes, its product range and its customer base. A comprehensive strategy also covers the adaptation or transformation of the company's operating model to meet future market conditions. With the acceleration of changes in the competitive environment, it becomes vital to synchronise changes in business processes, organisational structure and reward systems with appropriate shifts in the culture. Changing culture is therefore not about building a happy company – it is necessary to create an organisation that can deliver hard results.
>
> *Alex Mayall,*
> *CSC Research Service*

The cultural implications of strategy

> People did whatever it was necessary to do. Everybody did something, from maintaining the exterior of the building, painting, and so forth, to what we called 'snacktime' when someone had to cook and serve lunch. This was how interested everyone was in just being a part of it and watching it grow. It was fun – something that was in our blood, not just a job.

It sounds like a great place to work doesn't it? Interesting and fun! Well it would have been had you been in Detroit in 1962. This paragraph is a quote (Davis, 1991) from Raynoma Singleton, ex-wife of Berry Gordy, the founder of Tamla Motown, one of the most successful music corporations of its era. Motown became 'the voice of Young America', and produced hit after hit in the US and British music charts. The culture of the place is almost tangible from this description. And what a culture of success it proved to be.

The cultural implications of business strategy continue to be serious matters for those in HR. And there is evidence that cultural issues, always important, are now becoming more appreciated. First, understanding the culture of an organisation is a prerequisite to managing any sort of change. The organisational culture may be very different from that of Tamla Motown, but the point is no less important. Second, there is a massive undercurrent of change going on in attitudes to work and the impact that these new visions may have on the culture of the organisation. The reasons for this latter point are well understood and reflect changes in societal attitudes (work–life balance) as well as demographics. A view brilliantly articulated by Naomi Klein in her book *No Logo* suggests that organisations have moved from job creation to wealth creation – which has implications for loyalty and disloyalty (Klein, 2001).

Even a more moderate perspective shows that the world of work has changed and that those within it are faced with a whole new set of rules, both written and unwritten. It is with particular concern on the unwritten that the cultural implications of strategy focus. HR personnel have a major role to play as 'the voice of culture in the organisation' – analysing and articulating what it is, and doing something about it.

The previous chapters looked at the measurable inputs into the strategy, namely the supply and demand for people. These are the areas likely to generate a good deal of interest at business level. The business will want to know turnover and manpower flows, and their impact on the achievement of the strategy. This is 'HR stuff' that is hard and tangible. Less clear, and therefore less likely to be discussed, will be the cultural challenges of strategy-setting. And yet there is as much chance of problems being caused by the cultural implications of change as by almost any other area of HR. The key thing to remember when dealing with culture is not to get sidetracked into some kind of 'psychology-think'. This chapter looks at how the issue of culture might be dealt with in a meaningful way (a way that people can understand and do something about) during the SHRF process.

Figure 15 is a model of the process for analysing culture and for putting in place proposals for dealing with it.

The importance of understanding culture

Assessing the culture and style of the organisation – and how appropriate they are to the future business direction and strategy – is critical. It is, however, an area that is one of the softer aspects of human resource management. . .and as a result is often 'parked'. Nonetheless, it is incumbent on those

Figure 15 **ASSESSING THE CULTURAL IMPLICATIONS OF STRATEGY**

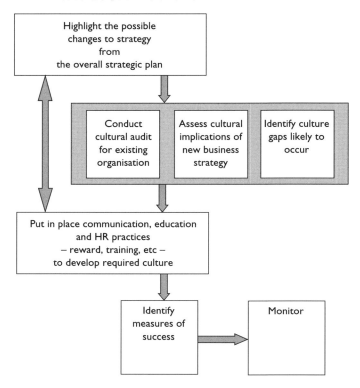

with responsibility for human resource management to emphasise how critical this particular activity is. A recent ethnographic study of the importance of culture in business planning (Bloodgood, 2000) reinforced this point when it concluded that

> the business planning processes of many companies need to change periodically in order to keep pace with changes in the business environment. Before any changes are made, however, the company's culture should be well understood to make sure that the alterations are appropriate. The culture of the organisation will affect the content of the changes recommended as well as how the changes are communicated.

When organisations fail to recognise cultural issues during the strategy-setting process, it has an impact on the ultimate success or failure of the strategy. There is evidence to support this. In studies of mergers and acquisitions (M&As), for example, it is often noted that organisational culture is one of the most critical factors for success or failure. This illustrates that organisational culture is a powerful force and can act either for or against the achievement of the business strategy. It is a conclusion reinforced by a study carried out on behalf of Hewlett Packard and Glaxo Pharmaceuticals. The study demonstrated that the identification and management of culture could be successful not by discerning what is apparently 'best practice' in this area but by giving careful consideration to contextual features, such as staff groupings, geographic spread, the number of divisions involved, and the exact outcome desired from the management intervention (Hope Hailey, 1999).

It is not just in mergers and acquisitions that the issue of culture is important. The issue of diversity, for example, is one that is increasingly seen as a great opportunity to harness the talent within the organisation in an inclusive way. The possibility of building a culture that values differences in race, gender and ability should enthuse everyone in organisations, whatever the sector. An organisation's culture is pervasive. It can be the critical factor for success. It can also stifle change and innovation if mismanaged or misunderstood. Organisational culture is a powerful force – and now there is a growing recognition that its management is an important facet of organisational success. If the door is not actually open, then at least it is ajar. The SHRF should include a section on 'assessing the cultural implications of strategy' as a valid part of the overall process. In some organisations this is in the form of a 'cultural audit', often as the precursor to some major organisational change such as merger or acquisition.

Definitions of culture

Most HR personnel will at some time have had to describe what is meant by 'culture'. And most will have reverted to Martin Bower's brilliantly apposite definition of culture as 'the way we do things around here' (Deal and Kennedy, 1982).

The challenge of dealing with culture as part of the SHRF is to articulate the important facets of 'the way we do things around here' in an analytical form that can be managed and measured. The intangibility of organisational culture sometimes induces cultural myopia on the part of business managers. Yet those CEOs who spend time working the culture will be more successful than those who do not in achieving sustained competitive advantage – *ceteris paribus*, of course! The SHRF process is an ideal opportunity to leverage the cultural elements of strategy onto the strategic top table. But why should we want to do this?

A few years ago the Hay Group, one of the world's leading consultancies in HR, outlined the cultural characteristics of successful companies. These were things that many successful companies did in common and consistently well. If such things could be emulated by others, there might be a better chance for them to succeed in their industry or sector. Of course, dealing with the organisation's culture is but one part of the overall HR package. Yet it is an important part, and one that has been 'under the radar' for too long.

So what *are* the cultures prevalent in 'the world's most admired companies'? The Hay research found that those companies that managed their cultural attributes well had certain key characteristics – as can be seen in Table 8.

If these are beneficial cultural characteristics, then we should use the SHRF to put in place frameworks that allow the organisation to understand and debate the organisational culture and, if possible, make changes that facilitate the

Table 8 CORPORATE CULTURES OF 'THE WORLD'S MOST ADMIRED COMPANIES'

More emphasis on	Less emphasis on
• encouraging teamwork	• achieving budgeted objectives
• delivering reliably on commitments to customers	• supporting top management decisions
• treating employees fairly and consistently	• supporting the decisions of one's boss
• maximising customer satisfaction	• maintaining existing customer accounts
• taking the initiative	• respecting the chain of command
• rewarding superior performance	• maintaining clear lines of authority and accountability
• encouraging innovation	• establishing clear job descriptions
• capitalising on creativity	• minimising human error

Source: Tunstall, 1998

achievement of strategy within an effective cultural climate. A key step in this process is to achieve a better understanding of organisational culture.

Every organisation has a culture, and the way that human behaviour expresses itself – in both speech and action – defines that culture. We might conclude that culture has a powerful, pervasive influence. Some would argue that it affects every corner of the organisation. Furthermore, it is unlikely to be a homogenous entity. We can see that these definitions and observations about culture suggest something that has elements of behaviour and history, that have a pervasive nature and that are articulated in words and actions. Recognising these characteristics may be an important prerequisite for the successful implementation of a business strategy.

There have been many analyses of culture and the various cultural norms detectable in an organisation. Handy attributes the different types of organisational culture to several factors including history, size, technology, goals and objectives, the environment, and of course the staff (Handy, 1988). He categorises several possible types, including culture based on power, based on role, based on task, and based on an individual. Others have tried to put a different perspective on culture. Howard Hills has emphasised the importance of culture in a team-based context (Hills, 2001).

Cartwright and Cooper listed observable ways in which culture shows itself in organisations (Cartwright and Cooper, 2000):

☐ the way in which people interact, their forms of address, and the language they use
☐ the dress code
☐ the way in which work is organised and conducted – eg production-line assembly versus cellular team arrangements
☐ the organisation's self-image and the dominant values it espouses, often through its mission statements, company and product literature
☐ the way in which it treats its employees and responds to its

customers – this is often reflected in the physical facilities provided by the organisation

☐ the rules for 'playing the organisational game' – eg the types of behaviour associated with being a good employee or effective manager.

In whatever way culture is defined in an organisation, 'the way we do thing around here' has significant implications for the way we *want* to do things around here. Understanding both the former and the latter is a key part of the human resources role. Furthermore, culture has both visible, overt characteristics as well as the tacit 'unspoken but understood'. Both types of cultural consideration must be addressed.

What issues should be raised in the strategic human resource forecasting process?

The strategic human resource forecasting process provides an ideal opportunity to raise cultural issues and for them to impact on strategy. There are several key points to consider during the cultural analysis:

☐ The first is to understand the physical setting, because an organisation will 'create a setting that makes a statement to the world about the company, both deliberate and otherwise' (Deal and Kennedy, 1982). This argument is one that many organisations would recognise. However, it is no longer a point universally accepted, and its relevance has to be tempered by the 'physical setting' that goes with the virtual world of dot.coms. What is the physical setting of an e-business? To get the right combination of 'clicks and mortar' is recognised as critical to the modern organisation, and this will be a key factor in the cultural analysis.

☐ The second is to gather existing statements about the organisation's culture. What is written already? What has been said in public meetings? What does the chief executive say when he or she is on visits to departments or sites? This will contribute to the 'cultural database' on which further analysis can be made.

☐ A third aspect concerns the image that the company

projects to the outside world, and how it is displayed in the behaviours of the individuals who do the projecting. This is more than the brand 'values' – it is how individuals express themselves in the context of the brand. So, for instance, an organisation might have the motto 'We try to be the best.' If the staff are evidently not the best in practice (in the actual performance to customers), then this is a powerful indicator that whatever comes out of the business strategy about striving to be the best is a waste of time. Unless, of course, the culture of the organisation is addressed as well as the financial investment in, say, new customer information systems.

The process for assessing the cultural implications of strategy

Following a brief insight into the importance of culture and how we might define it in an organisation, the next stage is to put in place a process for establishing just how culture and cultural implications affect strategy. This is one of the most difficult areas of HR in which to gain a foothold, even though it is an area that unless organisations recognise and deal with its implications can have far-reaching morale, motivation, and ultimately company performance implications. Having an effective process is the beginning of gaining this foothold.

Highlight the possible changes to strategy from the overall strategic plan

The initial part of the cultural assessment will be to identify the possible changes that might take place as a result of the strategic plans that are being formulated. Some examples of this are:

☐ The organisation decides to expand its business by merger or acquisition. In this strategy, several organisational cultures will be forced together into the new organisation. At this point there may be a 'cultural power-struggle' over which will prevail – the culture of the acquirer or of the acquired. Of all the issues on which mergers or acquisitions depend, cultural compatibility is increasingly recognised as the clincher.

☐ Outsourcing is proposed for non-core activities or support functions. In this strategy, a whole new approach to the support or service function is necessary. Whereas once, supply of service tended to be on demand, it will be replaced by a more formal process, requiring planning and forecasting on behalf of the user.

☐ Manufacturing is to be closed in one country and moved to another. The cultural challenge precipitated by this strategy is always immense. National cultures as well as organisational ones will have to be taken account of.

Each of these examples carries with it a possible change to the way of working, and this in turn may mean a change of attitude, process or value proposition. In each case there is a cultural implication, and the success of the strategy might depend on interpreting it and managing it accordingly.

Conduct a cultural audit for the existing organisation

This description sounds rather grandiose – the actuality need not be. There are various ways in which a cultural audit might take place. Indeed, it is likely that many of the components of such an audit already exist. Ways to achieve the desired output, one that indicates the cultural make-up of the organisation, include:

☐ staff attitude surveys
☐ interviews with employees within the company
☐ interviews with recent leavers and joiners
☐ an analysis of organisation structures
☐ a formal endeavour to understand how the career paths of people are decided
☐ an analysis of quantifiable people measures, such as staff turnover, length of service, etc.

A combination of these should be sufficient to describe the current cultural make-up of the organisation. What might come out of this? A whole range of cultural indicators. The attitude of the organisation towards diversity issues, for example, would be reflected in several of the measures. Whether the organisation had a marketing orientation, and whether customer service was regarded as a primary area would be brought to light. And so on.

Assess the cultural implications of the new business strategy

This aspect of the process means making a forecast of the type of culture that will be successful in the new strategic scenario. A classic case of this is when an organisation decides to merge or acquire. Statistics are claimed to decree that 70 per cent of mergers and acquisitions fail. Well, one of the reasons for this would be that there is a cultural mismatch. A step in the first stages of merger, therefore, is to ask the question 'What culture would we like to see in this newly merged organisation?'

Let us look at an example. Organisation A is a sales-oriented business successful because it is fast-moving and risk-taking. It merges with organisation B, which is financially conservative but has excellent risk management procedures. The two seem compatible in a business sense, but even in the brief description there are obvious differences in the type of organisation and probably in their cultures. The SHRF is an excellent opportunity to raise this as a strategic issue. Which culture is the more desirable? Is it that of organisation A or organisation B? Or is there perhaps a new culture that can emerge in the same way as Tony Blair's 'Third Way' for New Labour? It is very important to get this debate onto the strategic agenda – and much better to do so at this stage than when the company is being broken up because the merger has not worked. It is the role of those responsible for HR to ensure that the debate takes place.

Identify culture gaps

Once the assessment has been made, any gaps in the desired future cultural direction, compared with the current situation, can be identified, and plans put in place to close these gaps in a culture change programme. A way of doing this is to focus plans for culture change on the 'seven levers' that are held to create a culture of success. These are shown in

Figure 16 CREATING A CULTURE OF SUCCESS – SEVEN KEY LEAVERS

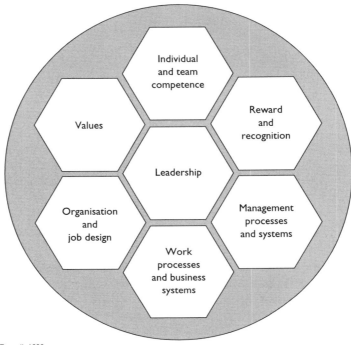

Source: Tunstall, 1998

Figure 16. The 'levers' demonstrate that changing corporate culture is not merely about communicating the desired state. It is much more complex than that, involving almost every part of the organisation, from its leadership to its processes.

So, for example, it is not sufficient to pull the lever marked 'work processes and business systems' and hope that the culture will miraculously change. Instead it will be necessary to work with several levers at once, and the co-ordinating of those actions will be a real challenge for HR, whose role will be to advise on which levers to pull!

Communication, education and HR practices to develop the required culture

In view of HR's role, it is essential that the methodology by which change is to be made and the explanations and the time-scales or 'road map' for doing so are all articulated in a coherently integrated way. This will require input for change at all levels. Furthermore, the entire management team will have to participate in the communication process if it is to be an effective cultural change medium.

In the first place the leadership team must engage in the new cultural requirements and 'walk the talk.' This will be no good at all, however, if the processes remain as they were previously and the reward mechanism is unchanged. So every single aspect of organisational behaviour has to be included.

The likely outputs are:

☐ new values statements and behavioural indicators

☐ reward strategies that reflect the desired future state rather than the current situation

☐ education and training in the new ways

☐ consultation with employee representatives to outline the new strategies and their cultural implications

☐ communication and engagement of all employees in the organisation.

Most organisations will have their own versions of these, and 'best practice' is probably not an effective approach. Yet it is worth noting that all the revised values statements in the world will be meaningless unless behaviours change accordingly.

Identifying measures of success

How will we know if the plans to change the organisation's culture have been successful? It is important once all the matters enumerated above have been taken care of, that measures of success are identified. These might be classified within two categories:

☐ *Business measures* – Has the strategy delivered the business benefits anticipated? Such measures would be constituted by sales, customer satisfaction indices, and so on.

☐ *Behavioural measures* – Have there been shifts in behaviour or attitude as measured by staff attitude surveys or a post-change cultural survey?

Because culture change must be sustained, processes for longitudinal measurement should be set up. This means taking regular checks against the measures. In general, two particular measures are recognised as the best for culture change: staff satisfaction and customer service indices. However, it is also possible to deduce culture changes from other people metrics, including staff turnover.

Monitor the cultural change

By identifying measures of success in this way, a foundation for future monitoring may be put in place. As mentioned earlier in this chapter, the 'softness' of culture and its quasi-mythical status mean that it has been difficult to raise as an ongoing management challenge. There are signs nonetheless that recognition of the importance of culture to organisational success is increasing. Some of the brilliant anecdotes that have accumulated on the subject of mergers and the cultural difficulties that accompany them have highlighted the importance of cultural shifts. (Many of these anecdotes have assumed the status of the apocryphal – one failure to agree a new corporate colour scheme is said to have been the final straw in the subsequent failure of a merger.) Yet proceeding on the premise that there is no smoke without fire, a key challenge will be to monitor the change in the culture.

The measures outlined above provide a benchmark. Staff attitude surveys monitored over time are a good indicator of culture change – as are other measures, including customer satisfaction ('We've moved to a customer-focused culture'), staff turnover ('It's a nicer place to work') and employee relations measures (in relation to such matters as absence and bullying).

All this, then, represents a proposal for assessing and monitoring the culture of the organisation, and providing an input into the strategy-setting process.

10 GAP ANALYSIS

Recognising the difference (the gap) between current and desired future states

Let me give you a definition of a 'gap'. It is from a publication of ancient sayings from the writings called 'The Master of the Demon Valley' (Cleary, 1994).

> A gap is an opening; an opening is a space between barriers; a space between barriers makes for tremendous vulnerability. At the first sign of a gap, it should be shored up, or repelled, or stopped, or hidden, or overwhelmed. These are called the principles of stopping gaps.

Gap analysis represents a final part of the strategic human resource forecast – although that is probably a misleading description in that there is no final part as such in a clear, sequential way. Instead, gap analysis brings together, at various times, the separate parts of the HR forecasting process into a holistic view of the HR implications of strategy.

In traditional manpower planning, gap analysis was the means of contrasting the current numerical size of the workforce against the size predicted in the strategic plan. That is still an important part of the strategic human resource forecast. However, it is now necessary to extend this simple but effective balancing act to include other factors, such as:

☐ training
☐ culture
☐ succession management.

These elements are increasingly of high profile because of the war for talent and its implications for recruitment and retention, and because of the need to keep a firm grip on cost management. It is necessary to include them as part of a holistic approach to strategic human resource forecasting. To quote Lynda Gratton (Gratton *et al*, 1999):

> gap analysis is at the heart of this dynamic model of human resource strategy. By understanding the alignment between future needs and current capabilities, the strategy for human resources can emerge.

Figure 17 shows that gap analysis can cover both short- and long-term initiatives. In the short term, any gap will be filled by objective-based reward and training. In the longer term a strategic perspective is necessary, requiring both organisation and workforce development.

So how should we go about identifying the gaps that might come out of strategy-setting? Figure 18 outlines the process

Figure 17 **THE PEOPLE PROCESS MAP**

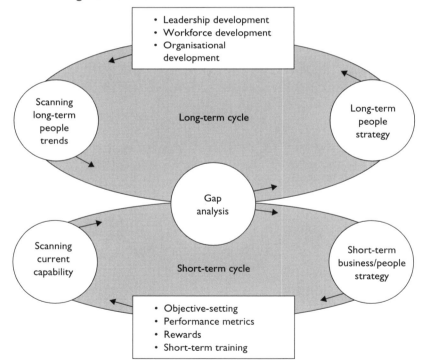

Reprinted by permission of Oxford University Press. Copyright © Lynda Gratton, Veronica Hope Hailey, Philip Stiles and Catherine Truss, 1999.

Figure 18 GAP ANALYSIS

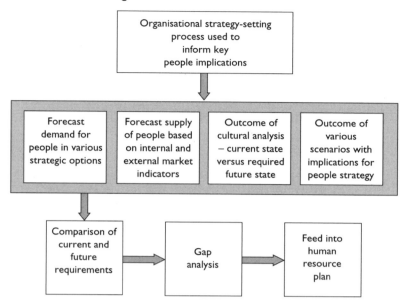

of gap analysis that this chapter uses. But before examining the process, it is essential first to fix a clear definition of the term, to understand how it operates in relation to people, and to see it in action.

Some definitions of gap analysis

A definition of gap analysis that is more contemporary than the ancient Chinese master's is provided by Hofer and Schendel (1986):

> Gap analysis – that is a comparison of the organisation's objectives, strategy and resources against the opportunities and threats in its environment to determine the extent of change required in the current strategy.

Hofer and Schendel find it possible to define this further by highlighting five subjects:

☐ First, the firm's past business portfolio must be assessed and its future position projected. . .

☐ Second, its past, present, and projected portfolios must be analysed in terms of their overall balance, growth and profit potential and level of risk.

☐ Next, these portfolios must be examined in order to identify individual SBU's that are expected to face major strategic issues and performance gaps during the firm's planning period.

☐ Then the impact of supplier, competitor and broad environmental trends on the firm's current and future port-folios must be assessed.

☐ Finally, the firm's future performance should be projected and compared with the desired levels of performance in order to identify performance gaps at the corporate level.

This is of course in a broader strategic context. The gap analysis is an opportunity for those in human resources to engage the senior management of the organisation in a strategic debate. It opens the door to identifying some of the major issues likely to arise in a people context.

Gap analysis in a people context

In a people context there are four critical areas in which gaps may be identified as part of the strategic human resource forecasting process. These are:

☐ in the supply and demand for labour – either as excesses of supply between current and proposed strategy (downsizing) or as excesses of demand (the war for talent)

☐ in the difference between the current cultural make-up of the organisation and that desired for the future

☐ in the difference between the current organisational structure and that indicated by the strategy debate

☐ in all aspects of organisational development, such as learning, reward, and employee relations.

The gap analysis as part of the strategic human resource forecasting process enables these elements to be identified, quantified and, most importantly, raised as 'issues' for strategic debate at board level during the overall strategy-setting process. The key here is for those responsible for human resources to make sure that such gaps are on the strategic agenda during the process rather than afterwards. It will be quite useless for the organisation to decide to adopt a strategy involving large human resource gaps without its both comprehending that there are such gaps and taking steps to fill them (a key part of the human resource plan). In one respect the gap analysis is the culmination of all of the other analyses in the SHRF. This does not necessarily imply a sequential approach, though, for gaps may be identified at any part of the process and 'real time' fixes put in place.

Examples of potential gaps and their implications for the people strategy

It might be useful, however, to glance at the kind of events that might lead those in human resources to flag up possible gaps for further debate:

☐ The organisational strategy is to open up the company's markets in Europe by setting up sales offices in Paris and Frankfurt. There are obviously facilities and marketing considerations in such a strategy, but the human resource implications are as critical. Are there people in the company with experience of the French and German market? If not, from where will they be sourced? Are the product designers aware of the different cultural variations of their designs? How can designs be integrated if they are not? What about European employment legislation? Does the organisation have the skills to develop employment packages for sales and support teams if this is the required route?

☐ The health authority decides to increase the number of nurses 'on the front line'. Are there enough nurses in the market as a whole? Can former employees be persuaded to rejoin the health authority? Is the reward package sufficiently attractive to compete with other careers for school- or university-leavers?

☐ The organisation decides to increase its customer service standards. Are there enough trained staff to facilitate this? If not, how will extra training be funded? Is the organisation's culture already customer-centric? If not, can an organisational development plan be implemented?

These are examples of where the organisational strategy towards its stated objectives may contain gaps for the human resource of the organisation – gaps that will have to be filled by means of an effective and focused people strategy. The solutions will, of course, cover the spectrum of HR responses. An example of how this might be achieved for the supply and demand of labour is included for reference in Table 9.

It may be informative to apply this concept to the health

Table 9 OPTIONS FOR MATCHING SUPPLY AND DEMAND

Labour shortage

a) INCREASE SUPPLY	b) REDUCE DEMAND	c) IMPROVE RETENTION
externally: • recruit differently • attract people of different age, sex, race, nationality, skill, qualifications, experience • advertise in different places • assess and select in different ways • improve terms and conditions • offer assistance in relocation, transport, childcare *internally:* • promote differently • train existing staff • redeploy existing staff	• redesign work • redesign job specification • use existing staff differently • subcontract work • relocate work • automate	• improve terms and conditions • improve management style and communications • improve promotion and recognition • improve training • improve inducements, bonus, etc • improve selection, placement and induction • monitor staff turnover

Labour surplus

a) INCREASE DEMAND	b) DECREASE SUPPLY	c) DISCOURAGE RETENTION
• increase markets for products and services	• early retirement • assisted career change • secondment, sabbaticals, etc • voluntary redundancy • compulsory redundancy	• short-term contracts • flexible working

Source: Rothwell, 1995

authority recruitment problem in the bullet list above. The first option is to increase the potential supply of staff. To date the staff have come almost exclusively from within the UK. By recruiting differently and advertising in different places, it should be possible to expand the source quite significantly. Similarly, a review of pay and location assistance could go some way to increasing supply and thereby reducing the gap.

How to prepare a gap analysis

It is important to note that the gap analysis is one of the main prompts for board-level dialogue. As such it should be concise and to the point. The other parts of the SHRF and the subsequent HR plan will be the detail. The gap analysis will also be an essential vehicle for instigating cross-functional HR debate. The responses to the gaps are likely to require 'joined-up thinking' on the part of HR, and the sooner this can be initiated the better.

The organisational strategy-setting process is used to inform key people implications

As with all other aspects of the strategic human resource forecast, the gap analysis starts with the organisational strategy, at the comparatively late stage of strategy-setting. By this time some ideas will have begun to emerge about the direction towards which the organisation will possibly be going. There will have been some scenario-planning, analyses of the labour implications of supply and demand, and a cultural audit of one sort or another. Those responsible for human resources should by now be getting a picture of issues that are likely to emerge from the strategy debate. It is at this point that the gap analysis should start to take shape.

The first port of call, then, is the organisational strategy, or more likely, the strategic options. These will give an indication of the possible demands that might be placed on the people within the organisation. HR personnel can begin to formulate ideas about the gaps that may present themselves.

How might this work?

In the first instance there will be enough evidence to suggest strategic options. Those responsible for HR ought already to have been involved in a high-level debate during several parts of the strategic human resource input to the strategy-setting process. Gaps should already be becoming evident. The organisation wants to become a global player? You have a dearth of managers with global experience. The strategy calls for a shift to enhanced customer service? You have inadequate training in place to allow for it. And so on. These responses will be registered as the process evolves, so that when the scorecard is reviewed, some indicators of gaps are already in place. These can be worked up into firmer contingency proposals during the gap analysis.

Demand and supply for labour is forecast and 'matched' in each of the strategic options

In order to get more detail into the gap analysis, a numerical view of the impact on the labour force is required. This will be presented in the form of contrasted demand and supply, and any resulting gaps will be shown. The development of strategic options (discussed in Chapter 5) and the analysis of demand and supply (Chapters 7 and 8) will be critical inputs at this point. Examples of possible outcomes include:

☐ The strategy requires the transfer of customer service to central contact centres (call centres) away from dispersed sites. The immediate gap is the lack of a workforce to man the call centres in the chosen region. Following the identification of this gap, a dialogue will be taken up about location, with the result that the gap starts closing. So we have a location but still no labour force. Then a recruitment or redeployment strategy can be considered, and plans formulated. There may also be gaps in the reward strategy, since a different pattern of reward might be proposed for the contact centre staff. A training need is also identified. And so on. The gap analysis is not about presenting solutions but about raising a dialogue and awareness, and making sure that the appropriate parts of the human resources function are aware of the gaps for their own technical plans that will be included in the overall human resources plan.

☐ An aspect of international growth raises the need to

expand the manufacturing operation outside of the base territory. There is a gap in the labour force numbers required to fill the new positions. There is also a labour shortage in the immediate area of the expanded factory. The dialogue raised by human resources using research on the local labour market will actually question the strategy. If those responsible for human resources can demonstrate through sound labour market analyses that the strategy is, in essence, flawed, it is as valid a position as coming up with a solution to fill the gap.

It is likely that the supply and demand for labour will be the most accessible and straightforward part of the gap analysis. It is tangible and measurable. It is also the area on which most of traditional human resource planning has focused. However, there are other less tangible but equally important parts of the analysis that can and should be raised at this point.

Cultural implications of strategy are identified and compared with the current situation

The strategic human resource forecast contains a section on the cultural analysis of the organisation (see Chapter 9). This will have demonstrated the organisation's cultural make-up, and will invariably have shown how complex and heterogeneous the culture is. It will also have raised the issue of the desired culture that has emerged from the strategic options. The gap between what employees say they want and what they are actually getting from their current jobs is growing. One aspect of this is reward. Another, which has been identified 'from Kobe to Kiel, from Moscow to Miami. . .is the ability to balance work and personal life and the feeling that they are secure in the future' (Johnson, 2001). Further studies have shown a clear gap between the employees' goals and those of the organisation, much of which can be attributed to a different cultural perception. The gap analysis is an opportunity to raise the issues that might arise from this into a board-level debate. Examples of the kind of things that might arise include:

☐ The organisation requires a directional change from a product focus to a customer focus. This has arisen in the past when an international competitor moves into what was previously regarded as a closed market. The UK tele-communications industry during the 1980s was very much this scenario. Companies manufactured products over which the consumer had little choice. When the markets were liberalised and newer products allowed in, manufacturers had quickly to have a more marketing/customer focus, which required a change of culture from the top to the bottom of the organisation. The gap analysis of the SHRF might have been a way of highlighting the possibility, thus enabling those companies affected to debate contingencies and prepare plans to satisfy the new demands.

☐ The trend towards outsourcing has also required a change of culture. Take for example a strategy to outsource web design to India from the home territory. How would this be achieved? The cultural analysis would have indicated a predominantly 'home'-based approach to web design, and that this would have to change if the full advantage of outsourcing was to be achieved. The gap analysis would raise this in a very specific way, identifying the people implications. Plans to change the culture would then be put forward. It sounds easy. Of course it is not, but it is important that the issue is raised during the strategic debate.

These are just two examples of the many cultural differences that might arise in the strategy-setting process, and that ought to be raised during the gap analysis.

A comparison of all aspects of people implications is prepared

What the above processes will do is to show the variances from the current position in the position proposed for the future across a whole range of people issues. The gap analysis will require all of these to be pulled together so that comparisons can be made across the spectrum. It is a stage that comprises more of a list than an analysis. It will allow those responsible for human resources to take a holistic view of all the people implications of the various strategic proposals. A simple 'one-pager' might be prepared under the key HR headings of:

☐ demand and supply

☐ culture

☐ organisation design and development

☐ learning training and development

☐ reward

☐ employee relations.

Possible gaps might then be highlighted in simple tabular form.

The gap analysis is developed

A more detailed analysis should then follow. What does this entail? Things that could be contained in it include:

☐ a statement of resource flows and the shortfalls/excesses in demand and supply of the labour force – eg 'We have a shortfall of 200 people to staff up the call centre in Glasgow.' This will then inform the resourcing plan with a corollary action 'Recruit 200 people in Glasgow'

☐ a statement of the cultural gap implied by the strategic options – 'We currently have a manufacturing culture: we need a sales culture to deliver the strategy.' Again this will allow the development of new people strategies and plans to deal with the identified gap, whether through training or through organisational development

☐ the proposed organisational design is very different from the present one – this effectively points up an organisational gap that will have to be dealt with in order to achieve the strategy

☐ a recommendation for a training needs analysis because of a perceived gap in the skills required to achieve the new strategies

☐ an analysis of the reward-based gaps that might arise as a result of implementing one of the strategic options – for instance, a plan to move to performance-related pay as a way of achieving the strategy might present a communications and employee relations gap if recommended

☐ the employee relations implications of strategy might also produce a gap if, say, outsourcing or wider employment in Europe (requiring the establishment of a European Works Council) are planned.

The output of the gap analysis should be a series of specific HR-function-related issues for which plans will have to be developed. This is the culmination of the strategic human resource forecast, and is the area that informs the development of a human resource plan.

Options and recommendations are presented for inclusion in the human resources plan

Although the gap analysis is not intended to include detailed plans for filling any gap, it is a good opportunity to test senior management thinking about possible options. Remember, the gap analysis is intended to be debated at board level, and it is therefore a good idea to get some direction – or at least rule out any options unlikely to be accepted.

The gap analysis is also a good vehicle for debate within the HR community. In that the whole point of the SHRF and HRP is to develop 'joined-up thinking' and actions from HR, opportunities for debate and dialogue between HR's generalists and specialists should be sought. Furthermore, there is often a 'gap' between the various areas of HR as each strives to deliver its own solutions. What a wonderful thing it would be if the reward specialist and the training specialist got their heads together before launching their strategies! The gap analysis and its associated process is an opportunity for them to do so.

Chartered Institute of Personnel and Development

Customer Satisfaction Survey

The more feedback we get, the better our books can be! We will send you a
FREE CIPD MOUSE MAT (UK addresses only) as a thank you for completing this card.

Name and address: ....

....

CIPD membership number: ☐ ☐ ☐ ☐ ☐ ☐ ☐ ☐

1   Title of book..

2   Date of purchase: month .... year ....

3   How did you acquire this book?
    ☐ bookshop   ☐ Plymbridge   ☐ CIPD website   ☐ other (specify) ....

4   If ordered from Plymbridge, when did you receive your book?
    ☐ 1 week   ☐ 2 weeks   ☐ more than 2 weeks

5   Please grade the following according to their influence on your purchasing
    decision, with 1 as least influential: (please tick)

	1	2	3	4	5
Title					
Publisher					
Author					
Price					
Subject					
Cover					

6   On a scale of 1 to 5 (with 1 as poor and 5 as excellent) please give your impressions
    of the book in terms of: (please tick)

	1	2	3	4	5
Cover design					
Paper/print quality					
Good value for money					
General level of service					

7   Did you find the book: covers the subject in sufficient depth   ☐ Yes   ☐ No
                             useful for your work   ☐ Yes   ☐ No

8   Are you using this book to help:
    ☐ in your work   ☐ study   ☐ both   ☐ other (specify) ....

If you are using this book as part of a course, please give:

9   Name of academic institution..

10 Name of course ....

11 Is this book relevant to your syllabus?   ☐ Yes   ☐ No

Call 020 8263 3387 for our latest books catalogue. Don't forget, CIPD members get 10% off!

2299/09/01

2 1

Publishing Department

Chartered Institute of Personnel and Development

CIPD House

Camp Road

Wimbledon

London

SW19 4BR

PART III

THE HUMAN RESOURCE PLAN

11 THE COMPONENT PARTS OF THE HUMAN RESOURCE PLAN

Chapters 4–10 dealt with the way in which HR could contribute to the development of the organisation's strategy. This was through the strategic human resource forecast and was presented as an *input* to strategy-setting. Once this process has taken place and the board or senior management team has given its approval to the strategic options, planning and implementation begins. From a people perspective, the key aspect of this is the human resource plan, which becomes the tool by which the people elements of the business strategy are effectively put in place. It is an *output* of strategy-setting.

To reiterate the definition of human resource planning as outlined in Chapter 3, the plan is:

☐ the output that arises from the process of business or organisational strategy-setting as it affects the people in an organisation. It contains quantitative analyses of HR data ranging from headcount and costs to qualitative analyses about culture, learning and knowledge management. The HRP is a dynamic entity that can be changed if turbulence or unpredicted extraneous factors affect the business strategy.

As with the strategic human resource forecast, this part of the book uses a process flow to outline the stages of the human resource plan. This is set out in Figure 7. The thrust of the HR plan, though, is to present something that has meaning to the management of the business or organisation. As a result, I made a number of assumptions as to what a typical organisation would want to achieve. It would want to:

☐ achieve effective resourcing to ensure provision of enough people in the right places with the right skills to deliver the strategy
☐ ensure that these people are rewarded and recognised in a motivational way
☐ ensure that employee commitment is secured in an environment of well-managed and equitable employee relations
☐ make training and development available to satisfy the needs of the organisation and the individual.

It is worth reiterating that no one HR plan fits all circumstances. What is being proposed here is a general framework that the reader could and should adapt to his or her own organisation.

The human resource plan should put in place processes and provide technical expertise that ensure that these objectives are fulfilled. It is also important to note that the human resource plan is not a stand-alone entity. It should be prepared as an integral part of the overall business plan, and as such will require 'checks and balances' at each stage of review. These should be provided by business managers as well as HR professionals in each of the specialist areas of the plan. Overall, the objective of the human resource plan is to provide a set of specific measurable implementation plans and 'roadmaps' for how the business strategy can be achieved through people. It will consist of a range of plans within the key HR activities that can be summarily grouped as:

☐ resourcing through specific organisational design, quantified HR plans and resource allocation
☐ employee commitment and relations
☐ learning, training and development
☐ reward and recognition.

How can we ensure that the human resource plan is regarded as an essential part of the organisation's planning process? When this book first talked about manpower planning, it was to note how it had evolved to human resource planning. The importance of planning was recognised, but the necessity to develop plans that were meaningful, added value and contributed to the overall success of the organisation was considered to be a real challenge. It is still a catch-up situation because we have not consistently achieved these objectives. A solution to that is to ensure that HR plans are seen to be integrated with overall business plans – that they are regarded as critical to the success of the organisation's strategy – and that key performance indicators (KPIs) include 'people'. The HR planning process proposed in this book attempts to add a broader dimension to the subject. If it is to succeed, it is imperative that those in HR gain access to the right debates. These are the ones concerned with the organisation's strategy-setting. If this is achieved, the human resource plan will gain its rightful place at the heart of the organisation's decision-making processes and not be left to founder in the C-drive.

So in spite of the growing recognition that good HR plans can make a difference to the chances of strategic success, it will require a good deal of professionalism on the part of HR to get them truly integrated and accepted into the overall plans of the organisation. 'In our research and consultancy visits with senior executives in organisations of varying sizes, we have found that asking for an overview of their HR plan can be a real conversation-killer' (Rosenfeld and Wilson, 1999). The preparation and successful implementation of a human resource plan will obviously require a significant amount of craft on the part of the HR professional.

Its possible that the push towards effective HR planning will gain a boost from other strategic business areas. The Business Excellence Model, for example, requires that resources are planned and improved. Issues to address include aligning the human resource plan with policy and strategy, developing people surveys, ensuring the fairness of employment, and using 'innovative work organisation strategies and methods to improve ways of working' (BEM, 1997).

It is becoming recognised that the inclusion of effective human resource plans are an important part of the overall planning mix, and should be of help to most organisations.

In the light of this, the human resource plan should contain evidence that the information from the strategic human resource forecast has been understood and that the strategic proposals are well founded on people issues.

The contents of the human resource plan

As we saw earlier, the human resource plan should contain sections on organisational design, resourcing, training, reward and employee relations. These should, however, be placed in an overall context that has two elements. One is a statement of direction for the plan (comparable with the dreaded mission statement), and the other comprises specific objectives for the human resource aspects of the strategy.

The directional (or mission) statement should define where the organisation is going in respect of its attitudes towards people. For example, such a statement might read:

> to provide a working environment for all employees that supports the achievement of the organisation's goals and the personal development and satisfaction of the individual.

The specific objectives outline what is to be achieved – for example:

☐ to provide learning, training and development opportunities for all employees

☐ to provide all employees with career opportunities

☐ to provide clear role specifications for employees

☐ to give reward that is linked to performance

☐ to launch flexible benefits programmes.

The key components and their constituent parts are discussed in the paragraphs below.

The quantitative human resource plan

The quantitative human resource plan highlights headcount changes that flow from the business strategy. The plan contains much of the detail that would have been included in the manpower plan. Its main features are:

☐ showing current or 'baseline' headcount and resource

allocation by group, division, business unit or project, by function, grade, gender and ethnic mix, by age, and by length of service

☐ including the key metrics of staff turnover, levels of recruitment and leavers, absence, ratios of part-timers to full-timers, and numbers of flexible workers

☐ showing changes against each project or business initiative that arise out of the strategic plan

☐ showing changes against 'business as usual' headcount patterns.

The output of this part of the human resource plan is a comprehensive, quantified assessment of headcount and other resource (financial and technological), and the potential shifts over the period of the plan.

Organisational design and development

The organisation and development plan shows current organisational structures and the possibilities for them in the future period covered by the plan. It highlights possible changes and gives recommendations on how these may be implemented using organisational development techniques. The key parts of the organisational design and development plan are:

☐ an assessment of how the business strategy will impact on current organisational structures

☐ a review of the strategic options for organisational design, and a proposal to the CEO or senior management team

☐ a transition plan showing how the changes might be made – including a review of the 'appointments and disappointments' process

☐ an identification of organisational development issues that might arise from the changes, such as cultural alignment and a proposal for communications and engagement in the new structure.

Designing and developing the organisation is an important part of the overall planning process. It is also the one that is likely to present the biggest challenge to those responsible for human resources – not because of a lack of technical knowledge on the part of those in HR, but largely due to the willingness or otherwise of senior managers to engage HR in organisational design at an early enough stage. HR personnel can overcome this by demonstrating the highest level of technical competence in organisational design and by having a battery of issues and options that can add value to the organisational design debate. Achieving the level of competence required to satisfy this part of the HR plan would seem to be critical.

The resourcing plan

The resourcing plan covers the practicalities of dealing with the demand and supply issues raised in the SHRF. The war for talent means that recruitment is now more difficult than for many years. This is likely to hold true even in an economic downturn, since some of the shortages are industry- or sector-specific. It will require smart, co-ordinated recruitment strategies and plans. It also means that there is a greater emphasis on retention in the modern organisation. In most organisations the war for talent applies to all levels – not just to actuaries, e-technologists and rocket scientists. Good resourcing strategies that embrace a wide range of HR concepts are essential to this part of the plan. The resourcing plan must also deal with the internal deployment of staff, and how exits are to be managed.

The key components of the resourcing plan are 'the four Rs'. These are:

☐ recruitment
☐ retention
☐ redeployment
☐ removal (by which I mean any kind of exit).

These four headings demonstrate the need for a truly integrated approach to resourcing. It is no good having recruitment and redundancy managed separately. The effects of converging activity in these areas can benefit both the morale of the organisation and its bottom line.

The learning, training and development plan

The learning, training and development plan has the objective of ensuring that all the learning needs at individual and organisational level identified in the strategic plan are addressed through the design and implementation of effective training and development plans. These will embody a multi-channel 'layered' approach and will take account of key external and internal influences. The plan's key components are:

☐ an identification of the main organisational and individual learning needs, such as new customer service emphases and a requirement for organisation-wide training, new team training, and possible culture-change programmes

☐ a statement of resource allocation for training and development on an organisational level, showing how this is to be allocated per training project and per business unit

☐ a definition of the target populations at which the plan will be directed

☐ a channel-delivery strategy for the training, covering face-to-face and web-enabled learning

☐ a process and the means to measure the effectiveness of the training once delivered.

The learning, training and development plan should have a strong business focus if it is to have any chance of being approved by the board. It should take account of such measures as return on investment, increase in sales, and improvement in productivity. It is up to those responsible for training therefore to incorporate business language and processes into the plan, and not to rely on any 'act of faith' on the part of those providing the funding.

The reward plan

In former times reward tended to be about the annual pay round involving a sequence of stage-managed offer-and-acceptance manoeuvres with employee representatives. Nowadays, however, reward is a much more comprehensive concept – and this should be reflected in the reward plan. It is critical that reward is linked to both organisational and individual performance if the strategy is to be achieved.

Furthermore, it is desirable that reward is also linked to career development, succession management and the overall 'deal' with the employee. This requires the reward plan to be a wide-ranging contribution to the overall human resource plan.

The reward plan therefore contains:

☐ an analysis of external influences on pay, including benchmarking against similar organisations or industry sectors, and government pay guidelines such as the minimum wage

☐ an analysis of internal factors that impact on reward, most notably the profit forecast and the amount available for reward

☐ a definition of what constitutes reward beyond the base pay: this includes bonuses and profit sharing, health benefits, and similar

☐ a statement of the principles by which reward will be implemented, such as performance-related pay, competence achievement as a pay management process, or a statement of where pay should sit within an overall market for that particular group of employees; it should include the levels of remuneration for directors and the senior management of the organisation; if there is a remuneration committee, a separate sign-off for this part of the reward plan will be needed

☐ a financial case for the allocation of the reward budget that will enable the board to understand the strategy and approve it

☐ a plan for communication with and engagement of the employees and their representatives in the principles and practice of reward.

The reward plan is an opportunity to revisit the whole question of the financial relationship that an employee has with the organisation. It is also a critical part of the new psychological contract, and goes beyond the transaction of pay for work. In this respect it includes far more elements than pay.

The employee relations plan

The final part of the human resource plan is concerned with how to engage the employees with the new strategy and its human implications. The employee relations plan takes account of external factors such as legislation and internal factors such as the make-up and diversity of the modern workforce. Its component parts are:

- employee relations, which cover a broad mix of people management practices and their effect on the overall employment relationship, including employee involvement, the psychological contract, and the growing interest in 'employee voice'
- industrial relations, which cover the more formal relationships between the employer and the employee representatives
- employee commitment, which identifies the current state of commitment through such things as staff attitude surveys and plans to ensure that commitment is maintained through periods of change while the business strategy is being implemented.

The employee relations part of the human resource plan is thus a comprehensive assessment of the state of play in the current environment, the likely impact that the strategy will have on it, and proposals for dealing with the issues that arise.

Other factors to consider

A final consideration in preparing the human resource plan is the application of knowledge management to people issues. There is a growing emphasis on knowledge work and knowledge workers in modern society. This, according to Scarborough and Swan (1999),

> suggests that the need to manage knowledge will endure as a core business concern, even if the label may change. There are clearly organisational trends which are aligned to this focus on knowledge assets. For example, a KPMG research report on KM opens with the words 'There is little doubt that we have entered the knowledge economy where what organisations

know is becoming more important than the traditional sources of economic power – capital, land, plant and labour – which they command.'

The advent of knowledge as a critical success factor in contemporary organisations means that planning and forecasting for knowledge requirements is as important as planning and forecasting for traditional areas (finance, marketing, etc). Because knowledge is normally associated with the human assets of an organisation, knowledge management becomes an important part of the human resource plan. In particular, the plan must take account of the need to acquire and retain knowledge and the implications of that need for the business. Knowledge will feature in the resourcing and reward parts of the plan but will also be a consideration in learning, training and development.

These, then, are the component parts of the human resource plan, which is a comprehensive statement of how the people implications of the business strategy are to be dealt with in a systematic way. Subsequent chapters look at each individual part in more detail.

12 THE QUANTITATIVE HUMAN RESOURCE PLAN

It is ironic that the quantitative part of human resource planning – for so long regarded as a waste of time – is back in vogue. The war for talent, the need to make preparation for succession, the recognition of diversity as a powerful competitive force, and significant demographic changes have converged to refocus the attention of managers on staff turnover, grade-mix and other quantifiable HR indicators. A sound numerical basis for HR decision-making is now perceived as a desirable objective. The likely advent of an HR scorecard is also going to focus our attention on more quantitative methods. Accurate information about how many people are needed to deliver strategy, the skills they require to do so, and where these people should be located make quantitative human resource planning more, not less, important.

There are some important reasons for a quantified analysis as part of the human resource plan:

- [ ] People deployment is a strategic issue, so a detailed understanding of the make-up of the labour force and its deployment is critical to the overall success of the organisation.
- [ ] Understanding human resource flows ensures well-informed decision-making.
- [ ] That means that the nature of the demand and supply of the organisation's human resource can affect business strategy.
- [ ] The cost of the management of human resource flows is significant, so understanding the plan will ensure that sufficient financial resource is allocated.

To make some headway into dealing with these issues, we thus need to get some core information. We need to know why the headcount is changing, and how that change will impact on the numbers, grades, skills, etc. And to do this we need to know as much as possible about:

☐ the required inputs of people into the organisation – the supply of labour

☐ the demand for people as a result of the organisational strategy

☐ the required skills mix determined by any changes to strategy

☐ the costs of running the human resource demand and supply flows.

This information will be gathered during the strategic human resource forecasting process.

Organisations will have to answer some critical questions about the people implications of the strategic options on which they have decided. In this respect the quantitative human resource plan will try to put dimensions on some of these questions:

☐ How many people will we need over the next three to five years?

☐ In which divisions or functions do we need them?

☐ What skills do we expect them to have?

☐ How will we manage succession?

☐ How much will the labour force cost?

In so doing we will move from the abstract to the very specific outcomes of strategy.

To help find answers to these questions, a range of human resource metrics is required. These might include comparative labour turnover, labour productivity, overall numbers of leavers and joiners, and so on. Such core data can then be used to inform decisions about people deployment. It is beyond the scope of this book to go into too much detail about how these metrics are calculated. There are numerous statistical sources that deal with such calculations. However, it is still up to those responsible for preparing the human resource plan to make themselves aware of which are most relevant to their organisations and to offer appropriate metrics accordingly (ie not to put forward multiple regression analysis when what is needed is a simple labour turnover figure).

It is important that the preparation and agreement of the quantitative human resource plan is seen as continuously progressive, being continuously updated. At best, the plan will be a snapshot of a moving car. As soon as it has been prepared it will have changed. Engaging those managers responsible for delivering the people elements is therefore critical. The process for this is shown in Figure 19. In essence what the quantitative HRP does is to put numbers to strategic options in respect of their people implications. It starts with an estimate of the level of demand for people (ie how many we need to be able to deliver the strategy) and the skills

Figure 19 **THE QUANTITATIVE HUMAN RESOURCE PLAN**

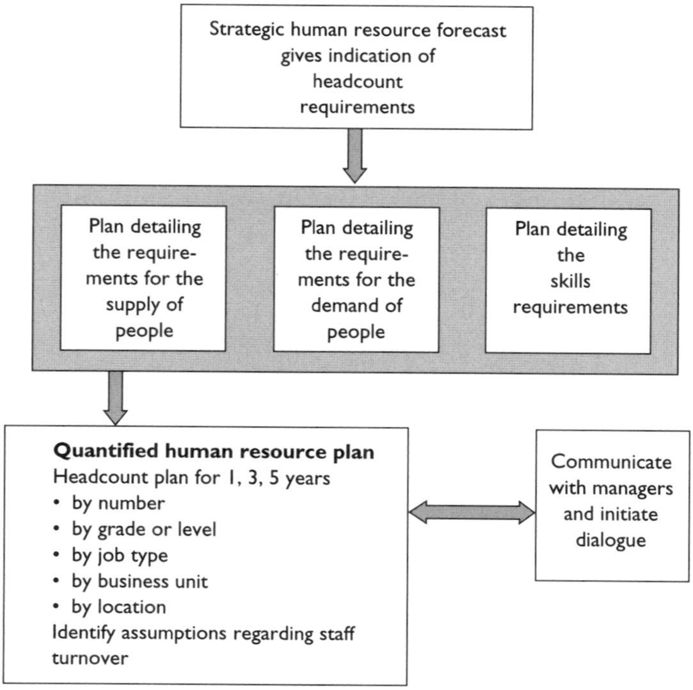

required (ie of what types). The quantitative HRP then matches this analysis with one of supply by type of job, grade, and so on, taking account of whatever staff turnover, sickness and absence levels are anticipated.

Data collection and preparation – preparing the base case

The first thing to do is to make sure we have access to information about the deployment of people in the organisation. Getting this information can be a nightmare – especially in organisations with more than one site or division. People join and leave, some work part-time, others are hired from agencies, some are temporary. Normally, people are on the move, and this makes tracking them difficult. So the only thing to do is to take a snapshot at a point in time. This will give a base case of:

☐ how many people work for the organisation, as a total
☐ how many work in each department or division
☐ their make-up in terms of gender, ethnicity and ability
☐ the grade-mix
☐ the skills or role-description mix (managers, sales, marketing, production, HR, finance, and so on).

The base case is the foundation of the future plan. It is the starting-point from which all other analyses are derived. How this data may be obtained varies from organisation to organisation. The payroll system is an obvious source, as are any reports that are produced on monthly headcount figures, budgets, etc. At the start of the preparation of the SHRF and HRP it is a wise thing for those in HR to take stock of their management information system to understand just how easy it is to access reliable information about the workforce. Obviously, the use of an HR information system (HRIS) makes this task somewhat easier. But the HRIS is only as reliable as the information put into it. Such information requires managers and HR to keep to the process and maintain the discipline to do so. Sometimes, the pace of activity means that data-processing is not always carried out in real time, and there can be a lag in accuracy.

Actually, this point reinforces the overall view about the HR role – that it will be taken seriously at strategic level only if it gets its act together at the administrative level. A thorough understanding of people metrics is one of these administrative challenges. The base case for the quantitative HRP is knowing how many people work for the organisation, into what job categories or grade they fit, where they work, how many are recruited on average per time-period, and how many leave. This is core data – an invaluable contribution.

The presentation of information

Before going into this in any detail, it is worth addressing the whole question of the analysis and presentation of information in the HR plan.

The first question here is how sophisticated to make the statistical analysis. The answer to this varies from organisation to organisation: it is the responsibility of those who are undertaking the analysis to read what is appropriate. The most critical elements here are:

☐ the output of the plan
☐ its implementation.

I once spent a lot of effort in a multiple regression analysis of economic and trade union activity and their relationship with wages and earnings. The output was an awesome piece of work. Unfortunately, I could come up with no answer to the very first question that someone asked me about it: 'What has this contributed to our knowledge, exactly?'

Too often the approach to manpower planning has focused on the sophistication of the tools and techniques of statistical analysis rather than why we are using them in the first place. Bear in mind, therefore, that preparing the statistics is not the objective. The messages, and the conclusions to which they lead, are.

The second concerns the importance of the presentation of the information in the quantified plan. It is important because we live in a media-aware society. On the one hand, turning up with badly presented plans – perhaps using inappropriate symbols and figures easily obtained from any computer's basic software – can have a detrimental effect on how the plan is received. On the other hand, turning up with pages of dense data massed together in Times Roman 8-point script because 'We present substance, not form' is probably as bad. For many, it seems as if form and substance are incompatible. They are not – and if any proof of this point it required, I recommend the reading of two excellent descriptions of the use of visual information. Both are by Edward Tufte, who declared quizzically in his introduction to one of them that 'The world is complex, dynamic, multidimensional; the paper is static, flat. How are we to represent the rich visual world of experience and measurement on mere flatland?' (Tufte, 1983 and 1990).

It is a point to consider as we present our own HR information. The challenge is to present the quantitative part of the human resource plan in a way that does not seem gimmicky in any way, yet that presents the information in a meaningful format that attracts attention. Remember the objective: we are trying to get the board members to understand the implications for people movements in the strategies they are formulating. We are doing this so that decisions are made with the people in mind. And while doing so we must now endeavour to attract rather more attention than has often been the case in the past. (Manpower plans have been known to disappear the moment after they have been agreed.) This requires a balance of sound financial and statistical presentation and an attractive format – attractive, that is, to the culture of the organisation.

Preparing the quantitative human resource plan

The fundamental point of the quantitative HRP, then, is to plan ahead for both the number of people and the skills that they will need to deliver the organisation's strategy. The output of this will be a form of human resource plan that contains detailed information about the deployment of headcount and any changes that are anticipated as a result of what might be described as 'business as usual' work. On this can be overlaid the effect of any strategic initiatives, such as merger or acquisition, downsizing, new sales outlets, and so on. The chart that is Table 10 is one way in which this can be summarised.

The objective is to fill in the chart with information from

Table 10 **THE QUANTITATIVE HUMAN RESOURCE PLAN – COMPILING THE DATA**

	Headcount at start of plan period	Business as usual		Strategic initiative		Headcount at end of plan period
		leavers	recruits	leavers	recruits	
Year 1 Manager Sales Manufacturing Clerical						
Total:						
Year 2 Manager Sales Manufacturing Clerical						
Total:						
Year 3 Manager Sales Manufacturing Clerical						
Total:						
Year 4 Manager Sales Manufacturing Clerical						
Total:						
Year 5 Manager Sales Manufacturing Clerical						
Total:						

the outputs of the SHRF. The chart makes provision for 'business as usual' and strategic initiative headcount changes. Looking at Year 1, we can see a starting-position for headcount based on a particular grade mix (manager, clerical, and so on). Anticipated business-as-usual staff turnover will enable us to fill in the leavers and recruits columns for Year 1. Then we can add or subtract changes because of any strategic initiative. (Opening a call centre would see a significant number of recruits in this area, downsizing HR would see a reduction.) A Year 1 headcount figure can then be calculated, and carried forward to the start of Year 2.

The model is very simplistic, and is intended only as a guide. In reality, the amount of backup analysis for each area will be significant. Each application will see variations on the theme, depending on the nature of the organisation. What should be consistent, though, is the 'at-a-glance' nature of the format which makes for attractively straightforward presentation.

This approach yields a statement of the expected demand for people as a result of the business strategy. By combining such elements as these, the first part of the quantitative plan can be compiled. However, we have already noted that the quantitative plan should include such elements as skills, costs and succession. Data on these will be derived from a detailed understanding of the organisation's strategic options. Examples of the kind of consideration here include:

☐ How do changes in the organisation's structure affect the quantities of people and skills? A switch to being a 'project-based organisation', for instance, requires the introduction and development of project skills. How many people are needed? What is the management structure? And so on.

☐ Can we be sure that there is continuity of management to deliver the new strategy? Do succession plans exist for the top 10 posts? What would happen if key people left suddenly? What are the plans for developing successors to key posts over time?

☐ How much will the changes in strategy increase the cost base? Say, for example, the organisation wants to launch a web-based product line. That would require the recruitment of a whole workforce experienced in the technology and marketing techniques of the web. But the return on investment is over a three-year period leading to an increase in labour costs over years one and two of the plan. What will this amount to, altogether? Has the senior management team understood the human capital implications of the strategy?

The process for deriving a quantitative analysis of human resources

We have seen the importance of establishing a base case for headcount and skills, and then applying statistical techniques for building on this to take account of anticipated changes to occur as a result of the strategy. Doing all this will require a comprehensive quantitative analysis. The components of a basic design for the process have been listed earlier (see Figure 19) – there is no model or format that can satisfy all needs, but the principles outlined are applicable whatever the organisational structure and culture.

The nature of this process stems from its being based on a quantifiable input to the overall strategic plan. It is subject to the same issues that arise from the nature of the human resource plan – issues emerging from the fact that quantifiable input is only one part of the process. Dialogue, continuously progressive updating and soft issues are equally important, and are key to achieving sustained corporate success.

Derive the changes to people requirements from the strategic human resource forecast

As we have seen, it is essential to establish a base case before embarking on any further analysis that stems from the quantitative HRP. Once the base case is established, the first part of the process can be applied. This should be an overview of the impact of strategy on people requirements. The whole process of the strategic human resource forecast will have been undertaken to reach conclusions about a series of HR issues, not least of which are headcount and skills. It is the role of HR personnel to quantify these along the lines mentioned above.

What might the result look like? Let us say that a bank decides to launch a new Internet banking division. It will require the creation of a new management structure, new support teams, marketing, finance and technology functions, product and compliance experts. From the strategy we will have to start putting domensions on these requirements: one managing director, one marketing director, 20 systems support technologists, 10 compliance officers, and so on. What we have done in this simple format is prepared a quantified human resource plan. The high-level understanding of the overall pattern of headcount requirements derived from the SHRF (itself derived from the organisational strategy) is the first point of the quantified human resource plan.

Prepare an analysis of the demand for people over the life of the organisational strategy

The two main components of the quantitative analysis are demand and supply. It is from this point that any of a variety of techniques might be used – techniques that have featured in most books on manpower planning published in the past 20 years or so. A selection is outlined below (quoted primarily from Dessler, 1994), but does not include computerised forecasting using proprietary programs.

Trend analysis

Trend analysis is the study of a firm's employment trends over the last five years or so in order to predict future trends. For example, you might compute the number of employees in your firm at the end of each of the last five years, or perhaps the number in each subgroup at the end of each of those years. The purpose is to identify employment trends that may continue into the future.

Ratio analysis

Ratio analysis depends on the ratio between some causal factor (like sales volume) and the number of employees required to deal with it. Such an analysis may help forecast other employee requirements.

The scatter plot

A scatter plot involves determining whether two organisational factors – a measure of business activity and the staffing levels – are related. If they are, and it is possible to forecast the measure of business activity, it should be possible also to estimate future personnel requirements.

Such techniques tend to be used in the business-as-usual forecasting process, but that should be overlaid with the 'strategic initiatives' and their headcount impact to give a complete picture. Applying such techniques to the organisational strategy might add some value to the overall process. It should be noted, though, that they provide material for internal analysis only. And in the meantime, whether multivariate statistical techniques have been used in analysing the information is not what the board or senior management team wants to hear, however clever the results might seem.

Demand, then, may be evaluated from a statistical analysis of trends and a forecast of changes expected to result from strategy. A note of caution for perfectionists should be sounded here. The figures derived can go up as well as down. Hence the need for constant monitoring and updating of these plans. If a plan is prepared and the output is placed into the files under 'planning', then this part of the process has already failed. The quantitative plan is intended to be a living document, not a historical record. Some organisations update their plans every three to six months through a reforecasting process.

Prepare an analysis of the requirements for the supply of people

In parallel with the demand analysis, there will be one for supply. The objective is to identify those issues likely to impact on the ability to deliver to the strategy (considerations that also featured in Chapter 8). Examples of the type of thing involved in the supply-side aspect of the quantitative human resource plan include:

- [ ] labour market trends for key sectors
- [ ] labour market trends for geographic sectors
- [ ] demographic implications.

How is the supply-side analysis used? Take, for instance, a proposal, after debate, to open a call centre in Glasgow. The supply of the specific type of labour required to work in the call centre has to be identified. Note that the important point here is the specificity of the supply-side estimate. We are now going beyond the general because we will have to match the supply figure against demand to identify any shortfalls (or excesses). This means finding an answer to the question, 'Are there enough people in the Glasgow labour market to recruit into a new call centre?' The answer requires an understanding of the labour market in Glasgow and its immediate catchment area. What we have done here is to move from the strategic debate that constituted the SHRF to the more specific kind of provision that is the human resource plan.

Outline any changes in the skills mix that might result from the organisational strategy

In addition to the actual changes in headcount that result from the business strategy there will be implications for skill mix. We noted in an earlier chapter the problems with skills shortages that are being experienced at national level. This section of the plan, therefore – suggesting how we mean to ensure that we have the right skill mix to deliver the strategy – is one that will become of increasingly high focus. The levels of skill required should be carefully quantified and articulated.

Examples of how skills issues might express themselves include:

- [ ] A manufacturing operation decides to introduce new production processes and new technology to increase productivity. The introduction of new technology requires new sets of skills. What types of skill will be required? From where are they going to be sourced?
- [ ] A retailer decides to undertake a new marketing push to make up for loss of market share in a particular division.

The introduction of a marketing focus might mean the separation of the sales and marketing function and the recruitment of people with new marketing skills, such as product managers, and so on. How many new sales and marketing employees will be required? Are new marketing skills needed? If so, will these be sourced internally through retraining or recruited externally?

☐ An organisation decides to go on the acquisition trail. It has a war-chest to do so – but does it have the right level of merger and acquisition skills in the organisation? What are its options? Consultants on contract, or a new in-house M&A unit?

The identification of changes to the skills mix as shown by these few examples is important and should be quantified in the plan.

Combine all elements into a quantified human resource plan showing flows and grade/skills mix

The co-ordination of all of the information relating to the supply and demand for labour as determined by the debate over strategic options can then be pulled together into an overall plan showing human resource flows and grade/skills mix. The latter should be seen as an equal factor. Grade-mix will have cost implications, and skills mix will impact upon both training and resourcing plans.

Communicate the quantified human resource plan to the senior management team and initiate a dialogue

It is at this point that the value of the quantified human resource plan really comes into its own. This is because the business managers will be able to see the implications of their proposed strategies on the organisation's human resources. We know what the big issues are in business. They are cash flow, profits, assets, and growth. These variables have inter-connections such that 'there is a balance that can be maintained between them and, from this balance, will come corporate value. It is corporate value that is the reason for most business activity' (Walsh, 1996). In this respect the people are key assets, and the quantified human resource plan enables those in HR to demonstrate the effect of strategy on these assets. Furthermore, because those responsible for HR are increasingly being asked to justify their expenditure by conventional financial means, such an analysis may be essential to justify recruitment or training budgets. Where resource is scarce (as in most places today), every area of the business or organisation will compete for that resource. In most, though not all, cases the proposals, projects or plans that have the best business return are likely to be more favourably received. Of course the return is not the only criterion for judging an HR proposal, and some proposals will receive the nod because of their sheer sense (as perceptibly mandatory requirements). But if HR can operate on a businesslike basis where possible, the sustainability of some of the key initiatives might be improved. The quantified plan should be a valuable weapon in the armoury of HR. It is less likely that (for example) training budgets will come under fire if a well-thought-out and well-presented plan clearly demonstrates how much of a gap there is in the skills needed to achieve strategic goals.

13 ORGANISATIONAL DESIGN AND DEVELOPMENT

Creating tomorrow's organisation

Emerging from the flux and dissonance of the 1990s, the shape of the traditional organisation has been indelibly changed by the nascent forces of IT, the province of people at work – characterised by new personal freedom allowing individuals to detach themselves from the traditional requirements of location and time – and the sphere of business strategy, where the fusion of the other two domains will offer a completely new organisational form and asset base.

The new age of future work will surface at organisational level, not as a result of government legislation or new working practices arising out of worker demand or experimentation, but out of the commitment and drive of its executives with an open and goal-oriented outlook. The rebirth of the networked organisation will be grounded on the key drivers of work being knowledge- rather than capital-intensive, of the most capable expertise no longer residing within the boundaries of the organisation, and of the interface between companies, individuals and units being increasingly co-ordinated by market mechanisms, not chains of command. This will feed through the traditional vertically-integrated supply chain, where financial domination of key elements will be replaced by a more fluid alignment between companies, within a network of trading arrangements.

As we enter the global marketplace, we are becoming increasingly aware that the current trading, employment and business legislation is based on a belief system unchanged since the Industrial Revolution. The need to break from these constraints too narrow to accommodate future pantheist business opportunity is a national and international challenge. Organisational structure, then, is the new competitive battle-field, where success will be based on a fusion of business need, customer focus, IT developments and HR issues, and underpinned by a theoretical basis for managing major change programmes.

Peter Cornwall,
Director, GetThere.com

Organisational design and development and the human resource plan

Organisations are going through dramatic changes, and those who work in them have a wide range of expectations. Anyone reading the novels of Douglas Coupland would recognise a very different world of work (in fiction at least). It was Coupland who wrote (1996):

> People of our age are abandoning the tech megacultures in droves, starting up their own companies, or joining small, content-based start-ups. There's a recruiting frenzy going on...multimedia craziness...and the big companies that aren't minting money are haemorrhaging brains. It's intellectual Darwinism.

A new generation of worker (*Generation X*, another Coupland novel) will not necessarily be willing to fit in with the boundaries and designs of its forebears. Setting up an organisation structure with immaculately designed 'sign-offs' for operating controls is one option – for a bank, maybe. It may not, however, be an ideal scenario for a Silicon Valley dot.com start-up. That is the message we are increasingly hearing. But for most people the 'org chart' is still a common feature of organisational life. It seems that when we come to the section of the HR Plan labelled 'organisational design and development' we are likely to face some tough choices. This is yet another very real challenge for those who work in HR. The human resource plan is an opportunity to surface some of the issues associated with organisational design and development. The good news is that those responsible for HR will have the advantage in that they are aware of these alternatives and can contribute to a dialogue that goes beyond the simplistic methodology of 'span of control'. A starting-point, then, for the HR community is to become expert on all aspects of organisational design and development.

The organisation's design and structure is the balance-sheet of the human resources professional. And yet it is an area in which HR has singularly failed to make a significant break-through. Similarly, the principles of organisational development are a way of integrating the mission or vision with a programme of culture change that transcends any individual department, function or business unit. Yet it is again a process that is not used as often as it might be. This is surprising, considering how the organisation's design and development can:

☐ determine whether a company achieves sustained economic success

☐ determine the prevailing culture

☐ inform training and development needs

☐ facilitate or block knowledge management and transfer

☐ impact on employee commitment and relations.

Most importantly, since 'structure is most noticeable to anyone who has anything to do with organisations' (Kakabadse *et al*, 1987), the organisation's design may determine the behaviour of those working in it – a point that has an impact across almost every aspect of people management. At the extreme ends of the spectrum, 'one tradition sees organisations as edifying forums, while the other, indicated by Michel Foucault, views organisations as controlled violence' (Weaver, 1997). Is it really possible for one organisation to resemble a scene from *The Sound of Music* and another a scene from *The Godfather*? If so, it really should make us sit up and take notice.

There is clearly something here that is a powerful entity. Those responsible for HR should see organisational design and development as a key to opening the door that gives access to strategic input. Similarly, organisational development work can operate in parallel with individual development, leading to a powerful and pervasive synergy between the two – something to which many of those in HR and the organisation as a whole would subscribe (Fisher and Torbert, 1995). The human resource plan should therefore make recommendations towards an appropriately designed and developed organisation – including processes and structure. The SHRF will have provided enough information about the implications on people of the business strategy. This information should now be translated into a proposal for organisational design and the subsequent development of the organisation to enable it to meet the strategic objectives set.

Those responsible for human resource management should see this aspect of their work as of particular importance. Organisational design and development is a competence that requires an understanding of behavioural and sociological theory and practice. It is a competence that is becoming increasingly useful in organisations, as rapid change in the environment brings with it the demand for a rapid organisational response. Yet it is the area that has traditionally proved to be the most difficult to break into for those in HR who want to. The chief executive officer and senior management team often take this activity upon themselves, without consulting HR for a 'technical' input as they would normally do on, say, industrial relations. There has also been a certain reluctance on the part of HR themselves to see this as a cause worth fighting for. They should, because it is. It is at the very heart of competitiveness.

An appropriately designed organisation, even if it follows contemporary patterns of matrices or networks, can contribute significantly to the overall chances of achieving sustained organisational success. The preparation of the human resource plan presents an opportunity for HR professionals to take the lead in the design and development of the organisation in a number of ways:

☐ by providing technical input into organisational development from expert knowledge of the implications of any particular organisational design

☐ by facilitating a debate about which organisational designs are appropriate to the business or the organisational strategies chosen

☐ by influencing the choice of organisational design

☐ by building processes into the organisational design that help in the quest for effective people management.

The process for the organisational design input to the human resource plan is depicted in Figure 20.

It assumes that a new structure is being proposed as a result of the business strategy. However, the principles on which a new organisation is to be designed can equally be based on those of the existing organisation if it is decided that they remain the most appropriate.

In any case, before examining the process in detail it is important to understand those principles on which organisational design and development are built.

Principles of organisational design and development

The subject of organisational design and development is one that has received a significant amount of 'air time' in both academic and business circles in recent years.

Figure 20 **THE ORGANISATIONAL DESIGN AND DEVELOPMENT PLAN**

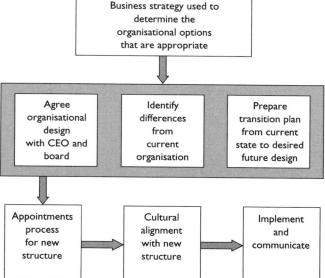

Henry Mintzberg asked the question 'What makes an organisation effective?' His response was (Mintzberg, 1991):

> For a long time we thought we had the answer. Frederick Taylor told us about the 'one best way' at the turn of the century, and organisations long pursued this holy grail. . . Then along came the so-called 'contingency theorists' who argued that 'it all depends'. Effective organisations designed themselves to match their conditions. They used those time-and-motion studies for mass production, they used strategic planning under conditions of relative stability, and so forth. Trouble was, all this advice never came together: managers were made to feel like diners at a buffet table.

Anyone who has managed an organisation during the past few years should be able to relate to this point. In large organisations during the 1990s, organisational design seemed to ebb and flow with the tides of academic fashion or environmental change – one year centralised, the next strategic business unit decentralised; one day re-engineered, the next re-processed; one day project-based, the next product-based. It was difficult to keep a grip on quite what was the thing to do. Mintzberg's solution was to be both 'Porterian' and 'Peterian' (Mintzberg, 1991). In some respects that is exactly what most organisations are like today: a dynamic mixture of chaotic design, start-up and innovation on the one hand, and a structured, systematic process-driven functionality on the other. This is probably the most difficult scenario one could imagine in terms of organisational design and development. It is, however, reality, and those responsible for HR will have to be able to put in some order and set up some parameters at least.

Two concepts will be important in preparing the human resource plan. Organisational design is clearly a critical element, and one that is most well known. The second is, however, increasingly talked about but not as well implemented – organisational development.

Organisational design

Most of those in HR have at some time been involved in organisational design – probably less than they would have liked, but involved, nonetheless. Invariably, this design would have centred on products or services: a new 'mobile phone division' perhaps, a 'retail banking division', or even a 'dessert topping division'.

If only the world was so simple that an organisation could always be designed around its products or services. But we know that this is not the case. For a start the evidence of history tells us that organisations are in constant flux. One analysis has demonstrated that commercial corporations are relative newcomers to the world and have not had the longevity of, say, educational or religious institutions. They have a high mortality rate. For example: of the 1970 *Fortune 500* corporations, one third were fairly rapidly acquired, broken up or merged (de Geus, 1997). There is also the small matter of new economy start-ups, project-based 'adhocratic' organisations and the 'clover leaf' suggested by Charles Handy. It is likely that many different forms of organisation structure are still to be found. It is also likely that many of them will exist in a state of flux. The challenge during the planning phase is to raise the issue of design to ensure a broad understanding of the implications of any one type on the chances of success.

So how do we go about designing an organisation?

It has been argued that there are two important aspects to an organisation's composition – its basic structure and its operating mechanisms. The basic structure encompasses (Huczynski and Buchanan, 1991):

☐ how the work of the organisation is divided and allocated between various individuals or departments – this is essentially the allocation of tasks and responsibilities

☐ how the various tasks and activities once assigned are co-ordinated – this relates to the system of reporting relationships, the hierarchy, and the various spans of control.

The basic structure is held together by processes that allow for delegation of authority within a set of operating mechanisms that consist of rules, procedures, controls and powers. Once these various elements are fully understood, it is possible to develop organisational designs that deliver the desired end-state for the organisation and its business strategy.

Figure 21 **THE FUNCTION-BASED ORGANISATIONAL STRUCTURE**

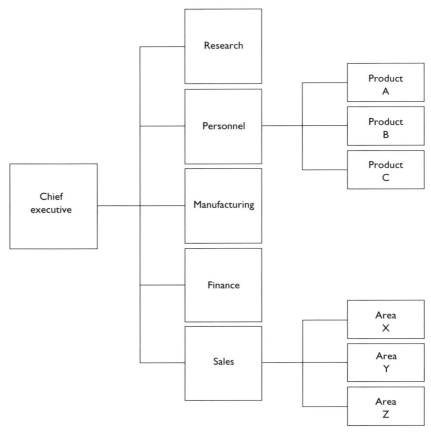

Source: Huczynski and Buchanan, 1991

Examples of types of organisational structure are presented as Figures 21–23, which show function-based, product-based and geography-based organisational designs.

In the light of the flux that seems to apply to organisational design nowadays, however, there are many more possibilities than these traditional three types. Anyone who saw Don Tapscott's incredible presentation at the Harrogate Conference in 2001 will be only too aware of the possibilities of networked intellectual capital and its implications for organisational design (Tapscott, 2001).

Figure 22 **THE PRODUCT-BASED ORGANISATIONAL STRUCTURE**

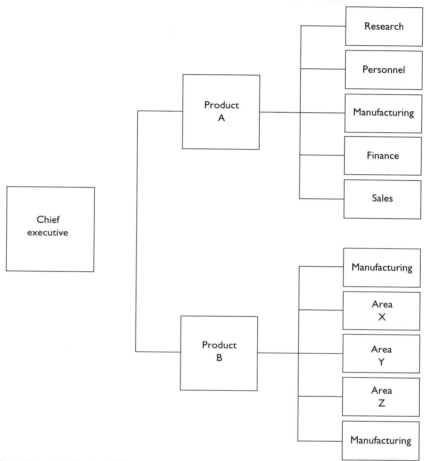

Source: Huczynski and Buchanan, 1991

Organisational development (OD)

The design of the organisation is a critical factor at this stage of the human resource plan. Having fulfilled that task of design – and having persuaded the chief executive officer that we, as HR, really do know what we are talking about in terms of organisational design – then the greater challenge will be to get organisational development on to the same agenda. This is one of the most talked-about but hard-to-implement areas of HRM, possibly because of the lack of clarity in its

Figure 23 **THE GEOGRAPHY-BASED ORGANISATIONAL STRUCTURE**

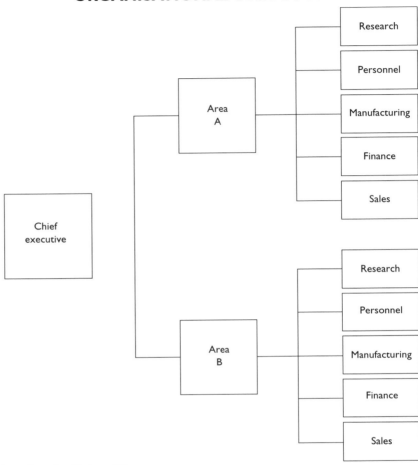

Source: Huczynski and Buchanan, 1991

definition and in exactly how those in HR should convert its concepts into practical, applicable methods. Lynda Gratton has noted that a 'focus on individual skills, motivation and commitment is central to the transformation of the organisation. At a macro-level there is a set of processes which support the transformation of the organisation' (Gratton, 1999). This is a particular view that is supported by the definition of OD as a way of increasing organisational effectiveness through interventions in organisational processes with the objective (according to Beckhard, 1969) of developing:

> a self-renewing viable system that can organise in a variety of ways depending on tasks. This means systematic efforts to change and loosen up the way the organisation operates so that it organises differently depending on the nature of the task.

In endeavouring to effect this, the quest will be to move towards an organisation that encourages collaboration rather than competition, deals with conflict, and ensures that decisions are made on the basis of knowledge rather than by reliance on any organisational role.

The characteristics of OD methods are that they are organisation-wide, that they have the support of the senior management of the organisation, that they are fully aligned with the organisation's mission, and that they are long-term in their nature. The main objective of OD is to change attitudes and behaviour through a broad range of HR interventions. These may be team-building initiatives as well as newer practices, such as 360-degree appraisal for senior managers. Organisation development, then, is a key HR tool aimed to ensure that the organisation achieves its business mission by recognition of critical people elements.

The process for preparing an organisational design and development plan

The process for preparing the organisational design and development plan has been outlined in Figure 20. Some key activities should be undertaken by HR *before* this, however, and these are:

☐ Identify and articulate the basis of the current structure. An understanding of the rationale for this is essential if changes are going to be made. For example: if the organisation is designed around its best-selling product range, then resource, budget and power are likely to be associated with that. The bulk of marketing spend, the design of technology systems and the location of distribution outlets will be geared to servicing the lead product. If, however, the organisation decides to diversify into new product ranges, the associated structure will have to be efficient enough to allow for such growth. Organisational design will be critical as to whether enough 'oxygen' is given to the new area or whether the new area becomes subsumed into the structure and processes of the current best-sellers – in which case there will be a whole series of further associated issues. Getting the structure right to support the new strategy will be critical as to whether the new strategy is successful.

☐ Identify and articulate the existing culture (or, more likely, cultures) of the organisation (see Chapter 9). This again will be critical to the success of any new design that is put in place. If, for example, there is a strongly centralised structure and the management of the organisation has been raised in this type of environment, then a proposal to decentralise will have ramifications. It is up to the HR community to draw the attention of strategic decision-makers to these issues and, most importantly, to put forward proposals for dealing with them.

☐ Finally – and this is the most basic of all points – make sure that a detailed headcount analysis is in place so that when the question is asked 'How many people work in finance in head office?', those in HR have the answer.

Once these preliminaries have been completed, the organisational design and development plan can be prepared. The following paragraphs describe how this may be done.

The business strategy is used to determine the organisational options that are appropriate

The starting-point for organisational design is the business strategy. It is imperative that the overall thrust is understood by those responsible for HR if the resultant organisational design is to make sense and be appropriate. The key factors to be sought from the business strategy are:

☐ plans to acquire or merge
☐ plans to expand the business organically into new areas
☐ start-up or incubator proposals

- ☐ proposals to combine departments (such as sales and marketing)
- ☐ proposals to set up shared services for support functions.

Each of these has its own implications for the structure of the organisation. Mergers or acquisitions, for example, present several organisational design options. The first is full integration of the two companies within a single organisational structure – but this is by no means the only way of integrating an acquired company. It is possible to leave the company's 'front office' activities (such as sales and marketing) as they were before, but combine the 'back office' and achieve economies of scale. This presents a different structural option. Highlighting such options is a key role of those in HR. (Once the organisation design has been outlined for discussion, the organisational development implications should then be put forward. If the HR function gets to this stage, it will really be on a winning streak!)

The organisational design is agreed with the CEO and board or the senior management team

How can we ensure that the chief executive and the board regard those in HR as a source of expert knowledge about organisational design? Some principles may help in such recognition:

- ☐ HR professionals demonstrate technical proficiency in organisational design and development
  - by outlining OD options early in the strategy-setting process
  - and by presenting the implications of these options (eg a matrix structure will require a governance process different from, say, a product-based structure's).

It is important, once a strategy looks like being agreed, that a dialogue takes place with the chief executive and board. This should be on the basis that several organisational designs are possible. Each has strengths and weaknesses, but one of them is probably appropriate to this particular strategy. The dialogue about organisational development with the CEO or others in the senior management team is one that is an essential part of the human resource planning process. Too often HR tends to be excluded until the later stages, by which time the organisational design has been agreed. And yet it is at this very point that crucial decisions – matrix or function, centralised or decentralised, short or long spans of control – are made. Influencing organisational design at early stage is an important success criterion for the whole of the HR plan.

A transition plan to take the organisation from current state to new design is prepared

The dialogue with the CEO should lead to an agreed organisational design. A transition plan has then to be formulated. How will the organisation get from its current state to the desired one by altering its organisational design? The pieces of the jigsaw required for that transition are:

☐ an appointments process for the top-level jobs in the structure, if they have changed

☐ HR support for this process

☐ a 'disappointments' process (for those who do not feature in the new design)

☐ a process for communicating 'no change' – often neglected

☐ a process for appointing into jobs at the next levels in the new structure

☐ communicating the new structure and inducting those individuals who have been appointed

☐ support for the development of the new teams.

The transition plan should be maintained by those responsible for HR until completion of the top three levels of the organisation. Then the process can be handed off to 'business as usual' arrangements. A point worth noting here is the necessity for speed. There is nothing more destabilising in an organisation than uncertainty about organisational change. In this respect a 'road map' giving dates by which key activities will have taken place is a possible means to alleviate some of the uncertainty.

The appointments process and HR policies for the new structure are set up

One of the most visible acts of organisational change is the way in which appointments are made. Getting this right or at least 'felt fair' can lead to success. The ramifications of getting it wrong can be disastrously complex. So, as outlined above, the transition plan must include details of the appointments process. Key characteristics of this process include:

☐ identifying the jobs in the new structure to be filled

☐ deciding whether they will be advertised or whether candidates will be nominated

☐ preparing a shortlist of candidates

☐ gathering information on each candidate

☐ agreeing dates on which interviews should take place

☐ agreeing who should do the interviews

☐ ensuring that individuals are told formally and properly of the outcome, and not on a fragmented department-by-department basis

☐ putting processes in place to ensure that those who are not successful are dealt with in the most equitable way.

The above guidelines do look basic. Unfortunately, even these are sometimes forgotten, which means extra work for the grievance-handlers and, in extreme circumstances, for employment lawyers at tribunals.

Cultural issues are identified for the purpose of alignment

Culture-change is included under the generic heading of organisational development. It is one of those 'soft' issues that, as we have already seen, are not for the faint-hearted. HR personnel will need a very hard profile to persuade the organisation that it is a serious cause for consideration. There is no single process for dealing with culture. In some organisations even the word 'culture' raised in a meeting about strategy will meet with concealed yawns or cries of 'Here come the tree-huggers in HR!' The robust response ought to be 'If you ignore it, the strategy will fail.' And if this response is met with incredulity, be sure to have to hand a case-study of a failed merger. There are plenty of them. Cartwright and Cooper have noted that some 40 per cent of joint ventures and strategic alliances record failure and 'between 50 and 75 per cent of key managers voluntarily leave acquired companies within the first two or three years post-acquisition' (Cartwright and Cooper, 2000). Not all of these failures are because of culture – but it is likely to have had a big part to play.

Identifying the cultural issues, then, is a key part of the organisational development role. If the organisational change involves the creation of new departments, the merging of different areas, outsourcing, or merger/acquisition, there are likely to be significant cultural issues. Cultural implications of strategy are dealt with in more detail in Chapter 9. However, key points that must be taken into account when organisational design is being considered include:

☐ Be aware of cultural differences: identify them and raise them as HR issues to be resolved. For example: do we have a sales culture when in fact we want a customer-relationship one (although the two are not necessarily incompatible)? If so, it will be necessary to emphasise the differences between the two, and to put forward HR solutions – reward, training, and so on.

☐ Be specific about culture. It is sometimes perceived as a 'soft' issue that can be avoided as of lesser importance than more tangible human issues. This is a fallacy. Cultural differences can be a competitive advantage if all parties are aware of them. They can also lead to the failure of a change. Does research into culture exist? Can staff attitude surveys be used to demonstrate any particular cultural leaning?

☐ Do not, however, throw in culture as a clever 'people' thing. Show how the culture will change because of changes in organisational design. It is not too difficult to persuade the senior team that if the strategy implies a move towards globalisation, it will require a different outlook on management than one focused mainly on a few territories. Give actual examples of change.

☐ Then provide some practical tools or recommendations

that can be used. The HR community will have a battery of team-building and personal development techniques that can help in the process of culture change.

Once the culture identification process has taken place, those in HR will have information applicable throughout the implementation stage.

Implementation and communication of the new structure

The importance of communication and 'engagement' is becoming increasingly recognised in HR. Organisational change is an area that requires the most professional of internal communication programmes, involving:

- [ ] agreeing the message that is to be communicated
- [ ] agreeing the medium/media and timing of the communication
- [ ] ensuring that a two-way feedback mechanism is in place.

It is particularly important that organisational structure change is communicated well. After all, the structure of the organisation affects everyone in it. HR people are often the messengers of organisational change, and getting the communication right is vital. Furthermore, achieving general understanding of and buy-in to organisational change should be seen as an HR priority. Implementing it will be a key aspect of organisational development.

A key element in the implementation of any structure will be to ensure that the workforce is made up of the right number of appropriately-skilled people. The subject of resourcing is therefore an important parallel process to organisational development.

14 THE RESOURCING PLAN

'Strategic' resourcing

Ask any accountant the plan for capital expenditure and anticipated return on investment and you'll get answers down to the last penny. Would that were the case of investment in human capital. The difference lies in traditional business planning, where the former is well understood, planned and audited, while the latter is frequently based on short-term reactions.

With mergers and acquisitions and globalisation on the increase, some sectors on the decrease, and technology demanding new capabilities and attitudes, it is little wonder there is a war for talent. Never was it more necessary to get and keep the right people while helping those outrun by progress to move on. Any board in its right mind will be more demanding about the plans for and returns from their significant investment in people. Every CEO and HR director needs to challenge current assumptions and think through their strategy for coping with an ever more complex and competitive battle for capable and loyal people.

And if they join, will they stay? What plans are in place to monitor attitudes and issues? Do you understand why people leave, where they go, whether they could have been saved? And do the stayers know you value them? What measures may be needed to lock people in by way of pay, benefits, stock ownership, pensions, and so on? Furthermore, does your style and culture encourage and reward people to want to stay with you because it's a great place to work?

There are times, of course, when the going gets rough that people may need to move on – to other jobs or other employers. The messages they take with them about their treatment upon exit are as significant as those you wish to convey to new entrants. It's all down to having plans in place that map out consultation and communication processes, retraining or outplacement provision, as well as compensation terms. At the same time, the survivors require no less consideration, since it is upon them the future of your business will rely.

These are hugely complex, demanding and costly issues that must receive strategic consideration on a regular basis to ensure that organisations continually limber up for the many challenges that present themselves. It is not good enough for any board to only really focus on people issues at the time of the annual pay review or when the request for new equipment to run personnel administration surfaces from the sea of other more exciting capex proposals.

Lesley James,
CIPD Vice-President

The growing importance of resourcing in organisations

Today, most organisations have to manage within a resourcing paradox. 'Companies hire even as they lay off' (*USA Today*, 26 June 2001) is not such an unusual headline. One commentator noted that 'Even as they kick them out the front door, they're bringing them in the back door – and that definitely causes a morale problem' (*USA Today*, 26 June 2001). It is hard to think of a time when resourcing has been more challenging than in the early years of the twenty-first century. There are labour shortages all over the place. The extreme elasticity of demand and inelasticity of supply that characterises the modern labour market has made resourcing tough. The global nature of many labour market sectors compounds this, and makes the solutions demanded from those in HR complex. There is a level of anticipation and planning required in resourcing that requires a strategic approach.

Clear examples of the basic organisational problems caused by labour market elasticity abound.

☐ A recent analysis of the US information technology market, for example, was headed 'While supplies last', and concluded that there was no end in sight to the pressure on employers as shown by unfilled IT positions at US companies – 843,328 in the year 2000 (Kuczynski, 2000).

☐ A recent *People Management* article claimed that Britain now relied on 'Spanish nurses, South African teachers,

Indian IT workers, and even a Swedish football manager. The media is full of tales about the introduction of talented foreigners to fill the UK's skills vacuum' (Johnson, 2001).

☐ Not to be outdone, an analysis of senior managers noted that 'across the range of industries, [organisation] sizes, [and enterprise] life cycles, virtually every company appears to be experiencing some form of executive leadership shortage, these shortages – in both number and type of leaders – acting as a constraint to corporate ambition' (Corporate Leadership Council, 1998).

But the shortage of labour has not precluded the necessity of closures, and the inevitable lay-offs that result. Disney were recently reported to be 'slashing 4,000 positions' while at the same time hiring 1,000 full- and part-time seasonal workers for the summer in Florida. Wal Mart and Hewlett Packard were further examples where simultaneous lay-offs and hiring was taking place (*USA Today*, 24–26 June 2001). Recruitment, retention and redeployment, the core components of resourcing, are significant issues for organisations. Those responsible for human resources will be at the sharp end of solving the problem. The profile of these issues has been raised as the war for talent extends across industry and commerce.

The importance of resourcing

The resourcing plan, then, is a critical part of the overall human resource plan and is likely to comprise an extensive review of a broad range of human resource activities. It has become more important in recent times because of:

☐ the war for talent
☐ the need to retain key talent
☐ the impact of redundancy and closure
☐ the need to redeploy.

It is important to understand these in order to make any sense of the forces that determine resourcing, and so they are examined in sequence below. They act as precursors to the preparation of the resourcing plan itself, which is depicted in Figure 24 (see below).

The war for talent

The war for talent has hit every part of industry, commerce and the public services hard. In some sectors, such as technology, this is because there are simply not enough people trained to do the work, and those who can are commanding high benefits and a great number of opportunities – the classic case of demand exceeding supply. It is likely that the war for talent will continue in spite of a recent spate of redundancy announcements. As Mike Johnson reminds us, the talent war has only just begun. 'Everyone, it would seem is trading up a rung on the employment food chain' (Johnson, 2001). In other cases it is just that low pay or lack of opportunity is driving people to other professions, again creating a scarcity.

I was struck how far this war had extended by a headline staring out at me in the branch of W H Smith's at St Pancras Station: 'TALENT DRAIN IS CRIPPLING DANCE'. This was the headline in *The Stage* of 14 June 2001. Here was yet another example of how the war for talent had hit a part of the service sector. Indeed, it is difficult to exclude any part of industry, commerce and public services from the debate over the talent war. A cursory scan of the recent HR press shows how widespread the effects have become:

☐ shortage of nurses – *People Management*, 8 March 2001
☐ IT skills shortages – *People Management*, 22 March 2001
☐ shortages in army personnel – *Personnel Today*, 1 May 2001
☐ shortages in the publishing sector – *Personnel Today*, 9 May 2001.

The war for talent has increased the need to make effective resourcing plans.

The need to retain key talent

A further force for change in the approach to resourcing is in the area of retention. In the light of the fact that key talent is at a premium across sector and grade, the retention of talent is a priority. The Corporate Leadership Council put this most eloquently (Corporate Leadership Council, 1998):

> No doubt many members first became acquainted with the employee retention issue several years ago, in the rich body of theory being developed around 'loyalty-based' business systems. The argument started with the felicitous links between stable employee populations, high customer satisfaction and repurchase behaviour, and stable investors in the company. That continues to be an intriguing inquiry into competitive theory. Our claim that there is a new business case for employee retention is based on new, pressing cost and growth constraints caused by the rapid increase in employee turnover hitting all companies, whatever their chosen competitive stance.

This issue is one that has lasted so far for around five years. As long as it continues to do so, the retention of talent will be a priority area for those concerned with resourcing in organisations, whatever their size.

The impact of redundancy and closure

The Loyalty Institute in Ann Arbor, Michigan, recently noted that 'employers that reduce their workforces can expect a sharp drop in commitment from the employees who remain' (*HR Magazine*, 2001). In yet another example of the contradictions that exist in a sharpened form in the modern organisation, redundancies are still a feature of the people landscape, however regrettable. Nowadays the effect on morale, the reputational risk and growing legal constraints have made the management of redundancy programmes extremely complex. The professionalism required on the part of those responsible for human resources must be of the highest calibre.

The resourcing plan is an opportunity to focus on the actions to be taken that minimise the risks to employers and employees of redundancy. What are the messages that come out of redundancy programmes in recent times?

The 1980s was a time of significant restructuring in British industry, and one outcome of this was the downsizing of whole industries such as coal, steel, and textiles. These actions brought with them the inevitable lay-offs and redundancies. At that time HR people would have seen this as one of the primary tasks, and were generally experienced in it – indeed, the implementation of redundancy programmes would have been a core competence. Unfortunately, it has not gone away, and those in HR are still expected to deal with lay-offs and redundancies effectively and sensitively. More importantly, they now have to be aware of the complexity of redundancy from both a legal and employee relations perspective.

When Motorola decided to close their manufacturing plant in Scotland, it evoked an 'argument over workplace consultation' (Taylor, 2001). This, together with Ericsson's announcement that it was to implement 12,000 job reductions worldwide, 'prompted renewed calls for firms to be compelled to discuss with employees such decisions before they are finalised'. Yet it was noted in an earlier section in this book that Ericsson was once actually praised for its work on recruitment – highlighting again the dichotomies that organisations have more and more to face. It is clear that redundancy is still a feature of organisations. Its effects can be catastrophic on employer and employee alike, and plans for its implementation must be well thought-through. The resourcing plan is an opportunity to do so.

The need to redeploy

At the two ends of the employment spectrum are recruitment and redundancy, both of which are proving to be extremely problematical. It is for this reason that the redeployment of the existing workforce is an increasingly attractive option in resource planning. Whereas once 'hiring and firing' were the hammer and anvil of organisational resource management, redeployment has become an alternative tool. If it is possible to redeploy, with all of its implications for retraining and relocation, it can often be an attractive option. Identifying redeployment opportunities is therefore important when undergoing the resource-planning dialogue.

Indeed, the need to redeploy has become so great in some organisations, both for cost-saving and for alleviation of the war for talent, that special units have been set up of which the sole purpose is to seek redeployment opportunities and to match those displaced by change with new jobs or internal vacancies.

The resourcing plan

The resourcing plan is prepared through a process of challenge and response with the business managers whose role will be to deliver the business strategy. It is important that plans are made for individual areas in the context of the overall plan, in order to ensure that there is co-ordination of activity between units such that cross-fertilisation of activity leads to optimum solutions. For example: a closure in one part of the business might coincide with the launch of a new product and recruitment needs in another. Given that there is a serious reputational and employee-relations risk in closure and that the war for talent might prevent success in the new product launch, there seems to be a possibility for a win–win situation by co-ordinating activity between the two areas. The resourcing plan (see Figure 24) will provide the links necessary for this desirable outcome.

Identifying the levels of recruitment, redeployment and redundancy from the strategic human resource forecasting process

The starting-point of the resourcing plan is the output of the strategic human resource forecast. This is to ensure that resourcing will be closely aligned to the business strategy.

At the early stages of the resourcing plan it will be necessary to identify whether recruitment, redeployment or redundancy are features of the strategy, where these are likely to take place in the business, and over what time period. And so on.

The steps for doing all this are:

☐ For each division or function identify the implications for recruitment, redeployment and redundancy in relation to the proposed strategic options. So, for example, the launch

Figure 24 THE RESOURCING PLAN

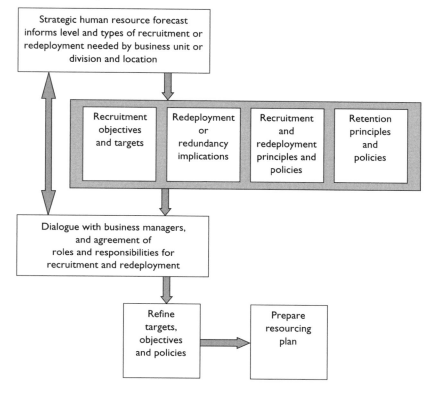

of a new product range in a division, combined with the wind-down of another, will have implications across the whole of the resourcing area.

☐ Quantify the implications for each area and derive net inflows and outflows. This will be manifested in terms of the number of recruits, the number of persons displaced, and the number of people who can be redeployed, giving an overall picture of the flows of labour.

☐ Cost the proposals for each of the activities. This will require a calculation of the cost of each recruit and each exit. Benchmarks and comparators are available for this but are not always applicable to the experience of specific organisations. The cost of resourcing is therefore an area in which some information analysis will pay off.

☐ Prepare a 'master resourcing plan' that allows a complete picture across the whole organisation.

This will be the first time in the strategy-setting process that a complete picture of the proposals as they affect both individual units and the whole organisation are presented.

Identifying key retention issues that arise from the forecast

In addition to the quantification and costing of the physical changes proposed, it is important to identify which individuals or groups of employees are critical over the life of the strategy. A recent example of this was the preparation for the year 2000. In this case most organisations had a strategy to ensure that their technology systems were 'Y2K-compliant' for a year or two before the change-over date. It was vital, therefore, to retain those technologists and their managers who were specifically working on legacy systems. For that very reason, organisations put in place retention packages for whole groups of workers as well as for senior managers.

Other staff in relation to whom retention might be an issue include:

☐ divisional directors or managing directors for key strategic areas

☐ key technical workers

☐ product marketing managers if a new product or range is to be launched

☐ high-potential employees.

The chief executive and board directors will of course be prime retention employees, and the remuneration committee will have to put in place packages to make sure that they stay put to see the strategies through. As the CIPD's publication on directors' pay explained (Conyon, 2000):

☐ Executive compensation arrangements are strategic tools used to attract, retain and motivate key employees in an increasingly international labour market.

☐ Typically, an executive compensation package for a director at a UK plc will consist of a base salary, an annual bonus and a long-term incentive payment.

Retention implications of the strategy are an important part of the resourcing plan, and these will filter through to other parts of the human resource plan, in particular training and reward (see Chapters 15 and 16).

Setting recruitment objectives and targets

Once levels of recruitment have been quantified, they will have to be converted into meaningful targets and objectives so that specific actions can be taken. Factors characteristic of this area of the resourcing plan are:

☐ an overall recruitment target for the company – This is derived from the analysis of flows of resource referred to earlier. For example: every division or function will have highlighted how many people require recruitment in each time-frame. These can be totalled so that an overall picture emerges. In taking this strategic perspective it can be advantageous to work with recruitment agencies. Negotiating a price per recruit is more favourable to the organisation if large numbers are involved over a long period, and at the same time, the agency will see advantages in large contracts for economies of scale in processing, advertising, etc.

☐ divisional or functional recruitment targets

☐ diversity considerations in gender, age and ethnic groups – Setting objectives in this area inevitably leads to debate. The pros and cons of targets for this type of area have been well articulated. The USA in particular has been through years of debate, and it is worth following up the subject before making a decision to set numerical targets.

☐ types of employee by working arrangement – A complete list is required of full-time staff, flexible workers, temporary or agency personnel, fixed-term contractors, and so on.

☐ the geographical areas where recruitment is to take place

☐ how the recruitment is to be managed – ie with an in-house team or through agencies

☐ the time-scales within which the recruitment is to be achieved.

There are now Investors in People standards for recruitment, which feature four basic principles (Investors in People, 2001):

☐ *commitment* to a strategic approach
☐ *planning* with clear aims and objectives for recruitment
☐ *action* to ensure effectiveness and efficiency
☐ *evaluation* of the effect of recruitment on performance.

Combining these four tenets with the considerations above will contribute to a recruitment plan that is both strategic in its overview of the whole picture and efficient in its tactical implementation.

Planning for redeployment and redundancy

Two further areas of the 'physical' resource plan are critical.

The first is that of *redeployment*. This occurs when one area of the organisation is expanding or has vacancies, and another is reducing its staff. Redeployment is an excellent option to achieve both objectives. It is cost-effective in that it reduces the cost of redundancy or recruitment, and it is beneficial to staff morale. Redeployment is growing in importance, and several organisations have set up a redeployment unit to act as a 'clearing-house' for employee movements.

The second area is that of *redundancy*. Inevitably, organisational change for strategic goals can bring with it closure and lay-offs. It is important that the resourcing plan tries to anticipate these and sets up processes for dealing with them efficiently. Factors to take into account are:

☐ employee consultation
☐ employee communication
☐ legal compliance
☐ the political implications
☐ financial provision – for both the organisation (ie was the cost of redundancy included as part of the strategy?) and the individual
☐ identifying opportunities for the redeployment of staff who have been made redundant.

When downsizing or redundancy is the likely option in the face of surplus resource in a particular area, there are several ways to mitigate either of these as an alternative to lay-offs. Some have been highlighted (Allan, 1997):

☐ freeze hiring and use attrition
☐ reduce or eliminate overtime
☐ pare contingent workers
☐ redeploy or transfer employees
☐ encourage voluntary terminations
☐ encourage early voluntary redundancy
☐ use work-sharing arrangements
☐ freeze or reduce pay
☐ call in contracted work
☐ retrain employees for new jobs.

Redundancy is a drastic action. Its effects can be catastrophic to the individuals involved and the communities in which they live. If redundancy programmes do have to be put into operation, therefore, those in HR should plan for all eventualities. Contingency plans should also be considered if industrial action is a possible outcome.

Setting up resourcing principles and policies

What are the organisation's principles and policies for resourcing? This is an important question that will be asked by the board, the managers who have to implement any resourcing plan, and those responsible for HR. In complex organisations there are sometimes different resourcing policies from area to area, which can cause confusion for cross-boundary strategies.

The principles that should be made widely available to managers and involve consultation with them are the company employment rules. If there is a 'people manual', it will form the basis of resourcing and will have to cover a wide range of policies. In particular, there will need to be a consistent source of reference for:

☐ pay rates for recruits
☐ benefits packages

- [ ] processes by which recruitment should take place
- [ ] qualifications to do each job
- [ ] reference satisfaction
- [ ] medical requirements
- [ ] redundancy calculations, including any pension rights
- [ ] grievance procedures for those who feel they have been unfairly picked on
- [ ] terms of redeployment on pay, relocation, and other benefits
- [ ] agreements with employee representatives.

In fact, most of this list amounts to headings that fall within what we might call 'personnel'. If these policies are already in place, then the task will be relatively straightforward. If they are fragmented, based on custom and practice, not in a formally printed form, and/or out of date, the resourcing planning process is an opportunity to rectify this problem.

The agreed terms should then be published, if they have not already been. The intranet or secure Internet is a good opportunity to ensure widespread coverage of terms.

Setting up and agreeing retention policies and practices

In the same way, the agreement of a common set of retention principles should be sought as part of the resourcing plan. Questions that require answering include:

- [ ] Who are the key individuals or groups of employees in relation to whom the organisation would want to put in place special retention arrangements?
- [ ] What will the nature of retention be? Options here include retention bonuses to be paid after a period of time, share options, or promotion opportunities after a specific project has been completed.
- [ ] What are the costs of the retention arrangements?
- [ ] Are different retention packages already in place in different areas of the business? If so, what are the implications for any new arrangements?
- [ ] Is there a single point of accountability for the management of retention?

These are important questions, and the resource plan is an opportunity to present some answers in the quest for a consistent, coherent retention policy.

Ensuring a dialogue with business managers to agree roles and responsibilities in the implementation of the resourcing plan

Effective resourcing is a joint venture between business managers and those responsible for HR. It is essential therefore that a dialogue takes place between the two groups at an early opportunity. The resourcing plan is a vehicle for this dialogue. Areas for discussion and agreement include:

- the levels of recruitment, redeployment and redundancy in each area of the organisation
- key retention targets
- the timing of the HR activity
- the roles and responsibilities of business managers to provide clear guidance on their HR requirements
- an agreement on targets in each area.

The aim of this dialogue is to make the achievement of the resourcing objectives easier by having a joint plan. It is important to move away from the view that these activities are 'HR's job'. They are not. They are instead a collaborative effort from which success will come by having clear objectives, accurate forecasts (both the role of the business managers) and excellent implementation (the role of HR).

Refining targets and objectives as a result of the dialogue

So we have a plan – a crucial first step. But it is a first step. In view of the nature of both the internal and external environments for labour, the resourcing plan is likely to be something of a movable feast. Plans will change. Targets will change. The law will change. It is important, then, that the resourcing plan is kept up to date. Of course there are no simple guidelines for this, other than to maintain a constant review. Otherwise, a monthly revisit of the resourcing plan is advisable.

To conclude, the resourcing plan is one that comes about as a combination of several of the other activities within

SHRF and HRP. The gap analysis that arises from demand and supply forecasts and the resultant implications for organisation design constitute some of these areas. The output of a resourcing plan provides a working model for recruitment, retention and redeployment throughout the organisation over the life of the plan.

15 THE LEARNING, TRAINING AND DEVELOPMENT PLAN

Why learning is crucial to earning – either as salary or as company profit

That training, development and learning are critical to good company performance seems almost an ethical tenet amongst HR professionals. In my view a company should consistently challenge its approach to development and learning to make sure that what is offered is both immediately useful to the employee and applicable in the working environment to the measurable advantage of the business.

Clearly, employees have to be trained to perform their role in a customer-focused, efficient and professional way. This applies just as much to the operative on the production line as to the manager of a professional team. Most companies train their operatives, but many make an assumption that a manager is appointed because he or she has superior managerial skills. Thirty-five years' experience working across a variety of industries persuades me that this is rarely the case. Maybe if all managers understood how to manage well there would be greater retention of key staff, and less harassment, disciplinary cases, ill health, and stress amongst the workforce.

In suggesting that companies go back to basics and challenge the status quo, I do not mean that advanced and technological methods of distribution of learning should be ignored. On the contrary, if they lower costs, improve throughput and performance, they should be used.

Any employee who has a skill in learning and who is able to transfer and apply what has been learned in different environments will be valuable indeed in a company where jobs and roles change with new technologies, new products and new markets. Such staff will be well able to look after themselves when it comes to the inevitable situation of redundancy or change of role. A company that invests in relevant training, development and learning support for its staff, and can measure the effect on the bottom line, will be a good place to work, and an environment in which the HR professional is treated seriously as a member of the business team.

Theresa Barnett,
founder of an HR consultancy business in 2000

The importance of learning, training and development

'The next big killer application for the Internet is going to be education. Education over the Internet is going to be so big, it is going to make e-mail use look like a rounding error', John Chambers, president and CEO of Cisco Systems – described as 'the world's most Internet-centric big company' – once said (*Fast Company*, 2000). How fitting that education and, presumably, training have received such a high profile. After all, it is generally assumed that investment in upgrading staff skills is key to success in the knowledge economy. It is not overstating the case to say that learning, training and development together are a most important factor in the success not only of commercial and public organisations but also of entire nations.

Furthermore, global competitive pressures, government policies and the sheer speed of the information society have converged in a short period of time to alter the shape of the landscape within which learning, training and development take place. In this fast-moving environment the effective harnessing and development of people skills are increasingly becoming a powerful source of competitive advantage. This is a significant factor and one that creates a huge responsibility for learning, training and development professionals. Not only do they have to meet the immediate needs of the organisation in terms of skills enhancement to satisfy short-term objectives but they also have a growing imperative to deliver strategic goals. The preparation of a training plan in such an environment thus has a higher profile than ever before.

There has been a lot of talk about this new, combined

operational and strategic role for training. Indeed, those in training have taken a good deal of criticism for focusing too much on the operational, as if it was no longer important. But it is all very well saying that training has to be 'strategic' if we know what that means and can deploy training resource accordingly. Such an understanding is perhaps a prerequisite to this part of the human resource plan.

The first and overriding point (in my opinion, at least) is that no single approach to training is more important than another. The emphasis at government level on work-based training and on its importance to national competitiveness shows that skill training remains a priority. Indeed, a recent CIPD-sponsored event drew attention to the proposition that 'the future of workplace learning appears fundamental to all "knowledge driven" scenarios' (Westwood, 2001). However, there is also a need to ensure that 'strategic' elements of the training arena – management and leadership development, human resource development, cultural and organisational development – become an integrated part of the overall people proposition. Strategic or human resource development is likely to be long-term and organisation-wide, and involve significant change management. Operational training, however, is more focused on the individual in the shorter term (Stewart and McGoldrick, 1996). In this respect, learning is the output of the overall training and development process, training is the operational/individual component of this, and development is the strategic/organisational perspective.

This chapter presents a methodology for 'learning, training and development' that acknowledges its/their position as a cornerstone on which other HR activity can be built. The diagram that is Figure 25 summarises the key processes for the plan.

There are three significant contributory elements to the preparation of the training plan.

1 An understanding of external influences – These might include government policy as well as demographic considerations (ie the availability of a trained workforce in the locale of the business activity).

2 Internal   factors   –   These   might   include   general

considerations, such as the budget, but also the availability of technology if web-enabled proposals form part of the training plan.

3 The process by which the plan is to be prepared – This point should not be underestimated. Bright ideas and innovative solutions need the buy-in of all the key stakeholders from the board through to the individuals who are going to receive the training.

Figure 25 **LEARNING, TRAINING AND DEVELOPMENT PLAN**

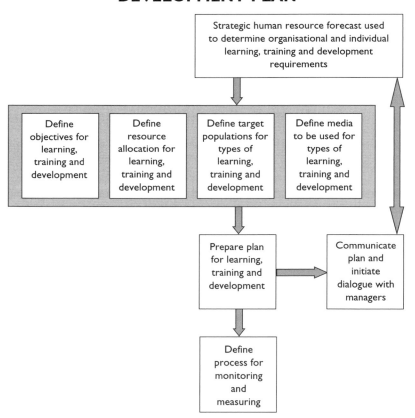

External factors

There cannot have been many times when training has been subject to so many external influences. Government interest in national competitiveness combined with a technological revolution has created a real need for those involved in preparing a learning, training and development plan to gain a full understanding of all these influences.

The role of government

Topmost in any consideration of external factors must be the views of government towards training. Its role is not only to set policy, to raise taxes and to provide national guidelines, but to form opinions in order to shape the right environment. Successive governments have been active in raising this as an issue (but with different solutions!). Tony Blair and New Labour were elected on the promise that education would be the number one priority, and the amount of debate that this subject has been awarded during this government is significant. Education and training have been given particular focus by an increasing emphasis on productivity – in particular, comparative productivity with the UK's main international competitors. The NTO Council noted that reinvigorating education and training was a priority for the UK (NTO, 2001), that government departments were responsible for developing policy and implementing strategy, and that government departments were committed to bringing about a significant change in both the quality and range of such provision. All together, this was intended to take account of:

- ☐ a greater emphasis on workforce development and linking learning to wider economic and employment needs
- ☐ increasing integration of post-16 learning structures in every nation
- ☐ a higher priority on the needs of individual learners, particularly those currently being excluded from mainstream education and those lacking in basic skills
- ☐ greater use of information and communications technology for learning and its assessment.

There was clearly something of great importance in the early part of 2001 that drew government attention to increasing national competitiveness through training. A variety of government initiatives to improve skills in the UK then followed, including the University for Industry, learndirect, Investors in People, Individual Learning Accounts, and the Learning and Skills Councils. It is useful when preparing the plan to incorporate these initiatives. As much as anything they are cost-effective. Understanding what forces contributed to creating this added impetus is also a good starting-point for deciding how any individual organisation should tackle its own training strategy and plan.

The role of technology

Yet this emphasis has not just been from the government. The private sector has been equally forthcoming in its views. A particular influence has been technology and its transformational potential for learning, training and development. The problem here is that technology has penetrated HR in widely differing ways. Some HR communities are able to offer a wide range of technological applications and platforms that can be harnessed for learning. Others have no technology. Yet others are a hybrid of new technology and very traditional infrastructures. Nevertheless, technology is already having a significant impact on the way learning is achieved. As Martyn Sloman has stated in his excellent review, 'By 2000 the relative growth of new technology as a delivery mechanism was far greater than other forms of training techniques' (Sloman, 2001). E-learning seems likely to be an exciting future channel of workforce development. It will be 'self-directed technology-based instruction that provides employees with just-in-time just-for-you training' (HR News, July 2001, Vol 20, No. 7, p. 8). This view is but one of many recent pronouncements on the use of technology in training.

It is hard to think of a training subject that has aroused so much interest as the Internet in recent times. Its potential to deliver 'anywhere, anytime learning', fast learning, and a whole range of other 'learnings' has stimulated fierce debate in the training community. If a benchmark for 'hot topics' in the world of human resources is the number of conferences devoted to a subject, technology in HR has surely achieved white-heat status.

The changing business environment

The availability of information, the sheer speed of its transmission, and the ubiquitous nature of access has created a change in the perception (if not the reality) of the economy. Whether a 'New Economy' exists or not is largely irrelevant. The fact is that there is a new approach available to run within the economy. This approach is technology-based and is centred on the Internet.

There have been some significant changes to the business environment accordingly. The Corporate Leadership Council has identified some of these (CLC, 1999) as:

☐ declining transaction and co-ordination costs
☐ declining economies of scale
☐ customer demand aggregation
☐ product unbundling
☐ digital substitution
☐ disintermediation
☐ cost competition.

This analysis had a particular technology focus – but any of the above factors, combined with globalisation, will create an urgency for a new learning, training and education response. The CIPD's view is unequivocal: it concludes that in increasingly knowledge- and service-based economies – characterised by intense internal and external economic pressures – the manner in which human effort is enhanced, developed and combined with investment in new technology is a key determinant of a nation's endogenous growth potential.

Such factors have had an impact on the question of how training is done, and where. The direction is towards 'an organisationally-based approach in which the competence and skills of knowledge workers become the major source of advantage to companies' (*CIPD Review of Training* portfolio. 2001).

Internal factors

We noted earlier that human resource strategy starts with the business strategy. So the learning, training and development plan starts with the needs of the business as identified in the strategy. However, these needs are not the only ones to be included. Indeed, the individual's needs are as important. Whereas once there was a maxim that 'If you train people, they will leave,' now it is more likely to be 'Unless you train people, they will leave.' It is an inversion of the traditional approach.

The business or organisational strategy

For most learning, training and development plans this is the prime source of 'need'. A good understanding of the business strategy is the base camp from which the direction of learning, training and development should be derived. I might put forward an example.

Let us say that in order to provide better links between the organisation's purchasing and invoicing processes – as part of a new strategy to improve the supply chain – a new finance system has been put in place. Its introduction is intended to lead to a systems training programme, a 'user' group programme, and ongoing training support for upgrades in software. A change in strategy has thus led to an operational training demand to be included in the learning, training and development plan.

This is the type of example that would satisfy the operational requirements of the business or organisational strategy. More problematic would be the introduction of knowledge management into a global consultancy using the company's worldwide information system. This would require more than technology training, although that would be important. It would also require a major programme of culture and attitudinal change in the consultancy, whose members and partners would now be required to disseminate their personal knowledge globally, thereby converting it into organisational knowledge. Such 'training' cannot be achieved through the use of workbooks or CD-ROMs. It requires a sophisticated multidisciplinary approach to learning, training and development that can be achieved by those responsible for the function only if they take a strategic view.

With reference to the business strategy input to the learning , training and development plan, those responsible for its preparation will have to be involved at all levels. This means going beyond the training intervention as a remedial measure to one where learning, training and development are regarded as strategic inputs as well.

The needs of the individual in the modern organisation

It is inevitable, perhaps, that the focus of the learning, training and development plan will be on the achievement of the business strategy. Training needs arise from the performance management system that traditionally uses competencies as its basis. However, there is an increasing awareness that the traditional psychological contract – the formal and informal relationship between the individual and the organisation – has changed. Because of this, there is an increasing role for the human resources function as a guardian of the wellbeing of the individual. Learning, training and development is one of the ways in which a new type of contract can be established.

To do this, the plan must reflect the learning, training and development needs of individuals *in their own right*. No longer is it enough to focus only on the business objectives. The success of the TUC's network of 2,000 learning representatives, and the dissemination of basic skills training, is perhaps testament to the recognition of this point (Rana, 2001). Training can be very powerful as a retention and motivation tool. Giving individuals recognised training qualifications or acknowledgement should therefore be seen as a critical part of the training plan. It will manifest itself in training objectives that include the provision of training that is recognised outside, as well as inside, the company. This contrasts with some of the attitudes towards training that were noted earlier (training to leave).

Yet it is wise, if not essential, to recognise that the provision of the transferable 'currency' of training through qualifications can be extremely motivational and, ironically, may prevent people from leaving the organisation. The thinking behind this latter point is that if people have confidence in their own position, because they are equipped with a recognised qualification, then they will have the confidence to deal with change, whatever the circumstances. I can already hear the voices of protest at this point. It is contentious. It is also something I believe those responsible for training should champion. There is a war for talent in play at the moment. It is essential that organisations retain the talent in which they have invested. Offering training that is excellent and prepares the individual for change is one way of achieving that.

Succession planning and management

One aspect of the talent management role of learning, training and development is succession management. This has become increasingly important as the war for talent has hit hard and first at the leadership and high-potential cadre. The power of the high-potential high-performing individual is recognised as a major asset. (When Stella McCartney took over as chief designer at Chloe, clothes sales rose 400 per cent.) The learning, training and development plan gives an opportunity to deal with succession management in two ways:

☐ by raising the dialogue about succession at board level
☐ by offering a methodology for dealing with it.

The role of the HR function in the question of talent and succession has been defined by the Corporate Leadership Council (CLC, 1997):

☐ Identify leadership competencies required to execute corporate strategy.
☐ Develop new organisational structures for identifying emerging leaders deep within the ranks and creating development paths across functional and business unit solos.
☐ Add or redirect formal development activities that align with the corporation's current challenges.
☐ Create diagnostic systems for monitoring the engagement,

loyalty and stickiness of especially critical talent in the organisation.

The management of talent and succession should, then, be a critical part of the overall learning, training and development plan.

The growth of corporate universities

One of the options becoming increasingly prevalent in larger organisations is the development of a corporate university. In the USA there are some 1,600 such bodies. There are fewer in Europe but they are becoming more common. They constitute a huge subject in their own right – but a reference here is necessary, since they are likely to be included in an increasing number of plans. If a corporate university is an objective of the learning, training and development plan, there are some principles that might be used in creating such a university. Meister has identified 'ten clear-cut goals and principles [that] lie at the heart of the corporate university's power to galvanise employees' (Meister, 1998). They are:

☐ Provide learning opportunities that support the organisation's critical business issues.

☐ Consider the corporate university model a process rather than a place of learning.

☐ Design a curriculum to incorporate 'the three Cs': corporate citizenship, contextual framework and core competencies.

☐ Train the value chain, including customers, distributors, product suppliers and the universities that provide tomorrow's workers.

☐ Move from instructor-led training to multiple formats of learning delivery.

☐ Encourage leaders to be involved with and to facilitate learning.

☐ Move from a corporate allocation funding model to one 'self funded' by the businesses.

☐ Assume a global focus in developing learning solutions.

☐ Create a measurement system to evaluate outputs as well as inputs.

☐ Utilise the corporate university for competitive advantage and entry into new markets.

In applying these principles, the organisation that decides on the use of a corporate university to brand its training will put in best practice based on experiences across the world.

The process by which the training plan is prepared

The component parts of the learning, training and development plan are shown in Figure 25 and are described below. But there is also a really excellent summary of the key factors involved in the planning process included in the 'Training wheel' proposed by Frances and Roland Bee, and shown in Figure 26. I particularly like this model. It is very comprehensive in defining how training needs analysis converts to actual training. As such it is a useful addition to the high-level process review included here. The Bees define a training plan (Bee and Bee, 2000) as:

> a statement of policy or direction for the period in question. A training budget setting out the financial implications of the proposed programme of training; an operational plan scheduling the training in terms of training, resources used – eg trainers, accommodation, etc.

Component parts of a learning, training and development plan are listed in the paragraphs below.

Determining organisational and individual learning

The output of the business strategy process has implications for both the organisation and the individual. These should be identified in the form of a series of learning, training and development imperatives. Until they are established it will not be possible to set corresponding objectives.

Both organisational and individual learning are important as part of this process. Organisational learning – key to competitive advantage – has been defined as embracing 'encoding and modifying routines, acquiring knowledge useful to the organisation, increasing the organisational capability to take

Figure 26 **THE TRAINING WHEEL**

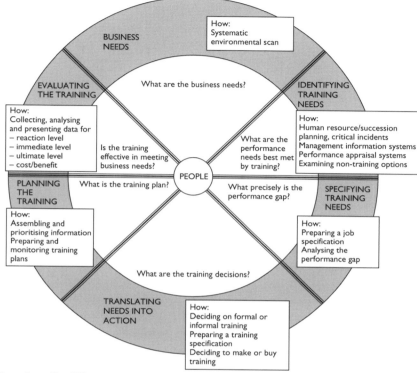

Source: Bee and Bee, 2000

productive action, interpretation and sense-making, developing knowledge about action–outcome relationships, and detection and correction of error' (Moingeon and Edmondson, 1996). Examples of the types of requirement encompassed by this definition include:

☐ The organisation wishes to move towards knowledge management and therefore requires a shift in attitudes between divisions or functions. This will require the managers of, say, sales and marketing to work closely with each other, share information and develop joint strategies. There is likely to be a training implication in this – if, for example, a new information system is put in place to facilitate such knowledge development – but also a development implication for teamworking and involvement across functions.

☐ The organisation wishes to improve morale in its work-force. Staff attitude surveys have seen a dip in the most recent periods. One response to this might be to offer training to all staff through a fixed training 'allowance'. There would be benefits to individuals from this in the improvement of their own skills, but benefits also to the organisation in that productivity and customer satis-faction increase with staff satisfaction.

☐ The organisation is going on the acquisition trail. Its skill base to complete the implementation and integration of acquired or merged companies is limited. This represents both a training need and a recruitment opportunity.

The above is by no means a definitive list of the types of implication that can arise from the business or organisational strategy. The point at which the training plan starts is under-standing the training implications of the outputs of the business or organisational strategy.

Defining objectives for learning, training and development

As soon as the identifying of both organisational and indi-vidual implications of strategy has taken place, those responsible for preparing the training plan can move to set training objectives. These should follow the overall process of objective-setting in the company. An excellent example of how learning, training and development objectives might be set is that published in the DfEE document *The Learning Age*. Once the overall objective had been established to make the nation more competitive by better training in the work-place, specific objectives and strategies could be put in place. National objectives for training were set and subsidiary objec-tives then prioritised. In setting this process out the document provided a clear focus against which other activity, such as budget allocation, could be agreed. So, for example, the Learning at Work section of the report gave priorities for early action as (DfEE, 1998):

☐ establish Investors in People as the general standard for employers

☐ set new targets for workplace learning

- establish a skills taskforce
- encourage workplace partnership between employers, employees and their trade unions to promote learning
- develop benchmarking of employers' investment in developing skills and the publication of more information on employers' investment in learning
- require TECs to produce development plans.

These are a mix of both objectives and strategies (the 'what' and the 'how'). In theory, all of the investment of the government should be within this framework. It is the same in an organisational training plan. Once objectives have been set, resource can be allocated accordingly, and little will be dedicated to activity outside of these objectives, making the resource allocation more efficient. The outstanding item in the objectives listed above is the measurable targets, which will have to be formulated. For example, the objective to make Investors in People the general standard might be made firmer by adding 'to ensure that 50 per cent of employers achieve IIP status by the year 2002'. As soon as the objectives have been agreed within the learning, training and development plan, budget and resource allocation can be determined.

Defining resource allocation for learning, training and development

The allocation of resource is only possible once the business strategy, its human resource implications, and the training strategy have been identified. Resource can then be allocated. In practice, those responsible for preparing the training plan should essentially formulate a business plan that outlines:

- the training required – in general, and more specifically by way of a detailed training needs analysis
- how it is going to be delivered – face-to-face, coaching, web-based learning, etc
- whether the organisation's own trainers or developers will be leading the training or whether the training is to be carried out by external consultants
- where the training design is to be completed

□ how the effectiveness of the training will be monitored, immediately and over time.

In most organisations 'resource' usually means headcount or budget. Often the training allocation has been made as an act of faith, involving little by which to measure return on the investment. This is unlikely to continue. Those responsible for training will be required to provide figures that show a return on the investment made in training as it competes with other projects and budgetary requirements. Two types of basic measurement might be used:

□ headcount or people requirements
□ measures of financial performance.

The calculation of headcount required for any aspect of the training strategy and training plan should be a mix of both internal resource and external consultants and trainers. The mix is determined by the type of training need that has been established.

So the development of a new leadership cadre might be satisfied by some in-house coaching and mentoring by senior executives, but also (for example) by the Insead, Harvard or London Business School business programmes. The management of such a programme will be dependent upon the number of potential leaders that have been identified – a calculation that should be inserted into the training plan. On the other hand, the organisation might decide to go for IIP accreditation across the board. To do so will require a resource that will act as interface between the organisation and the IIP body, but will also require training plans to ensure that compliance with standards is met. This might mean the introduction of a new performance management system, an agreement to ensure that all members of the organisation achieve, say, NVQ level 3 or equivalent, and so on. Once the various strands of the training plan have been assessed for their headcount implications, these can then be totalled to derive an overall resource requirement, and this becomes the training resource for the duration of the business strategy.

The financial implications of the learning, training and development plan – its business case – will come under increasing scrutiny. This is because organisations are applying the same financial disciplines to training as they do to other investment requests. It will be essential for those who are responsible for training to articulate their plans on a business basis – that is, to include such measures as return on training investment, sales increases per unit of training spend, productivity improvements through training, and reduced costs of staff turnover. Once again these should be prepared for each segment of the training plan where it is possible to do so (and it is notoriously difficult to measure the effectiveness of training investment in anything other than short-term skills training). When both headcount and budget have been agreed, they can be presented as a total resourcing plan for training.

Defining target populations for learning, training and development

Market or customer segmentation is a process used within the marketing profession for ensuring that its activity is targeted in the most effective way to those populations for whom the product or service is being developed. It is an approach that can also be adopted in the development of the training plan. Just as marketers segment, target and position their own offerings, HR might want to do the same.

Any of three types of segmentation may be used for the training plan:

☐ *Horizontal segmentation* – This means taking particular groups of employees at the same grade or level of service and developing programmes specifically for them. There are advantages in so doing. It is probable, for example, that such training will be highly focused. So a development programme 'for middle managers' can be set in a way that is more likely to reach the needs of middle management than would a programme 'for managers'. The downside is, of course, that there may not be as much diversity in the programme, and this could inhibit the development of a wide range of views.

☐ *Vertical segmentation* – This is when a 'slice' of the organisation is targeted for some type of training intervention.

The achievement of IIP is a classic example. Division X or company Y or department Z is chosen. All members of that area have to comply with the demands of IIP accreditors, and the training proposals therefore have to ensure that the whole vertical segment is covered. This is an ideal way to gain buy-in at every level.

☐ *Segmentation into units of one* – This means designing training that is totally transparent to all those in the organisation – ie it is not intended for any particular group but for all as individuals, who will each have a personal development plan and unique solutions. The use of web-enabled training is critical to the success of this approach in the light of the vast range of possible requirements of individuals. The great advantage of looking at training in this way is that it will be possible to provide a totally customised means of training – any time, anywhere, anyhow. It will provide a solution to the constant issue of the best learning style. Training will be customised to unique styles.

It is very important that the target populations are segmented into manageable groups (in technological terms, 'objects') for the training plan to achieve its objectives and the efficient allocation of resource.

Defining media to be used for learning training and development

The options open to those responsible for preparing the training plan, and, indeed, its subsequent delivery in respect of the medium or media used, are great. The fantastic progress made by the introduction of new technologies and the potential of the web have been discussed briefly here. To those responsible for training there is now a mass of information available on the subject of alternatives in training design and delivery. The CIPD training and development survey 2001 showed how broad the use of different types of training media actually was. The details are included in Table 11.

In any learning training and development situation, those responsible will be faced with the challenge of recommending the most appropriate type of medium to be used. In the contemporary organisation the probability will be that a 'layered'

Table 11 **THE EXTENT TO WHICH ESTABLISHMENTS USE DIFFERENT TRAINING METHODS AND FACILITIES**

	regularly	sometimes	never
One-the-job training	87.3	11.4	1.4
Face-to-face	84.3	14.7	1.0
Coaching/mentoring	59.4	32.1	8.6
Formal education	49.6	46.2	4.2
Conferences	43.4	50.2	6.4
Non-electronic open learning	34.7	51.8	13.5
CD-ROMs/DVD	28.9	47.6	23.5
Video	26.1	54.0	19.9
Intranets	23.7	34.5	41.8
Other computer-based learning	22.7	43.2	34.1
Internet	16.5	38.0	45.4
Action learning	14.7	36.5	48.8
Audio	8.4	38.8	52.8
Extranets	7.4	23.3	69.3

Source: CIPD, 2001

approach will be available. This means using a combination of face-to-face ('F2F'), e-learning and coaching. The CIPD survey has shown that those responsible for training are being highly proactive in this area: it is important that the momentum is maintained.

It is unlikely that e-learning will replace F2F. Indeed, there are many situations where it is inappropriate to use such a method. Equally, those responsible for training should not cling to the traditional classroom approaches in situations where other media are available and probably more fitted to learning. We live in an age of anywhere, anytime learning, and to respond to the needs of the diverse customer base that constitutes the modern organisation requires a sophisticated approach to 'channel management'. There is an exciting array of approaches for the training profession in the contemporary organisation. Imagination and creativity can make for exciting and value-adding learning, training and development if they are used in a coherent and integrated way.

Defining the process for monitoring and measuring

Evaluation is a critical part of all aspects of the human resource plan, and of none more so than training. In the past, much of what has been allocated to training in the annual budget round has been an act of faith. The training budget has not always been subject to the same hurdle rates of return as some other investments. However, there are signs that this approach is beginning to change – and it is certainly possible that all training investment will henceforth require a return calculation before it is approved. In terms of the training plan, therefore, it may be necessary to prepare metrics that demonstrate performance improvements. The purposes for doing so are (Bee and Bee, 2000):

☐ to improve the quality of the training: in terms of the delivery (eg the trainer, methods, length of training) and the training objectives (content, level)

☐ to assess the effectiveness of the overall course, trainer, training methods

☐ to justify the course: to prove that the benefits outweigh the costs

☐ to justify the role of training: for budget purposes, in cutback situations.

It is a worthwhile activity to develop these metrics. Much of the training may in any case be covered by trainer satisfaction measures, and these should be given a high profile. Yet they may not be enough, so more detailed financial analyses could well be worth looking into.

This concludes the section on the preparation of the learning, training and development plan. Of course, everyone has a view on this. Training continues to be a popular pastime for many managers in organisations, and it is encouraging that they take such an interest. That is why the learning, training and development plan should be inclusive, not exclusive. Learning, training and development is a necessity for everyone who works in the organisation. And although surveying the products of the leading international business schools is a fascinating thing to do, it should not be done at the expense of deciding on the best way to train those on the shop floor for their benefit and for the possible survival of the company.

16 THE REWARD PLAN

> The 1990s were a decade of unprecedented change in the whole area of reward. The change has been dramatic and transforming.
>
> The areas of major change have been:
>
> □ the decreased incidence of collective bargaining
> □ the wider scope for discretion in setting individual pay levels
> □ pay and performance linkage – organisation, team and individual
> □ market-driven pay.
>
> In future the reward strategy will be integrated with other areas of HR and the business.
>
> *Vicky Wright,*
> *CIPD Vice-President – Reward*

The reward plan

The 'fat cat' stigma at one end of the spectrum and pressure for a minimum wage at the other have prompted a new focus on reward that has caused it to become part of the responsibility of the wider HR community rather than of a few actuarially-trained specialists. Reward is a mainstream HR activity, and as such is likely to feature very prominently in the strategy-setting process.

Reward is at the heart of good human resource practice. It is a fundamental part of the relationship between the employee and the organisation. It affords the employee rights and recognition. It is also a key employer lever in a) providing incentives towards the achievement of strategy, and b) cementing the psychological contract. In the blended workplace, in which virtual and actual organisation structures combine, reward programmes can be used to 'promote a single set of objectives and provide reinforcement for success on common goals' (Randall and Wallace, 1997). On the downside, the failure to put in place strategies for dealing with reward can result in real cost, production and morale problems – especially during significant strategic change, as for instance during a merger or acquisition (Mercer, 2001). But reward is no longer just about money. It is about a complex set of options that include non-financial benefits. Developing a reward strategy is therefore an essential part of the human resource professional's activity, and the reward plan is a statement about achieving both the objectives of the business and those of the individual.

The preparation of the reward plan should be based on a broad range of inputs including the business strategy and the organisation's approach to performance management. The key stages of this process are outlined in Figure 27.

Reward and strategy

But what is the link between reward and strategy, and why is it so important? Vicky Wright, group managing director of Hay and the CIPD's Vice-President for Pay and Employment, has noted four themes that are shaping the strategic approach to reward (Wright, 2001):

☐ a desire to increase employees' engagement with their organisations in order to staunch high staff turnover

☐ a concern with managing skills shortages

☐ a recognition of the large differences in contribution made by effective teams and individuals

☐ a wish to move all staff up the performance curve.

It is perhaps not surprising then that research by Towers Perrin and Watson Wyatt, two leading HR consultancies, has shown that a clearly articulated strategy and plan for reward is a growing feature of organisational strategy. It can bolster and support the achievement of strategy and cement the relationship between individuals and the organisation.

It is essential for HR professionals to be instrumental in

Figure 27 **THE REWARD PLAN**

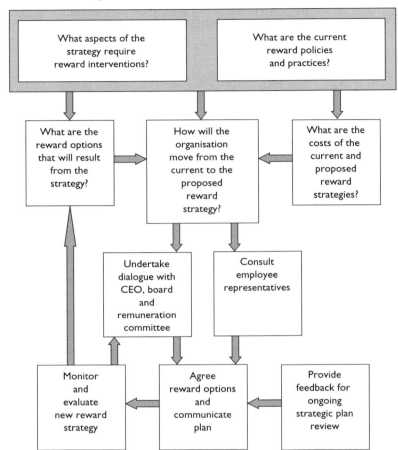

shaping the reward strategy and articulating it within a reward plan, because 'the balance between corporate objectives and the need for the remuneration and incentive package to support those objectives falls clearly within the HR brief' (Hubbick, 2001). Reward has to be seen as a strategic component of HR as well as a tactical solution to short-term demands (typified by the pay round).

The aim of the reward plan is thus focused on supporting the achievement of both long- and short-term goals. It provides that support through a variety of means. In addition to

the traditional use of compensation for value added to products and services (more commonly known as wages!) reward
can be used to communicate and reinforce values and
behaviours. Furthermore, it can 'motivate all members of the
organisation, promote teamwork and flexibility, provide value
for money, and achieve fairness and equity' (Armstrong and
Murlis, 1998).

The plan is an opportunity to align reward to wider organisational objectives. In doing so, four key elements are
necessary. These are: 'defining strategic objectives for both
the organisation as a whole and individual business units;
setting performance indicators; matching human resource
assets to these; [and] aligning compensation and rewards'
(Ashton, 1995). The paragraphs below deal with these in more
detail.

Output and objectives for the reward plan

To help in the achievement of these rather stretching goals
for the reward plan, it is important to have clear objectives.
For example, the plan might contain:

☐ a statement of the likely reward implications of specific
   strategic initiatives that might require one-off arrangements, such as an acquisition

☐ a statement of objectives for the employer

☐ a statement of objectives from the employees' perspective

☐ a specialist view outlining the technical options available
   to the organisation.

How reward links in to the objectives of both the individual
employee and the employer is a fundamental part of the
reward plan and, indeed, is critical to the success of the overall
organisational strategy. Research (Ashton, 1995) has suggested that:

> if pay, individual performance and career are not reviewed,
> redesigned and linked to organisational performance and out-
> comes, change programmes at best will secure half-hearted
> support from individuals and under-par contributions. At
> worst, unique talents will be lost to other employers, which

directly threatens competitive capability from within, and pro-grammes may well fail.

Employee and employer objectives

When considering objectives, there are two particularly relevant questions:

- ☐ What are the things that the employee will want to get out of the reward relationship with the employer?
- ☐ What does the employer want to achieve by the reward strategy and plan?

These can be effectively summarised as in Table 12 (Torrington and Hall, 1991).

When putting together the reward plan, therefore, both sides of the employment equation should be considered. In this way a more balanced set of options can be presented for the senior management of the organisation to consider. Increasingly, the linking of reward to performance is something that has been growing in importance. It is worth repeating here that reward requires more than a 'technical' input from the reward specialists within the human resources function – important as these are. Its fundamental position in the success of the people relationship means that there is a need to put reward in an overall context. These objectives are the basic constituents of the reward plan.

Table 12 **REWARD-RELATED EMPLOYEE AND EMPLOYER OBJECTIVES**

Employee objectives	Employer objectives
Purchasing power	Prestige – the endeavour to become
Terms and conditions that are 'felt fair'	known as a good payer
Guaranteed employee's rights	To pay competitive rates
Retention of relativities between groups	To maintain control of operations
and/or individuals	To provide pay that motivates and
Recognition of personal contribution	increases productivity
Composite compensation – variable	To minimise costs
make-up of the reward package	

Information required when preparing the reward plan

In advance of preparing the reward plan, then, certain key information is needed. It is useful to spend time gathering as much information on current reward arrangements as possible. Information required includes:

Reward by

- [ ] organisational division
- [ ] regional variations
- [ ] functional variations
- [ ] age-group
- [ ] gender
- [ ] level of responsibility.

Breakdown of reward by

- [ ] salary or wages
- [ ] overtime
- [ ] pensions
- [ ] benefits (cars, health, flexible benefits)
- [ ] employee share ownership.

Key reward indicators

- [ ] movement in earnings
- [ ] labour turnover
- [ ] recruitment and retention rates.

External influences on reward

- [ ] legislation
- [ ] competition for labour in industry or market rates
- [ ] benchmarking against competitor or similar organisations.

These are the basic data required as the reward plan is put in place. The nature of this general description of reward inevitably precludes any specific industry or market considerations: it is up to those responsible for preparing the reward plan to ensure that these are taken into account.

Preparing a reward plan – the process

A process for preparing and developing a reward plan was presented as Figure 27. It is worth noting here that the methodology of reward planning is very much a matrix type of activity. Specific strategies have reward implications that run 'vertically' down a division or function (eg a sales incentive scheme). However, there will also be an overall organisational approach to reward that is perceived to run 'horizontally' through the whole organisation (eg equal pay). The reward plan must ensure that the interfaces between the two are recognised and accounted for. This is expressed diagrammatically in Figure 28.

How does it apply in practice?

Let us say that an organisation has four divisions, each of which has its own unique reward needs. As is visible in the

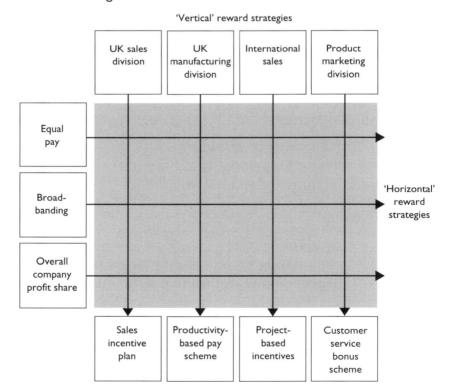

Figure 28 **THE REWARD MATRIX**

diagram, the sales division wants its own sales incentive scheme, manufacturing focuses on productivity, international sales – which has a longer lead time – wants to reward against the achievement of project objectives (for example: sales of high-value multi-million pound capital equipment may take years, so a way to use reward as a motivator is against some measurable objectives other than sales – the completion of a tender, a presentation to the board, shortlisting, or whatever), and finally the product market division wants to reward against customer satisfaction indices. Yet the organisation *as a whole* has reward policies that it wants to apply to all the divisions. Equal pay is a good example of this.

The reward plan has to take account of the cross-points of the matrix if both divisional and organisation-wide reward strategies are to be implemented successfully.

Outlining current practices on reward throughout the organisation

The obvious starting-point for the reward plan is to understand what is currently in place. A critical part of the dialogue will be a comparator basis with existing reward schemes, strategies and policies. This is an important part of the reward plan. In particular, any changes that are proposed are likely to have cost implications in relation to existing arrangements. A clear statement of comparison is therefore a useful inclusion in the overall planning process.

Examples of this might include:

☐ details of current share ownership schemes if new ones are being considered

☐ details of pay rates in different employee areas – for example: how do sales incentive schemes currently operate? Again, this is important information if new sales targets or new products are to be introduced. It is essential to show the links between terms, or, indeed, why the current schemes are being replaced

☐ details of current bonus arrangements

☐ details of benefits packages including health, cars, product discounts, etc.

It is also essential that equality of pay is seen as a key part of the overall reward plan – and at this point an equal pay review might be conducted. This issue is one that has been raised by both the TUC and the Equal Opportunities Commission. The CIPD view is that the 'key to making significant progress on equal pay is raising awareness of the issue and convincing employers that the problem is more widespread than they might realise' (CIPD, 2001). The Equal Pay Task Force has outlined the steps for this (Paddison, 2001):

☐ Stage one – Identify all jobs that are done by both men and women, calculate average pay, compare average basic pay between men and women, check gradings to ensure a like-for-like basis, analyse any differences, monitor and review information regularly.

☐ Stage two – This is designed to review 'whether men and women have equal access to each element of pay, and whether they receive equal outcomes for equal work'. It involves a review of the design of the pay system and of how it has been implemented.

☐ Action plan – This uses the information gained in Stages one and two to identify any inequality in pay and make proposals to put it/them right.

The intention here is to provide a reward foundation on which to build the new strategies. This stage in the process can then be used to inform thinking about any future proposals on reward.

Identifying reward policies and strategies that are part of the overall organisational strategy

Having identified the base case, so to speak, we can then look at the implications on reward of the strategic options that have been proposed. In the first instance we will want to look at the overall picture. This is the horizontal part of the reward matrix (Figure 28), relating to policies that apply across the whole organisation. Examples include:

☐ 'We want to pay in the third quartile' to attract a particular calibre of employee.

- □ 'All employees will have performance-related pay' to ensure that there is a customer focus as part of our strategy to enhance service.

- □ 'We will pay profit share at 10 per cent' to ensure that there is a shareholder focus as part of our strategy to deliver enhanced shareholder value.

- □ If a merger or acquisition is planned, it will require sophisticated reward planning. For example: what will be the basis of reward in the new company – will it be that of the acquirer or acquiree? Which of the merged company reward schemes will predominate? Will a new scheme be instituted?

- □ In order to rationalise the different schemes in different divisions, a flexible benefits programme is being considered. What should be included in the programme? Should it apply to all staff?

The above are examples of reward implications that apply to the organisation as a whole as a result of strategy-setting. Other factors to take into account here are performance management policies that impact on all employees, broad requirements for the minimum wage, profit share, and so on. Share ownership schemes will also have to be included since 'the extent to which any scheme will address the broader objectives of the company must be considered' (CIPD, 2001). The wider reward policies of the organisation must be inserted into its plans for reward.

Highlighting how a specific organisational strategy is likely to require reward interventions

This is the vertical part of the reward matrix (Figure 28). The initial input to the development of the reward plan is, of course, the organisational strategy. It is important to review the strategy in the context of reward as much as of any other area of people practice. Examples with some possible implications might include:

- □ The organisational strategy requires a move to the idea of shared services by grouping together functional areas such as HR, finance and technology – ie taking them out of individual business units into a central grouping. This will have reward implications for the managing directors of the business units whose objectives may change from profit to sales volume or lower costs per unit produced. The reward basis of the managing directors will have to be changed accordingly, and this will have to be reflected in the reward plan. Each division or business unit will have new, specific business targets, and these will have to be planned *individually*.

☐ The organisational strategy involves the launch of new products onto existing customers by one of the sales divisions. It will require a new incentive scheme. The reward plan will highlight the options for this scheme. Is it based on current incentives, for example, or will there be a special scheme put in place?

These examples show how an understanding of the specific organisational (ie divisional or business unit) strategy is a key foundation on which the reward plan may be built. The HR community will have to dissect the organisational strategy piece by piece in order to get a full understanding of the implications for reward. This reinforces the point made throughout this book – that HR must be fully integrated into the strategy-setting process.

Identifying reward options that result from the strategy

Once the implications of both the organisational and divisional strategies have been identified, the options for reward may be articulated. There are usually a number of things that an organisation might do in its reward plans. Rarely is there one right answer and, even more importantly, legislation may compel changes anyway – as it has done with current profit-sharing schemes. The reward plan is an opportunity to present the options and their implications for the CEO, board and (if appropriate) remuneration committee to debate. The issue of performance-related reward strategy is clearly one that should feature here. The objective of linking reward to business strategy and performance will be a key part of the overall plan.

It will require a really good understanding of the strategy

and of how reward can be used in its achievement. A dialogue with the divisional leaders, an understanding of the costs of the reward proposals, and a good communication plan once agreed are three of the essential success factors.

So what are the major questions that might arise from the reward debate?

☐ Literally at what level should share options be given? The basis for calculating this might be, say, a Hay point scale – eg if an employee is above a certain level, he or she receives a discretionary quota of share options – or it might be that all employees receive share options through Sharesave schemes or the equivalent.

☐ At what level should the bonuses be set for both senior managers and all other employees?

☐ What should be the relativity of pay in the organisation – more, or less, than competitors', for example?

Such options provide a basis for dialogue with business managers.

Whatever options are chosen, however, it is important to have good design principles for them. In this respect some important principles ought to be followed when designing proposals (Marchington and Wilkinson, 1998).

☐ Design reward systems so the desirable performance is rewarded, and the relationship between performance and reward is clear.

☐ Design tasks and jobs so that employees can satisfy their needs through work.

☐ Individualise the organisation, reflecting different needs for different people (different valences); this includes not only the work but the benefits they receive, and might point to a system of cafeteria benefits.

Increasingly, flexible benefits are being considered as an option for reward strategy. This method of reward does allow a range of strategic options to be accommodated, and serious consideration should be given to their applicability in this section of the plan.

Outlining how the reward strategy might move the organisation from current to proposed options

After the options have been presented, a key question will be 'So how are we going to get there?' The reward plan should therefore contain a 'reward roadmap' outlining the key stages in the proposed plan. If we take the example of the sales division and a new sales incentive scheme, we can identify some of the features on the roadmap. It will contain:

☐ a statement of the present reward situation – which might be as simple as 'Our current reward schemes do not give the right level of focus on sales of the new product range'

☐ a proposal for the reward plan – 'To deal with this, the organisation will introduce a new sales scheme that will give additional commission for the new product range'

☐ a note of key changes being proposed – the note will give details of the new scheme and how it will affect each individual, as well as the total projected costs

☐ a statement of who will be affected and how – in particular, the effects on each sales person and the impact on the package

☐ a proposal on how engagement and buy-in will be obtained – 'We plan to communicate at our sales conference in May'

☐ the dates by which key events will take place – 'The scheme will be introduced in June, with the first payments in the July salary.'

Of course there will be some overlap with the communications part of the reward plan that will appear later, so a summary is all that is required here.

Quantifying the cost of making these moves

Once the options and plans are decided, it will be necessary to quantify the costs of the reward plans and their benefits. Measures that might be included are:

☐ the overall cost of reward to the organisation pre- and post-reward-plan

☐ benchmarks against other organisations or functional groups

- □ the cost-income ratio analysis and the changes likely as a result of implementing the reward plan
- □ the phasing of reward and ongoing costs (is there a three-year pay deal? a sliding scale of bonuses? possible one-off buy-outs of existing reward arrangements? and so on)
- □ any quantifiable benefits of the new reward plan.

The result of this analysis will be a 'balance sheet' of reward. On one side of the balance sheet will be the costs of the reward plans. On the other the measurable benefits (say, commission versus additional sales, productivity improvements, and so forth).

Understanding the cost of reward proposals is important to those responsible for putting in new reward plans. It is likely that when these are presented, the chief executive officer or the board will have questions about the benefits to the organisation in implementing new plans. Those in HR will have to have answers to such questions. Calculations that might be made therefore include:

- □ the forecast increase in sales and margin of the new incentive scheme
- □ the total cost of putting in new equal pay proposals
- □ the cost of profit share and potential increase in profit by offering a range of percentages
- □ the cost and benefits of flexible reward arrangements.

In fact, it is useful to prepare as much information on this type of analysis as possible before the dialogue takes place.

Instigating dialogue with the CEO and the board or remuneration committee about the options

At this point we have the basis of a reward plan (founded on the strategies and the reward plans that support them) that can then be presented to the senior management of the organisation and any reward governance committees. HR will lead the debate about reward, but it is important to remember that it is not HR who is responsible for the decision on the reward strategy. HR makes recommendations in varying strength, but at the end of the day the decision on which of the reward options is chosen is a management decision in which HR professionals are but one constituent part.

The dialogue with the board therefore requires HR to play two roles:

☐ that of technician – providing expert input to the reward plan

☐ that of facilitator – outlining the possible implications of each of the reward options, their costs, any legal implications, any employee-relations ramifications, and so on.

It is this latter role that is the strategic input of HR as part of the human resource plan.

The dialogue with the remuneration committee is different. The remuneration committee 'is charged specifically with the design and management of the remuneration of the directors of a company' (Hubbick, 2001). The main consultation will therefore be about changes in the packages for the directors. In particular, these might include new bonus or share-ownership arrangements. It is essential corporate governance to gain approval for this type of change by the committee.

In both of these activities, rigorous preparation is required by those in HR. For the dialogue about the overall reward plan, financial, legal and employee-relations information is essential. For the remuneration committee there will have to be a very detailed analysis of and justification for any proposals. The non-executives on the committee will want to ensure that any decision has a sound basis – especially since director reward will be made public, being published in the report and accounts (and increasingly in the financial pages of both broadsheets and red-tops).

Consulting employee representatives

Given the sensitivity that surrounds the whole question of reward, it is important to make full use of the consultation and communication process. Consulting with employee representatives on reward is not really an option but a necessity. Whatever process the organisation has for employee consultation should therefore be instituted for the reward plan. That

will vary from organisation to organisation. Where trade
unions act as employee representatives, a formal consultation
process is likely to be in place which can be adopted for the
reward strategy. Consulting with the support of a confiden-
tiality agreement is common practice. Feedback – via a pay
round – can be used to modify the reward plan if necessary.

Where trade unions are absent from the workplace, other
less formal and bureaucratic ways of consultation should be
used to inform employees of the direction of the reward plan.
In modern industrial relations this is seen as good practice.
It will also form part of the employee-relations plan dealt
with in the next chapter.

Increasingly, however, pay is being negotiated on an individual basis. In spite of this there is still a need for
consultation. In large organisations with hundreds or thou-
sands of employees, this is done through broad-banding or
flexible benefits. Such schemes allow a wider range of negotiation possibilities with individuals in relation to their own
packages.

Agreeing on an option and communicating with employees

Once the process has been followed, a reward plan can be
approved by the senior management, and communication to
employees can follow. This is not just a one-way communication exercise, however. More importantly, it is about
gaining buy-in to the proposals and the engagement of
employees to the direction in which reward will take them.
This task should not be underestimated. Lack of understanding about the need for engagement is one of the most
common errors made in relation to the many aspects of organisational strategy. None is more commonly made than in
relation to reward. It has been noted that 'presentation of the
pay plan and organisation-wide communication are critical
issues. Successful organisations put considerable effort into
this, since employees usually need to be convinced about
purpose, outcomes and whether an undeclared agenda exists'
(Ashton, 1995). The need to communicate in a way that is
understood gives two-way feedback, results in information
that can be cascaded and repeated throughout the

organisation, and is a really important part of the human resource plan in general and of the reward plan in particular.

So how might we achieve this? First and foremost we should take account of Jay Conger's telling comment, 'If ever there was a time for businesspeople to learn the fine art of persuasion, it is now. Gone are the command-and-control days of executives managing by decree' (Conger, 1998). The communication of reward is as much about persuasion as direction, and Conger's four essential steps to effective persuasion – establish credibility, frame for a common ground, provide evidence, and connect emotionally – are as good a guide to communicating reward plans as you will ever see. So apply them as part of this process.

Monitoring and evaluating the level of engagement

We are increasingly being told that 'If you can't measure it, you can't manage it.' Whatever your feelings are at this particular adage, even the sceptical among us would see some merit in trying to monitor the success of the reward strategy. There are several ways to monitor whether engagement is being achieved:

☐ One particular route is through the staff attitude survey – and it is one well respected. It is recommended here that a special survey is undertaken if a new reward plan is being proposed. The results of the survey can be compared at, say, one-, three-, six- and 12-month periods to gain a real understanding of the level of satisfaction with the reward plans.

☐ A further attitudinal measure might derive from focus group analysis. This is an increasingly common route to the understanding of staff attitudes. Such analyses can be either conducted formally and be facilitated, or informally, often through senior manager visits and presentations. The 'site visit' can be a great source of intelligence about attitudes.

☐ Measures of recruitment and staff turnover are good indicators of reward. Is 'pay' one of the reasons for successful recruitment? This is a question that should be high on the agenda of HR. Equally, 'Are people leaving because of pay?'

will give further evidence of the success or otherwise of the reward strategy.

Clearly, the success of the reward plan is as much about the way it is communicated and sold in as about the plan itself. It is no use providing for extra pay or bonus if the engagement of the employees is not part of the deal. Measuring that engagement is therefore a key part of the overall process.

Feeding back results and amending the plan accordingly

The final part of the process is something common to all aspects of the human resource plan: feedback. In the light of the fundamental assumption that the plans are not static, any results should be fed back into whatever process is in place for strategy and planning reviews. If things are not working according to the reward plan, proposals may be put in place to change them.

This process is one being put forward as a template that might be adapted to fit the prevailing needs of any and every organisation. It is not intended to be cast in stone. It is intended to evolve, based on the experience of implementing the plan. At this point it is important to reinforce the fact that the preparation of the reward plan and its implementation are more than technical 'reward' responsibilities. Reward is a key part of organisational development, and this should be reflected in the reward plan. Reward is used to influence attitudinal and behavioural issues, and therefore forms a key component of culture change when this is required. Furthermore, reward is a strategic issue in the people management of an organisation. It is not the sole responsibility of the reward specialists. Its development is part of the overall human resource function, and not a separate entity.

17 THE EMPLOYEE-RELATIONS PLAN

The 2001 May Day Parade might perhaps act as a metaphor for employee relations so far in the 21st century. The marchers consisted of traditional Labour Party members and followers of New Labour. There were representatives from the Socialist Workers Party and, surprisingly, a Communist Party group. Glassworkers, public service workers and engineers were well supported. But there were also cyclists, environmentalists and a band of marchers dressed as Cavaliers. This was no Cromwellian New Model Army but a gathering of many diverse groups, each with a different perspective on work and society as a whole. An attempt at a common theme 'People before Profit' was only moderately effective.

Two things stood out. First, how committed the marchers were to their diverse causes: they were very vocal about many different issues – creating a cacophony of causes. Second, how diverse the 'labour movement' was in modern society. Understanding these two points determines our approach to employee relations as we include this aspect in the human resource plan.

Transfer this May Day march into today's working environment and there is a real challenge to the effective management of people unless the diversity of the modern workforce is understood and reflected in the principles and practices of employee relations. It is less likely that the great bodies of trade unionists, united behind a single theme, will be present. However, the role of trade unionism remains an important characteristic of the modern organisation, albeit that that role is somewhat different from manifesting the confrontational policies that characterised industrial relations until the 1980s. It is no less important, but requires a radically different approach on the part of human resources and business managers. This makes employee relations a complex affair. Furthermore, the challenge of employee commitment is likely to become a very big human resources issue in the 21st century.

The subject of employee relations is one that has grown in scope in recent years, moving from the narrow confines of traditional industrial relations to one that now embraces a broad range of human resource issues. At its core is the fundamental contract that an employer has with an employee in the contemporary organisation. This contract is one that encompasses the very tangible legality of employment and all of its implications as well as the less tangible psychology of the relationship. It also encompasses the need to tap into the business benefits of diversity, as the quest for competitive advantage in global markets gathers momentum. To deal with this complex subject in a comprehensive way, this chapter covers not only the process of the employee-relations plan (see Figure 29) but also a more detailed analysis of some of the main employee-relations trends under three headings:

☐ *employee relations* in its broadest sense
☐ *industrial relations*, which includes the more formal relationship with trade unions or employee representatives
☐ *employee commitment*, which is likely to dominate the whole field of employee relations for the foreseeable future.

An understanding of these is an important part of the preparation of an employee-relations plan.

Employee relations and business strategy

It is likely that almost every aspect of change associated with the business strategy will have employee-relations implications. Take mergers and acquisitions, for example. When Lloyds and TSB got together in 1995/1996, the human implications of doing so were significant. Some idea of the scope of employee-relations issues can perhaps be grasped from an

Figure 29 **THE EMPLOYEE-RELATIONS PLAN**

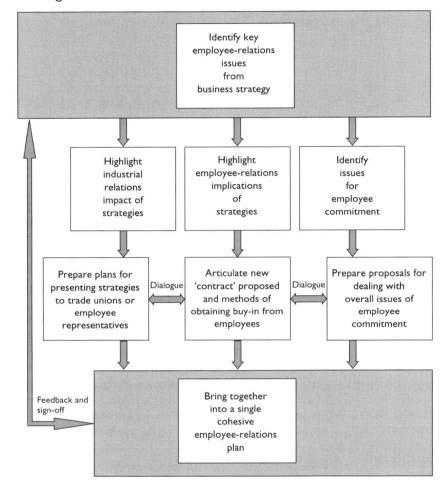

analysis of the 'Heads of Agreement' that were reached with the trade unions involved. These are included in the form of Table 13. Peter Chadwick, head of employee relations, faced with the challenge of managing the employee-relations issues in a multi-union environment, noted that HR was an integral part of the merger from the start (Chadwick, 2000). The Heads of Agreement reflected the wide scope of employee relations – and this is an important indicator for what should and should not be included in the employee-relations plan.

Given the potentially broad scope, are there any particular areas on which those preparing the employee-relations plan should focus?

The modern workforce – understanding diversity

The first focal point is the nature of workforce diversity. Some would argue that it was less complicated (but still not easy to deal with) when 'employee relations' really meant 'industrial relations' – when the issues of the workforce were dealt with through the rigid structure of the various agreements reached with trade unions. As Salamon has noted of one case study, 'any attempt to bypass this structure would be seen as an attack on trade unions and collective bargaining' (Salamon, 1987). In the traditional industrial relations approach:

☐ Stage 1 was the presentation of both sides of the case.

☐ Stage 2 was negotiation and agreement – or led into.

☐ Stage 3, failure to agree.

☐ Stage 4 was arbitration.

☐ Stage 5 was either a ballot of the members or a strike.

The process was invariably confrontational but usually easy to understand. There were two 'sides', who either agreed or disagreed. These were the good or bad old days, depending on your perspective.

Now, though, the situation is far more complex, and those responsible for human resource management require a new set of competencies to deal with the modern workforce. These involve a level of understanding and sophistication previously unknown. In non-unionised environments, the challenge is to gain agreement and commitment from every member of the workforce as individuals. In unionised environments, understanding the complexities of the diverse workforce is compounded by the need to satisfy the trade unions involved. And of course there are now four very different groups of workers in Generation X, Generation Y, Baby Boomers and 'Matures'. In any organisation there are likely to be employees who are into the Bangles, Britney Spears, the Beatles and

Table 13 HEADS OF AGREEMENT IN THE MERGER OF LLOYDS AND TSB

1. Union recognition
The banks will present the union with a draft recognition and procedural agreement which will protect existing levels of recognition and will be developed upon the following framework:

1.1 *General principles*
- The banks and the union will have a shared commitment to the prosperity of the bank for the benefit of all stakeholders (customers, shareholders, employees), recognising the value of the speedy management of change in responding to competitive pressures.
- The banks and the union will commit to an open exchange of information and spirit of co-operation.
- The banks will extend the principle of equal treatment to each recognised union.
- The banks will commit to developing positive and stable working arrangements.
- The banks will encourage employees to join one of the recognised unions and will encourage a statement of this within the staff regulations/staff manual.
- The banks will negotiate separately with each recognised union.

1.2 *Collective bargaining*
The banks will provide collective bargaining rights to the union for members in bands 2 to 8 (or equivalent) on harmonised terms and conditions, with the following matters being negotiable:
- recognition arrangements
- grading and salary structures
- basic pay
- holiday entitlement
- sick pay scheme
- overtime rates
- regular allowances
- shift pay
- provision of cars
- provision of medical insurance
- health, safety and security
- mobility
- staff benefits
- equal opportunities
- TSB salesforce pay productivity arrangements
- job security terms
- discipline and grievance procedures
- changes to pension scheme rules
- job evaluation process
- hours of work.

The banks will propose and agree with the union appropriate machinery for collective bargaining.

1.3 *Consultation*
The banks will extend to the union the opportunity to be consulted where changes may affect members in bands 2 to 8 on harmonised terms and conditions. The banks will consult the union over the following matters:
- business results and changes
- staffing arrangements arising from organisational change
- changes to work practices
- performance management
- general pension scheme matters.

Source: Chadwick, 2000

Bobby Darin. One size does not fit all. This is a complex scenario requiring a multi-level employee-relations plan.

Employee relations

This is the broadest area and contains much that is general about the overall relationship an individual has with the organisation. The CIPD has outlined its position on employee relations, defining the main characteristics. The Institute noted that in the working environment a successful relationship could be established if there was employee trust, perceptions of fairness, and 'delivery of the deal'. Further evidence of good employee relations practice was presented (CIPD, 1997):

□ Key elements of good people management are job design, skills development and a climate of regular, systematic involvement.

□ Good people management practices are associated with a positive psychological contract based on trust, fairness, and delivery of the deal.

□ An organisation culture in which employees believe their employer will look after their interests has positive outcomes for work performance.

The issue we face in dealing with employee relations (ER) as part of a wider HR plan is that it is possible to include almost every aspect of human resource practice as part of the employee-relations proposition. The ER aspect of the plan can thus become too generalised. It is critical to have objectives for the ER plan that are specific and unique to ER. Otherwise, a critical success factor within organisations – namely, how people are treated in their day-to-day relationship – will be lost in a morass of generalisations. So the focus of the ER plan has to be to identify those aspects that are unique, and to present plans for their enhancement or delivery. Such plans might include:

□ proposals for employee involvement
□ proposals for presenting the psychological contract in a way that is understood and accepted

☐   a suggestion on how employees can have a voice in their employment conditions.

Employee involvement

In his book *The Employee Revolution*, Thomson noted that in order to do anything that needs some form of persuasion, it is necessary to find what creates or reinforces the 'need' for employees 'to want to act in a positive and motivated way' (Thomson, 1990). And yet so often business strategy is implemented in a way that does not take account of the needs or the views of employees. Marcus Buckingham of Gallup recently noted that over 80 per cent of employees were not 'engaged' at work – ie they were not psychologically connected (Buckingham, 2001). This stance is no longer tenable. In the modern organisation the employee expects to be consulted about both the strategy and how it is implemented. This applies in both unionised and non-unionised environments. A key part of the employee-relations plan must be to outline exactly how it is to be achieved.

Employee involvement can be achieved in at least two ways – first by deciding how employees can become involved in the way work is organised, and second by deciding how they can have a greater influence on factors that affect the organisation as a whole (CIPD, 1997).

The psychological contract

Much has been written about this area. The CIPD's research on people management and business performance has concluded that 'a positive psychological contract based on trust and respect supported by progressive people management' can contribute to higher levels of business performance (CIPD, 2001). The psychological contract has been defined as 'the set of expectations held by the individual and specifying what the individual and the organisation expect to give to and receive from one another in the course of their working relationship' (Schemerhorn, Hunt and Osbourne, 1991). The fact is that relationships have changed in organisations. This has caused problems for both employer and employee. As one commentator (Ettore, 1996) has noted:

We see that the rules have changed. But we haven't figured out how to conform. Most of us are at least vaguely aware that there is a new employment contract, a new set of assumptions that affect how we relate to our managers and vice versa. We know that the old arrangement which assumed lifetime employment is dead. . .*requiescat in pace*, say the experts. We're not sure about that because we still believe our companies owe us something. Maybe not a job for life. But what?

The question posed here is one with which many organisations have wrestled. The employee-relations-planning process is an opportunity to surface some of these issues.

So what are we to do now? As *The Economist* noted as long ago as 1993, 'Unless we find new ways to motivate those who have survived the purges of professional ranks, most big firms may never achieve the gains that are supposed to justify such wrenching changes' (*The Economist*, 1993). This point is still relevant but has an added complication – not by way of those who have survived purges but in those who have thrived on staff shortages brought about by demographic change. This is the 'double whammy' of the employee-relations scene in the 21st century. We need a new psychological contract that fits those who see themselves as survivors of the massive change of the previous decades, and those who have seen only opportunity because of these changes.

The employee-relations plan is itself an opportunity to raise the level of understanding about the new contract that organisations must put in place to satisfy a diverse, discerning and educated workforce not prepared to believe in the tenet, 'Your career is your responsibility.' They will want some clarity about how and why their employment relationship is important to the employer.

Employee voice

Employee voice is a way in which employees can actually participate in decision-making. But what does it involve? Marchington has defined employee voice as (Marchington, 2001):

☐ a two-way communication/exchange of views

- ☐ upward problem-solving
- ☐ collective representation
- ☐ employee engagement
- ☐ having a say about issues.

The means by which this may be achieved are many and varied. Most notably, the attainment of IIP requires extensive employee participation – and proof that it has happened! However, there are other mechanisms that might be used. Quality circles have been around for some time and continue to be an excellent means of employee participation. There is also a greater emphasis on teamworking now as a method of achieving employee participation.

Yet there is an opportunity, now that technology is available, to get real-time participation. Web-enabled employee voice therefore adds a new dimension to the traditional staff attitude survey, which is normally a one-way ticket. It allows information to flow both ways quickly and effectively. The employee-relations plan should therefore include and explain how this two-way movement of information is to be achieved.

The first part of the employee-relations plan has thus to deal with the softer aspects of the relationship between employer and employee.

Industrial relations

The second aspect of the employee relations plan concerns industrial relations (IR) and the associated implications. Those who have worked in HR for the past few years will be only too aware of the significant changes that have taken place in this area. Radical reform, started by the Conservative Government during the 1980s and 1990s, was only tempered by New Labour and a growing body of European Union legislation. The overall thrust towards what might be seen as modernisation has continued apace. The current industrial relations environment is very different from the one that pitched IR professionals against the massed ranks of militant unionism. The 'sophistication of steward organisations' (Marchington and Parker, 1990) has contributed to a more complex scenario on both sides. Recently, the TUC urged its unions to increase their recruitment efforts in the dot.coms.

For the purposes of the employee-relations plan, then, it is necessary to understand both the organisation's experience and its definition of IR as well as external factors.

'Industrial relations' tends to refer to the formal relationship between employer and employee. The objectives behind such a formal relationship might be (Marchington and Wilkinson, 1998):

☐ minimising disruption at work and reducing the likelihood of overt conflict

☐ achieving greater stability in employee relations by channelling discontent through agreed procedures

☐ increasing co-operation and commitment so as to increase the likely acceptance of change

☐ increasing control over the labour process.

These are aspects of industrial relations that occur largely in the workplace, and the context within which they take place is often the result of government intervention through law. The CIPD has been proactive in this area during the past few years, its involvement providing an indication of some of the complexities of modern IR of which those responsible for working on the HR plan ought to be aware. These include (James and Emmott, 2001):

☐ disciplinary and grievance procedures published by ACAS

☐ Part-Time Workers' regulations that came into force in July 2000

☐ the establishment of European Works Councils

☐ the operation of employment tribunals (ETs)

☐ the code of practice on the use of personal data

☐ the regulations on collective redundancies

☐ the EU Directive on fixed-term work

☐ the Working Time Regulations.

These issues centre on a rich and complex body of legislation and consultation that forms part of the industrial relations picture and is further compounded by legal frameworks that have also to be considered as part of the overall human resource plan.

Employee commitment

Let us now examine two case studies that show just how challenging the issue of employee commitment can be.

During 1997 two industrial disputes took place which surprised many observers. In the UK, British Airways – one of the most successful airlines in the world – got themselves into a dispute over proposals for changes in the terms and conditions of their staff. 'BA ACCUSED OF BEHAVING BADLY', 'BA REFUSE TO EAT HUMBLE PIE', were some of the headlines. There was a three-day walk-out by 313 members of the cabin crew. However, another 1,983 staff remained off work, listed officially as sick. It was reported that 'claims have been made by cabin crew that during the three-day walk-out they received telephone calls from BA managers demanding to know whether they were part of the strike. Cabin staff claimed to have been so scared by BA's threats to prevent their return to work...that they phoned in sick' (Croner, 1997). Eventually the strike cost £125 million and led to the setting up of a senior team to rebuild 'morale, motivation and trust' (*Personnel Today*, 1997).

At about the same time in the United States, UPS, the $22 billion revenue distribution company, suffered a stoppage involving 185,000 of its workers, many of whom were members of the Teamsters Union. The stoppage lasted 15 days and cost millions of dollars in lost income. It involved serious picketing and received extensive media coverage throughout the country. The causes of the dispute were again ostensibly terms and conditions – in this case, changes in benefits based on potential cost savings and outsourcing. The Teamsters' president Ron Carey characterised the strike as a struggle against part-time labour. President Clinton and Labor Secretary Alexis Herman refrained from ordering the Teamsters back to work but 'nudged both parties back to the negotiating table' (*Washington Post*, 1997). Eventually the two parties settled.

In both BA and UPS the overt causes of the disputes were

economic – cost reduction and workforce flexibility. However, there were strong feelings on both sides, which, to an outside observer, seemed to imply a deeper underlying issue in the relationship between employer and employee. In the UPS case there was apparently a good deal of public support for the strikers because the issue of part-time working 'resonated with a lot of people' (*Washington Post*, 1997). It was later reported that the 'UPS strike gives all firms a bad name' (*Personnel Today*, 1997) because it had raised the issue of the extensive use of part-time staff. What made these disputes particularly surprising was that both companies had implemented business strategies that ought to have been the pride of the business gurus. Mission statements had been published and competitive advantage had been achieved. 'Clover-leaf' operations consisting of specialist full-time staff and flexible part-timers had been put in place, making both companies extremely profitable – indeed, world leaders in their respective fields. Both organisations had spent a good deal of effort in handling staff concerns. BA had stated, for example, that 'the motivation and commitment of all employees continues to play a major part in [our] success,' and they had made steady progress in increasing the number of women in senior management, put in place new training and development initiatives, and backed all of this up with a 'comprehensive internal communications programme to ensure that all employees are well informed about the business and the airline industry in general' (*Inside British Airways*, 1997). Yet when the crunch came, a gap appeared between the employer and employee which seemed out of place with the business strategies that had been implemented.

The cases of BA and UPS highlight the fact that the challenges facing employers and employees during times of change are immense. They illustrate the point that underlying issues surrounding the fundamentals of the human relationship can serve to negate success in the economic relationship – that achieving mutuality of interest between employer and employee is a complex task. To quote Tony Watson, 'Economic goals can be pursued only through the orchestrating of social co-operation and the exercise of political skills and moral insight' (Watson, 1994). So we might conclude that achieving competitiveness does not necessarily sit easily with the challenge of maintaining loyalty and motivation in the workplace. Acknowledgement of this point is important when considering employee relations, its strategy, and its inclusion in the human resource plan.

What, then, are the component parts of the employee-commitment element?

☐ an understanding of the current state of employee commitment through the use of staff attitude surveys – key questions are those such as 'Would you recommend the company's products to a friend?' or 'How highly do you regard the company's position on social responsibility?'

☐ an understanding of the metrics that might act as a proxy for employee commitment, such as staff turnover, length of service, etc – by segmenting the staff base it is possible to detect different attitudes of various types of employee that might be indicators of employee commitment.

The employee-relations-planning process

These are the factors that are critical to the preparation of the employee-relations plan. The challenge is to prepare a plan that is not so general that it crosses other areas of HR and therefore becomes difficult to convert into specific action. The key elements are outlined in Figure 29 and discussed in more detail below.

Identifying the key issues in the business strategy that are likely to affect employee relations, industrial relations and/or employee commitment

It is very important, as in other parts of the human resource planning process to align employee relations to the business strategy. Let us examine an example to see how this might develop.

The business strategy requires a focus on the core business and the outsourcing of some non-core functions. The following knock-on effects will have to be taken account of during the employee-relations-planning process:

☐ legal issues and the Transfer of Undertakings (Protection of Employment) Regulations 1981 (TUPE)

☐ industrial relations and the need to brief trade unions or other employee representatives

☐ morale issues for those being outsourced and the need to ensure an effective 'employee voice' in the process

☐ communications issues and the need to explain the rationale for the strategy.

Those responsible for preparing the employee-relations plan will have to consider the implications against each of the headings (ER, IR, employee commitment) and come up with appropriate and timely solutions to the issues.

Highlighting the overall employee-relations implications of these strategies

Once the issues have been identified, it will be necessary to look at the implications for employee relations. Again an example can demonstrate the point.

The business strategy calls for the increasing use of telephones for customer contact – which means the opening of a new call centre. This is bound to carry with it a range of changes in the employment relationship – changes that might include new ways of working, new terms and conditions of service, and/or a new mandatory training programme for which plans will have to be made, agreements with employees and their representatives reached, and a new contract, psychological as well as legal, implemented. The HR professional will have to work through the business strategies and identify, in each of them, the core issue and appropriate HR action.

So the process will be:

☐ for the overall organisational strategy, to highlight the employee-relations implications

☐ to identify these in three areas – employee involvement, the effect on the psychological contract, the implications for ensuring employee participation (employee voice).

This will provide a systematic understanding of the effects of strategy on employee relations in its broadest context.

Identifying the industrial relations implications for which formal agreement from employee representatives will be sought

A manufacturing operation closure will clearly involve complex negotiations; an expansion or change in the European strategy will involve consultation with the European Works Council; and so on. There will also be legal requirements to be satisfied if radical change in employment is implied by the strategy. Each of the strategies will have to be tested very rigorously against the industrial relations requirements. This is a unique responsibility for HR. A successful interpretation can lead to the successful implementation of strategy. A failure can lead to serious setbacks or, indeed, the failure of the whole business strategy.

One procedure for identifying industrial relations implications is:

☐ Identify how the organisational strategy will affect the fundamentals of the formal employee relationship (eg a move to flexible contracts to take account of different hours of working).

☐ Cross-refer these effects against the formal agreement with employee representatives.

☐ Cross-refer against any legal implications of moving to the new strategy.

The output of this part of the employee-relations-planning process is a thorough understanding of industrial relations issues that can later be taken into account when the time comes for finding solutions.

Ensuring that the issue of employee commitment is identified and a plan put in place to engage the workforce

This is by far the most difficult part of the employee-relations plan. How to ensure employee commitment during times of strategic change is a challenge that faces most organisations. If a new strategy is being proposed, how is it going to be communicated? And once it has been communicated, how is the organisation going to get the buy-in and commitment of its employees? The best strategy in the world will fail if the employees are not engaged in its implementation (as witnessed particularly during mergers and acquisitions, which highlight the subject of employee commitment).

A process is needed to bring the issue of employee commitment to the table. What sort of process would it take?

☐ First and foremost make sure that employee commitment is actually seen as an issue. Too often the need to engage and eventually carry employees along with the strategy is not given enough air time. The employee-relations plan is a perfect opportunity to do so.

☐ Identify the current status of employee commitment using staff attitudes measures. Where are the hotspots? If these are about resourcing, training to do the job, the performance of local management, or even (God forbid!) the performance of senior management, they need to be identified.

☐ Then show how the implementation of a new strategy will impact on the current commitment. For example: if a new customer relations management system is to be put in place, will there be enough training to ensure its effectiveness? Will employees take to the new processes, and are local managers strong enough to persuade their teams of the merits of the new system?

In raising employee commitment in this way, enough time and resource can be built into the plan to ensure that issues are dealt with effectively.

Articulating the new 'contract' proposed and methods of obtaining buy-in from employees

This is particularly important in that it embraces the problematic area of the fundamentals of the employment relationship. The psychological contract is a subject often talked about as critical. If it is, then the employee-relations plan should recognise it as such, and put in place actions for resolving issues and taking the employee to the point proposed by the strategy.

Language is important here. Referring to a 'psychological contract' probably will not get far in business-focused organisations looking for relevant solutions. So those in HR will have to be smart in putting the point across.

How can it be done? What are the questions to be raised?

☐ When outlining the plans, take account of employee expectations as well as the expectations of other stakeholders (shareholders, for example). What are the implications of the strategy for jobs and careers?

☐ How will the strategy change the working relationship? If, for example, terms and conditions of service are to be harmonised during a merger, are there winners and losers in the harmonisation? If so, it will be essential to deal with this up front in a mature way.

☐ Does the strategy demand more flexibility and change? If so, it will almost inevitably affect the 'contract' – especially in organisations where stability has been the norm (although there are very few of those these days).

Each of these examples demonstrates a change in the contract – psychological or otherwise – and will require explanation, persuasion and engagement. This can be initiated through the employee-relations plan.

Preparing plans and strategies for presenting to trade unions or employees' representatives

It is critical that the employee representatives are engaged in and back the business strategy. One way of gaining general buy-in is to ensure that the plans are communicated to and understood by the employee representatives. It is equally important that this is a two-way process. In some countries, worker representatives on the board have access to and participate in the strategy of the organisations in which they work at a very early stage. In others, works councils are used as sounding-boards and an opportunity to hear the organisation's plans. Where such ER mechanisms do not exist, the principles of two-way engagement of strategy must be fulfilled in a way appropriate to the organisation in question. One thing is constant: the necessity for it. The employee-relations plan should make provision for the different requirements in ensuring that it is achieved.

Bringing it all together into a single, cohesive employee-relations plan

Finally, the joining-up of employee relations is as important as of any other part of HR, and the human resource plan is an opportunity to do this. In this respect the three areas of employee relations, industrial relations and employee commitment should be presented within a holistic approach. These activities will bring with them plans involving consultation, communication and engagement. It is important to ensure that these are co-ordinated in an integrated way.

The employee-relations plan, then, is the final part of the human resource plan. It is an appropriate concluding section in that it embodies a pervasive aspect of HR. Many areas of both business and HR strategy have an impact on the way the organisation interfaces with its employees. The ER plan is an opportunity to make sure that employees understand and are engaged in the strategy, and that their representatives are able to support such strategies.

PART IV

CONCLUSION

18 CONCLUSION

HR has a key role in bringing strategy to life. How do we know this? Well, for one thing chief executive officers are asking more and more questions about the people aspects of their organisations. For another, the gurus of management are increasingly emphasising the importance of people in the delivery of strategy. When Robert Kaplan spoke at the CIPD Conference about the principles of the strategy-focused organisation, he enjoined people to 'make strategy everyone's job', and 'mobilise change through executive leadership' (Kaplan, 2001). This was a testament to the importance of people to delivering organisational strategy from a man who started life as the expert on 'the balanced scorecard'. Strategy had gone from an abstract concept to one that was alive through the actions of the people in an organisation. It is up to HR to make sure that people strategies are aligned to business strategy, and to have enough imagination to achieve the transformation being sought in organisations throughout the world. Can HR deliver this on massive expectation?

There is no doubt that HR is being transformed – and the process is nothing short of a revolution. The demand from organisations for solutions to complex people issues – such as how to align people satisfaction and customer satisfaction – is increasing, and those in HR are gearing up to deliver such solutions. We now have evidence to show that the adoption of a range of HR practices is good for business. In particular (CIPD, *Performance through People*, 2001):

☐ Managers should expand progressive people management practices.

☐ The general principle must be 'the more the better', since the impact of any single practice in isolation is likely to be small.

☐ The most effective practices or combinations of practices are those concerned with skills acquisition and development, knowledge management, motivation, commitment, job design and involvement.

☐ Effective execution of the practices is as important as their number, meaning that management skills are vital.

☐ Learning at all levels should be thought of as fundamental to people management processes, both as an outcome and as an input to the next round of continuous improvement and strategic capacity enhancement.

The way that HR supplies services to meet these challenges is undergoing a radical review. And the growth of business-oriented HR methodologies from people such as Ulrich, Huselid and Guest has provided a professional set of tools, techniques and arguments. The ingredients are there for HR to produce a superb product. But the ingredients need a catalyst if they are to blend together in an optimal way. The catalyst is the change in the personal profile of the HR professional. This requires clarity of thinking and a focus on objectives that we have yet to deliver in any sustained way. The chapters of this book are intended to provide at least part of this catalyst by focusing on the strategic elements of human resource forecasting and human resource planning.

But this is only a start. Those in HR have to make sure that their role in the strategy-setting process is understood and accepted by the organisations in which they work, because 'If you are not crystal clear on the role of the HR function, you cannot expect line managers to understand and respect what you do' (Mooney, 2001).

It is just incredible that after 50 years of providing an invaluable service to organisations in both the public and private sector we have to have this role-clarity debate. But if we do have to have such a debate, now is as good a time as any – because it is clear that unless organisations get the people things right, they are unlikely to get anything else right.

How should we go about this task? We can start by having

a well understood and valued role in the strategy-setting process of the organisations in which we work, getting HR on to the top table with a voice that is equal to other professional functions'. In fact, it is our obligation to do this, since there is hardly an area of the strategy that does not have an impact on people. And so the objective of this book is to present a process for ensuring that HR can genuinely participate in strategy in a way that no other function can. Strategic human resource forecasting deals with issues for which a professional and proactive input from those in HR is mandatory. Later, the tools and techniques for human resource planning provide a continuum of involvement at the implementation stage.

What we need to do is to put forward a great strategic human resource forecast followed by a great human resource plan. In this respect Sahlman has advised us that the way to do great planning is to understand and analyse systematically four interdependent factors. These are *the people, the opportunity, the context* and *risk/reward* (Sahlman, 1997). We should not forget these four elements when preparing our forecasts and plans. In Part One of the book we looked at both the people and the opportunity by analysing what strategy actually was and why it was important. We then outlined a role for HR in this arena. In Part Two we looked at the context of HR strategy in areas such as scenario-planning and the demand/supply axis that was such a critical feature of modern employment. In Part Three we looked at how effective strategy could become rewarding by the implementation of excellence in the human resource plan.

So the ingredients are there to reinforce the HR role. But on the issue of 'strategic HR' there is some way to go. It still occasionally feels as though one hand is tied to the tightrope walker. So how can we break free from this? Those in HR need to demonstrate solid professionalism in developing strategies to help the organisation to achieve sustained performance – to get off the tightrope and once and for all show how the HR profession can really add value. This will require more than good models and interesting graphs. It will require a personal commitment on the part of HR professionals to engage in strategy-setting.

But we know that it can be a complex affair. Strategy-setting is mostly a long march, sometimes as tough as boot camp, and requiring a wide range of business and personal competencies. And things can be pretty chaotic. Balancing short-term business as usual with longer-term strategic investments is not straightforward. So is there any way that we can hope to get an HR strategy that is achievable and, most importantly, understood by the people who have to make it work? The answer is Yes. It is possible to point the organisation in the right direction through good processes. What is needed are information, ideas and luck. The strategic human resource forecasting and planning processes were about the first two. You will have to make your own luck.

In the previous chapters, I have tried to present some tools and techniques that should help in gathering and providing information to make sure that people inputs are taken into account during the strategy-setting process and that HR is able to engage at the right level. What I have not provided is a panacea, nor would I claim that all of these tools and techniques are relevant to all organisations. I would claim, though, that the *principles* are. There is a window of opportunity for HR. It is important that we climb through it and close it firmly behind us. Then we shall no longer have to endure the unhelpful debates about the actual role of HR. People issues are high on the corporate agenda. The HR function is expert in such issues. It is our business, after all, and it is up to those in HR to make sure that these issues are dealt with in the most professional way possible, using techniques unique to HR and its practitioners. All this stuff about HR's being transplanted by technology is clearly nonsense when viewed from the above position. HR is about providing information and insight. Technology can never do both.

Is there anything that might stop HR from getting onto the strategic agenda? Only probably HR itself, by failing to engage in the strategic debate. We can overcome this by making sure that we understand business issues, strategies and methodologies before we add our own HR contribution. Then when we do intervene, we do so with tools that add value. The first stage is to get to grips with some of the concepts of strategy. The second is to provide interventions that make the organisation sit up and take notice, that make others in the organisation realise the unique contribution of HR and its professionals. It is time to get up and at it. Even the more reflective practitioners cannot afford to wait too long, to be over-cautious, in taking this step.

A final thought. HR is at present a composite function. It is increasingly involved in the strategy of the organisation but still has to mop the brows of those affected by change. It is judged by both activities. 'Getting strategic' will not dispense with the need to do operational things excellently. The two stand together, and if we forget that simple point, we may never ascend to greater heights. The future may be different. Today is about delivering to these dual account-abilities. Both sides now. In doing so, I hope you have the time of your life.

REFERENCES AND FURTHER READING

ALLAN P. (1997) 'Minimizing employee layoffs while down-sizing: employer practices that work'. *International Journal of Manpower*, Vol. 18, Nos 7 and 8.

ARMSTRONG M. *and* MURLIS H. (1998) *Reward Management*. London, Kogan Page.

ASHTON C. (1995) *Pay, Performance and Career Development*. London, Business Intelligence.

BEARDWELL I. *and* HOLDEN L. (1997) *Human Resource Management: A contemporary perspective*. London, Pitman Publishing.

BECKHARD R. (1969) *Organisation Development*. Reading, Massachusetts, Addison Wesley Publishing Company.

BEE F. *and* BEE R. (2000) *Training Needs Analysis and Evaluation*. London, CIPD.

RAHMAN BIN IDRIS A. *and* ELDRIDGE D. (1998) 'Reconceptualising human resource planning in response to institutional change'. *International Journal of Manpower*, Vol. 19, No.5, pp343–357.

BLOODGOOD J. M. (2000) 'Understanding a firm's culture before changing the business planning process'. *Strategic Change*, 9 Vol. 4, June–July, pp237–248.

BRAMHAM J. (1988) *Practical Manpower Planning*. London, Institute of Personnel Management.

BRITISH AIRWAYS (1997) *Inside British Airways, Our People*. Internet, September.

BRITISH QUALITY FOUNDATION *and* EFQM (1997) *Guide to Self-Assessment*. London, The British Quality Foundation.

BUCKINGHAM M. (2001) 'Building a strength-based organisation'. CIPD National Conference, Harrogate.

CARTWRIGHT S. *and* COOPER C. L. (2000) *HR Know-How in Mergers and Acquisitions*. London, CIPD.

CHADWICK P. (2000) 'Life after merger: managing change at Lloyds TSB'. *IRS Employment Trends, 709.*

CHRISTENSEN C. M. (2001) 'The past and future of competitive advantage'. *Sloan Management Review*, MIT, Vol. 42 No.2, Winter.

CIPD (2000) *Effective People Management*. London, CIPD.

CIPD (2000) *Raising UK Productivity: Why people management matters*. London, CIPD.

CIPD (2001) *The Case for Good People Management*. London, CIPD.

CIPD (2001) *Compensation Forum Handbook*. CIPD, London.

CIPD (2001) *Employee Share Ownership*. London, CIPD.

CIPD (2001) *The Future of Learning for Work*. London, CIPD.

CIPD (2001) *Performance through People*. CIPD, London.

CIPD (2001) *Training and Development Survey Report*. London, CIPD.

CLEARY T. (1994) *Thunder in the Sky*. Boston, Shambhala Publications.

THE CONFERENCE BOARD (1997) *Managing Knowledge for Business Success*. New York, The Conference Board.

THE CONFERENCE BOARD (1997) *Investing in Profitable Customer Relationships*. New York, The Conference Board.

THE CONFERENCE BOARD (1997) *The Value of Training in the Era of Intellectual Capital*. New York, The Conference Board.

CONGER J. A. (1998) 'The necessary art of persuasion'. *Harvard Business Review*, May–June.

CONYON M. J. (2000) *Directors' Pay in UK Plcs*. CIPD, London.

CORPORATE LEADERSHIP COUNCIL (1999) *Transforming the Human Resources Function*. Washington, Corporate Advisory Board.

CORPORATE LEADERSHIP COUNCIL (1998) *Workforce Turnover and Firm Performance.* Washington, Corporate Advisory Board.

CORPORATE LEADERSHIP COUNCIL (1998) *Forced Outside, Leadership Talent Sourcing and Retention.* Washington, The Advisory Board Company.

CORPORATE LEADERSHIP COUNCIL (1997) *The Next Generation, Accelerating the Development of Rising Leaders.* Washington, The Advisory Board Company.

COUPLAND D. (1996) *Microserfs.* New York, HarperCollins.

COWLING A. *and* WALTERS M. (1990) 'Manpower planning – where are we today?' *Personnel Review* 19, 3.

CRONER (1997) Industrial Relations Briefing, *Industrial Relations Law*, Issue No.56, 12 August.

DAVIS S. (1991) *Marvin Gaye: I heard it through the grapevine.* Edinburgh, Mainstream Publishing Company.

DEAL T. E. *and* KENNEDY A. (1982) *Corporate Cultures.* Reading, Massachusetts, Addison Wesley Publishing Company Inc.

DE BOTTON A. (2000) *The Consolations of Philosophy.* London, Penguin Books.

DEPARTMENT FOR EDUCATION AND EMPLOYMENT (1998) *The Learning Age.* London, The Stationery Office.

DESSLER G. (1994) *Human Resource Management.* London, Prentice Hall.

DIXON P. (1998) *Futurewise.* London, HarperCollins.

DRUCKER P. F. (1992) *Managing for the Future*, Oxford, Butterworth-Heinemann Ltd.

ELIN R. (2001) 'Think ahead to avoid nasty surprises'. *Sunday Times*, 29 April.

ETTORE B. (1996) 'Empty promises'. *Management Review*, July.

FISHER D. *and* TORBERT W. R. (1995) *Personal and Organisational Transformations.* London, McGraw Hill.

FOSTER R. N. (1986) *Innovation, the Attacker's Advantage.* London, Pan Books.

FOUCAULD J. B. DE (1996) 'Post-industrial society and

economic security'. *International Labour Review*. Vol. 135, No.6, pp675–682.

FYFE J. (1986) 'Putting the people back into manpower planning equations'. *Personnel Management*, October.

GARRATT B. (2000) *The Learning Organisation*. London, HarperCollins.

GARRATT B. (ED.) (1995) *Developing Strategic Thought*. London, McGraw Hill.

GARRATT B. (2000) *The Twelve Organisational Capabilities*. London, HarperCollins Business.

GHEMAWAT P. (1991) *Commitment, the Dynamic of Strategy*. New York, The Free Press,.

GIBBON E. (1994) *The History of the Decline and Fall of the Roman Empire*. Vol. 2. London, Penguin Books.

GRATTON L. (2000) 'A real step change'. *People Management*, 16 March.

GRATTON L. (1999) 'People processes as a source of competitive advantage'. In L. Gratton, V. Hope Hailey, P. Stiles and C. Truss, *Strategic Human Resource Management*. Oxford, Oxford University Press.

GEUS A. DE (1997) 'The living company'. *Harvard Business Review*, March–April.

GUEST D. (1999) 'Do people strategies really enhance business success, and if so, why don't more organisations use them?' Institute of Personnel and Development National Conference, 27–29 October.

HAMEL G. *and* PRAHALAD C. K. (1994) *Competing for the Future*. Boston, Harvard Business School Press.

HAMLIN B., KEEP J. *and* ASH K. (2001) *Organisational Change and Development*. Harlow, Essex, Pearson Education Ltd.

HANDY C. (1998) *Understanding Organisations*. London, Penguin Books.

HANKE J. E. and REITSCH A. G. (1989) *Business Forecasting*. Boston, Allyn and Bacon.

HENDRY C. (1995) *Human Resources Management*. Oxford, Butterworth-Heinemann.

HILLS H. (2001) *Team-Based Learning*. Aldershot, Gower Publishing Limited.

HININGS C. R., THIBAULT L., SLACK T. *and* KIKULIS L. M. (1996) 'Values and organizational structures'. *Human Relations*, Vol. 49, No.7, July.

HOFER C. W. *and* SCHENDEL D. (1986) *Strategy Formulation: Analytical concepts*. St Paul, West Publishing Company.

HOPE HAILEY V. (1999) 'Managing culture'. In Gratton, Hope Hailey *et al*.

HUBBICK E. (2001) *Employee Share Ownership*. London, CIPD.

HUCZYNSKI A. and BUCHANAN D. (1991) *Organisational Behaviour*. New York, Prentice Hall.

INSTITUTE OF EMPLOYMENT RESEARCH (2000) *Projections of Occupations and Qualifications, 1999/2000*.

INVESTORS in PEOPLE (2001) *The Recruitment and Selection Model*. London, Investors in People UK.

IPD (1997) *Employment Relations into the 21st Century*. London, IPD.

IPD (1999) *Workplace Learning, Culture and Performance*. London, IPD.

JAMES L. and EMMOTT M. (2001) 'Employment regulation'. CIPD internal paper, June.

JARRELL D. W. (1993) *Human Resource Planning*. New Jersey, Prentice Hall.

JOHNSON M. (2001) *Winning the People Wars*. London, Financial Times/Prentice Hall.

KAKABADSE A., LUDLOW R. and VINNICOMBE S. (1988) *Working in Organisations*. London, Penguin Books.

KAPLAN R. (2001) 'The strategy-focused organisation'. CIPD National Conference, Harrogate.

KENNEDY P. (1988) *The Rise and Fall of the Great Powers – Economic change and military conflict from 1500 to 2000*. London, Fontana Press, p693.

KLEIN N. (2000) *No Logo*. London, Flamingo.

KOYS D. J. (1997) 'Human resource management and Fortune's

corporate reputation survey'. *Employee Responsibilities and Rights Journal*, Vol. 10, No.2, June.

KROMBEEN K. (1988) 'Managing the organisational change from a multinational to a global company'. In J. F. McLimore and L. Larwood, *Strategies. . .Successes. . .Senior Executives Speak Out*. New York, Harper & Row.

KUCZYNSKI S. (2000) 'While supplies last'. *HR magazine*, Vol. 45, No.6, June.

LEGGE K. (1995) *Human Resource Management – Rhetoric and Realities*. London, Macmillan Business.

LEOPOLD J., HARRIS L. *and* WATSON T. (1999) 'Strategic human resourcing'. London, Financial Times Management.

LUNDY O. *and* COWLING A. (1996) *Strategic Human Resource Management*, London, Routledge.

MARCHINGTON M. (2001) 'Employee voice'. CIPD National Conference, Harrogate.

MARCHINGTON M. *and* PARKER P. (1990) *Changing Patterns of Employee Relations*. Hemel Hempstead, Harvester Wheatsheaf.

MARCHINGTON M. *and* WILKINSON A. (2000) *Core Personnel and Development*. London, Chartered Institute of Personnel and Development.

MCBEATH G. (1992) *The Handbook of Human Resource Planning*. Oxford, Blackwell Publishers.

MCFADZEAN E. (2001) 'Critical factors for enhancing creativity'. *Strategic Change*, Vol. 10, No. 5, August.

MCKENZIE J. L. *and* MELLING G. L. (2001) 'Skills-based human capital budgeting, a strategic initiative not a financial exercise'. *Journal of Cost Management*, Vol. 15, No.3, May–June.

MEISTER J. C. (1998) *Corporate Universities*. London, McGraw Hill.

MINTZBERG H. (1987) 'Crafting strategy'. *Harvard Business Review*, July–August.

MINTZBERG H. (1991) 'The effective organization: forces and forms'. *Sloan Management Review*, 54, Winter.

MINTZBERG H. (1994) *The Rise and Fall of Strategic Planning*. London, Prentice Hall International.

MINTZBERG H., AHLSTRAND B. *and* LAMPEL J. (1998) *Strategy Safari*. London, Prentice Hall.

MOINGEON B. *and* EDMONSON A. (eds) (1996) *Organisational Learning and Competitive Advantage*. London, Sage Publications.

MOONEY P. (2001) *Turbo-Charging the HR Function*. London, CIPD.

NTO NATIONAL COUNCIL (2001) *Towards a Stronger Skills Framework*. London, April.

ORPEN C. (1997) 'The downside of downsizing: managing an organisation to its right size'. *Strategic Change*, Vol. 6.

PADDISON L. (2001) 'How to conduct an equal pay review'. *People Management*, 14 June, pp58–59.

PATTERSON M. G., WEST M. A., LAWTHOM R. *and* NICKELL S. (1997) *The Impact of People Management Practices on Business Performance*. Institute of Personnel and Development.

PETTIGREW A., FERLIE E. *and* McKEE L. (1992) *Shaping Strategic Change*. London, Sage Publications.

PHILPOT J. (2001) *Raising UK Productivity: Why people management matters*. CIPD, January.

PORTER M. E. (1980) *Competitive Strategy*. New York, The Free Press, Macmillan.

PORTER M. E. (1985) *Competitive Advantage*. New York, The Free Press, Macmillan.

PORTER M. E. (1990) *The Competitive Advantage of Nations*. London, Macmillan Press Ltd.

PORTER M. E. (1996) 'What is strategy?'. *Harvard Business Review*, November-December.

PORTER M. E (2001) 'Strategy and the Internet'. *Harvard Business Review*, March.

PRICE J. L. (1997) 'Handbook of organisational measurement'. *International Journal of Manpower*, Vol. 18, Nos 4/5/6.

PURCELL J. (2001) 'Personnel and human resource managers: power, prestige and potential'. *Human Resource Management Journal*, Vol. 11 No.3.

RAJAN A. (1994) *Winning People*. Tunbridge Wells, Create.

RANA E. (2001) 'Low skills, low interest'. *People Management*, 13 September.

RANDALL N. F. *and* WALLACE M. J. (1997) 'Inside the virtual workplace: forging a new deal for work and rewards'. *Compensation and Benefits Review*, January–February.

RAPPAPORT A. (1986) *Creating Shareholder Value*. New York, The Free Press.

REIGO B. (2001) 'How to overcome the know-how shortage in a fast-moving Telco'. *Human Resources Solutions for Europe*, HR Summit Conference, Montreux, February.

REILLY P. (2000) *HR Shared Services*. Institute for Employment Studies.

RHINEHART L. (1993) *The Search for the Diceman*. London, HarperCollins.

RICHARDSON R. *and* THOMPSON M. (1997) *The Impact of People Management Practices on Business Performance: A literature review*. Institute of Personnel and Development.

ROSENFIELD R. H. *and* WILSON D. C. (1999) *Managing Organisations*. London, McGraw Hill.

ROTHWELL S. (1995) 'Human resource planning'. In J. Storey, *Human Resource Management*, London, International Thomson Business Press.

ROUSSEAU D. (1995) *Psychological Contracts in Organizations*. London, Sage Publications.

RUCCI A. J., KIRN S. P. *and* QUINN R. T. (1998) 'The employee-customer-profit chain at Sears'. *Harvard Business Review*, January–February.

SAHLMAN W. A. (1997) 'How to write a great business plan'. *Harvard Business Review*, July–August.

SALAMON M. (1987) *Industrial Relations: Theory and practice*. New York, Prentice Hall.

SCARBOROUGH H. *and* SWANN J. (ED) (1999) *Case Studies in Knowledge Management*. London, Institute of Personnel and Development.

SCHEMERHORN, HUNT *and* OSBOURNE (1991) *Managing Organisational Behaviour*. London, John Wiley & Sons.

SCHWARZKOPF H. N. (2001) *Vision of Leadership for*

Tomorrow. HR: The Sky's the Limit, 53rd Annual Conference and Exposition, San Francisco, California, 24–27 June.

SENGE P. (1990) 'The leader's new work: building learning organisations'. *Sloan Management Review*, Vol. 32, No.1.

SHELL (2000) 'Global scenarios, 1998–2000' at shell.com.

SKINNER W. (1981) 'Big hat, no cattle'. *Harvard Business Review*, Sept–Oct.

SLOMAN M. (2001) *The E-learning Revolution*. CIPD, London.

SMITH D. *and* RUSHDIE D. (2001) 'It's the taxis, stupid'. *Sunday Times*, Business Focus, 13 May, p5.

STAINER G. (1971) *Manpower Planning*. London, Heinemann.

STEFFENS-DUCH S. (2001) 'Employee commitment – evaluation, analysis, and enhancing as condition for economic success'. *Human Resources Solutions for Europe*, HR Summit Conference, Montreux, February.

STEWART J. (1991) *Managing Change through Training and Development*. London, Kogan Page.

STEWART J. *and* McGOLDRICK J. (EDS) (1996) *Human Resource Development, Perspectives, Strategies and Practice*. London, Pitman Publishing.

STOREY J. (ED.) (1995) *Human Resource Management: A critical text*. London, International Thompson Business Press.

TANSLEY C. (1999) 'Human resource planning'. In J. Leopold, L. Harris *and* T. Watson, *Strategic Human Resourcing*. London, Financial Times/Pitman Publishers.

TAPSCOTT D. (2001) 'The new economy'. *People Mean Business*, CIPD National Conference, 24–26 October.

TAYLOR C. (2001) 'Motorola closure revives debate over consultation'. *People Management*, 3 May.

THOMSON K. (1990) *The Employee Revolution*. London, Pitman Publishing.

TORRINGTON D. *and* HALL L. (1991) *Personnel Management*. Hemel Hempstead, Prentice Hall (UK) Ltd.

TRICKER B. (1995) 'From manager to director: developing corporate governor's strategic thinking'. In Garratt *op.cit.*

TUFTE E. R. (1990) *Envisioning Information*. Cheshire, Connecticut, Graphics Press.

TUFTE E. R. (1983) *The Visual Display of Quantitative Information*. Cheshire, Connecticut, Graphics Press.

TUNSTALL S. (1988) 'Corporate cultures of the world's most admired companies'. Hay International Conference, Barcelona, November.

TURNER P. (2000) 'Professional development into the new millennium'. CIPD Professional Standards Conference, Warwick University, 10–12 July.

TYSON S. (1997) 'Human resource strategy: a process for managing the contribution of HRM to organizational performance'. *The International Journal of Human Resource Management*, Vol. 8, No. 3, June.

TYSON S. *and* DOHERTY N. (1999) *Human Resource Excellence Report*. London, Financial Times Management.

ULRICH D. (1998) 'A new mandate for human resources'. *Harvard Business Review*, January–February.

ULRICH D. (1996) *Human Resource Champions*. Boston, Harvard Business School Press.

VAND DER HEIJDEN K. (1997) *Scenarios, Strategies and the Strategy Process*. Nijenrode University Press, Breukelen, the Netherlands, www.library.nijenrode.

VERHOEVEN C. J. (1982) *Techniques in Corporate Manpower Planning*. The Hague, Boston, London, Kluever Nijhoff Publishing.

VISHWANATH *and* HARDING (2000) 'The Starbuck's effect'. *Harvard Business Review*, April.

WALSH C. (1996) *Key Management Ratios*, London, Pitman Publishing.

WARNER M. (1997) 'Review symposium: from human relations to human resources'. *The International Journal of Human Resource Management*, Vol. 8, No. 1, February.

WATSON T. (1986) *Management, Organization and Employment Strategy*. London, Routledge.

WATSON T. (1994) 'Management flavours of the month: their role in managers' lives'. *The International Journal of Human Resource Management*, 5, 4 December.

WATSON T. J. (1994) *In Search of Management*. London, International Thomson Business Press.

WEAVER W. G. (1997) 'Dewey or Foucault? Organization and administration as edification and as valence'. *Organization*, February, pp31–49.

WEST A. (1992) *Innovation Strategy*. Hemel Hempstead, Prentice Hall, UK.

WESTWOOD A. (2001) 'Drawing a line – who is going to train our workforce?' In *The Future of Learning for Work*. London, CIPD.

WILLEY B. (1997) 'New industrial relations with old rules'. *Croner Industrial Relations Briefing*, Issue No.59, 11 November.

WILLIAM M MERCER (2001) *People Issues and Mergers and Acquisitions*. London, William M Mercer.

WRIGHT V. (2001) 'The current state of pay'. *People Management*, 17 May, p53.

ZEFFANE R. and MAYO G. (1994) 'Planning for human resources in the 1990s: development of an operational model'. *International Journal of Manpower*. Vol. 15, No.6, pp36–56.

INDEX